HOW AND WHY WE STILL READ JUNG

How and Why We Still Read Jung offers a fresh look at how Jung's work can still be read and applied to the modern day. Written by seasoned Jungian analysts and Jung scholars, the essays in this collection offer in-depth and often personal readings of various works by Jung, including discussion of:

- Ambiguating Jung
- Jung and alchemy: a daimonic reading
- Chinese modernity and the way of return
- Jung: respect for the non-literal.

Including contributions from around the world, this book will be of interest to Jungian analysts and academic Jung scholars globally. With a unique and fresh analysis of Jung's work by eminent authors in the field, this book will also be a valuable starting point for a first-time reader of Jung.

Jean Kirsch is a Jungian analyst practising in Palo Alto, California. A graduate of Stanford University Medical School, she is a member and past president of the C.G. Jung Institute of San Francisco. She is a member of the training faculty at the C.G. Jung Institute.

Murray Stein is a training and supervising analyst at the International School of Analytical Psychology in Zurich (ISAP Zurich). He is a former president of the International Association for Analytical Psychology (IAAP) and of ISAP Zurich.

HOW AND WHY WE STILL READ JUNG

Personal and professional reflections

Edited by Jean Kirsch and Murray Stein

Routledge
Taylor & Francis Group
LONDON AND NEW YORK

First published 2013
by Routledge
4 Park Square, Milton Park, Abingdon, Oxon OX14 4RN
605 Third Avenue, New York, NY 10017

Routledge is an imprint of the Taylor & Francis Group, an informa business

British Library Cataloguing in Publication Data
A catalogue record for this book is available from the British Library

Library of Congress Cataloging in Publication Data
How and why we still read Jung : personal and professional reflections / edited by Jean Kirsch and Murray Stein.
pages cm
1. Jung, C. G. (Carl Gustav), 1875–1961. 2. Jungian psychology.
I. Kirsch, Jean. II. Stein, Murray, 1943–
BF109.J8H69 2013
150.19'54092–dc23 2012047450

ISBN: 978-0-415-68647-1 (hbk)
ISBN: 978-0-415-68648-8 (pbk)
ISBN: 978-0-203-50753-7 (ebk)

Typeset in Garamond
by Wearset Ltd, Boldon, Tyne and Wear

CONTENTS

CONTRIBUTORS

Paul Bishop teaches German and comparative literature at the University of Glasgow. He has written a series of studies on Jung's intellectual affinities with major figures in German literature and thought, notably Nietzsche (in *The Dionysian Self*, 1995), Kant (in *Synchronicity and Intellectual Intuition*, 2000), and Goethe and Schiller (in *Analytical Psychology and German Classical Aesthetics*, 2008/2009). In addition to more specific studies of Jung's *Answer to Job* and Jung's theory of midlife crisis, he has also published a wide variety of articles examining Jung's place in the German tradition and the reception of Jung by, among others, Thomas Mann and Hans Trüb. More recently, in the form of a series of articles he has been investigating the significance of *The Red Book*.

Betsy Cohen PhD is an analyst member of the C. G. Jung Institute of San Francisco. She teaches in the analytic training programme and public programmes. She is the author of *The Snow White Syndrome: All about Envy* (1987) and articles in *Jung Journal: Culture & Psyche* on "The Intimate Self-Disclosure" and "Emmanuel Levinas and Depth Psychotherapy". Her current interest is bringing the ancient wisdom of the Torah and the erotic dialogues of Plato to contemporary psychoanalysis.

George B. Hogenson PhD is a Jungian analyst in Chicago and Oak Park, Illinois. He is the author of *Jung's Struggle with Freud* and numerous papers on Jungian theory and the history of psychoanalysis. Originally trained in philosophy at St Olaf College and Yale University, he is a graduate of the C. G. Jung Institute of Chicago and past president of the Chicago Society of Jungian Analysts. He is on the editorial board of the *Journal of Analytical Psychology* and a member of the Executive Committee of the International Association for Analytical Psychology.

Jean Kirsch is a Jungian analyst practising in Palo Alto, California. A graduate of Stanford University Medical School, she is a member and past president of the C. G. Jung Institute of San Francisco, where she was instrumental in establishing its International Student for Analytical

Psychology programme, through which mental health professionals from countries with no formal training opportunities may spend two years at the San Francisco Institute studying Jungian theory and practice. She is a member of the training faculty at the C. G. Jung Institute. Her publications include professional articles, reviews, and contributions to several collections of essays

Thomas B. Kirsch MD is a Jungian analyst, Past President of the Jung Institute of San Francisco, and Past President of the International Association for Analytical Psychology. He is the author of *The Jungians, A Social History of the Jungian Movement* (2000); he was co-editor of the Jungian section of the *International Encyclopedia of Psychoanalysis, Psychiatry, Psychology, and Neurology* (1977), co-editor of *Initiation: The Reality of an Archetype* (2007), and consulting editor to the book *C. G. Jung–James Kirsch Correspondence* (2011). Kirsch has written numerous papers on the history of depth psychology, the analytic relationship, and dreams. He is presently working on a memoir and co-editing with George Hogenson, *Papers from the Red Book.*

Shiuya Sara Liuh PhD, a licensed psychotherapist in Taiwan, taught at Tungkung University Graduate School of Counseling Psychology. She is the founder of Shiuli Memorial Foundation, which offers seminars and training programmes in various psychotherapies in Taiwan. She is one of the founding members of Taiwan Jungian Association, which later became the IAAP Taipei Jungian Developing Group. She is currently a candidate in analytic training at the International School of Analytical Psychology (ISAP) in Zurich, Switzerland.

Stanton Marlan PhD, ABPP, LP, is an archetypally oriented clinical psychologist and Jungian psychoanalyst in private practice in Pittsburgh, Pennsylvania, an adjunct Clinical Professor of Psychology at Duquesne University, and a training and supervising analyst with the Inter-Regional Society of Jungian Analysts. He is also President of the Pittsburgh Society of Jungian Analysts. He holds diplomates in both clinical psychology and psychoanalysis from the American Board of Professional Psychology. He has published numerous articles on Jungian psychology and alchemy and is the editor of *Archetypal Psychologies: Reflections in Honor of James Hillman* (2008) and other books. He is the author of *The Black Sun: The Alchemy and Art of Darkness* (2005) and is currently working on a new book on the philosopher's stone. Marlan has lectured widely at Jungian and archetypal conferences in the United States and abroad, including the First International Conference on Jungian Analysis and Chinese Culture, in Guangzhou, China; the IAAP International Congresses, in Cambridge and Barcelona; the first conference for the International Society for Psychology as the Discipline of Interiority, in Berlin;

and the Guild of Pastoral Psychology, in Oxford. He has taught at the C. G. Jung Institute of Zurich and elsewhere and has a long-term interest in archetypal psychology, the psychology of dreams, and alchemy.

Susan Rowland PhD is Core Faculty at Pacifica Graduate Institute and Associate Chair of Hybrid Programs. Previously, she taught at the University of Greenwich, UK, where she became Professor of English and Jungian Studies. First chair of the International Association for Jungian Studies (IAJS) 2004–6, her work takes Jung into literary theory and literature into myth with an emphasis on gender. Her books include *Jung: A Feminist Revision* (2002), *Jung as a Writer* (2005), *C. G. Jung and the Humanities* (2010), and *The Ecocritical Psyche* (2012). She lives in California.

Mark Saban MA is a senior analyst with the Independent Group of Analytical Psychologists and practises in Oxford and London. He has written and lectured on Dionysus, the body, drama, and alterity. Recent publications include "The Dis/Enchantment of C. G. Jung", *International Journal of Jungian Studies*; "Entertaining the Stranger", *Journal of Analytical Psychology*; and two chapters, "Fleshing Out the Psyche: Jung, Psychology, and the Body" and "Staging the Self: Performance, Individuation and Embodiment", in *Body, Mind, and Healing After Jung: A Space of Questions*, edited by Raya Jones and published by Routledge in 2010.

Murray Stein PhD is Past President of the International School of Analytical Psychology in Zurich (ISAP Zurich) where he is a training and supervising analyst. He is the author of *In Midlife*, *Jung's Treatment of Christianity*, *Jung's Map of the Soul*, and many other books and articles. Most recently he edited and published *Jungian Psychoanalysis* in collaboration with an international team of Jungian psychoanalysts.

Craig Stephenson is a Jungian analyst (C. G. Jung Institute, Zurich), a psychodrama practitioner (the Institute for Psychodrama, Zumikon), and an independent scholar (with a PhD from the Centre for Psychoanalytic Studies, University of Essex). His books include *Possession: Jung's Comparative Anatomy of the Psyche* (Routledge, 2009) and *Anteros: A Forgotten Myth* (Routledge, 2011), and he has edited a collection of essays on Jung and Moreno entitled *The Theatre of Human Nature* (Routledge, forthcoming, 2013). He worked on the editorial board of the *International Journal of Jungian Studies* and serves on the Executive Committee of the International Association for Graduate Analytical Psychologists (AGAP). He teaches in Canada and Europe and recently lectured on Jung and Gérard de Nerval at the Bodmer Foundation.

David Tacey is Professor of Literature and Psychoanalytic Studies at La Trobe University, Melbourne. Tacey was born in Melbourne and grew up in Alice Springs, in central Australia, alongside Aboriginal cultures. It was the influence of Aboriginal cultures and philosophies that predisposed him to studying Jung's psychology, with its emphasis on the unseen world. He studied literature, psychology, and philosophy at Flinders and Adelaide Universities in the 1970s and, in the 1980s, completed post-doctoral studies in archetypal psychology and culture in the United States, under the direction of James Hillman in Dallas. He is the author of 12 books, including *Gods and Diseases* (2011), *Edge of the Sacred* (2009), *The Spirituality Revolution* (2003), and *ReEnchantment* (2000). Five of his books are on Jung and the psychology of religious experience, and these include *The Jung Reader* (2012), *The Idea of the Numinous* (2006, co-edited with Ann Casement), *Jung and the New Age* (2000), and *How to Read Jung* (2006). His books have been translated into several languages, including Spanish, Cantonese, Korean, and French.

ACKNOWLEDGEMENTS

We would like to thank the Scholarship Committee of the C. G. Jung Institute of San Francisco for the grant that helped defray the editing costs for this book. We are grateful, too, to LeeAnn Pickrell for her fine work in copy-editing and organizing the text. Kate Hawes, our editor at Routledge, has been most encouraging throughout the project. Finally, we would like to acknowledge the many scholars whose readings of Jung are not included here, but whose works have been an inspiration for us and for the authors of the essays in this collection.

Jean Kirsch and Murray Stein

INTRODUCTION

Jean Kirsch

The idea for this collection of essays came to me at the IAAP Congress in Montreal in 2010. Knowing of his interest in the variety of contemporary readings of Jung, I presented it to my good friend Murray Stein. He became enthusiastic as we discussed the possibility of inviting a group of prominent authors on Jung to contribute essays about why and how they read Jung's oeuvre, and he also agreed to co-edit the book with me as well as to contribute an essay. Together, we assembled the present collection. We asked the authors to be personal in their accounts, in addition to showing how they read Jung from their own perspectives. Let me explain where this idea came from in the context of my own experience of reading Jung's works.

I was introduced to Jung's writings in 1967 by my then husband-to-be, Tom Kirsch, one of the authors in this book. At the time I was in my fourth year of medical school at Stanford and intending to train in plastic surgery under the guidance of a professor whose specialty was the reconstruction of injured hands. Jung once made a comment that applied so well to me at that time, when he wrote about the mindset of doctors and the challenge they face when they try to understand his psychology.

> I have often found that the medical psychologists try to practice their art in the routine manner inculcated into them by the peculiar nature of their studies. The study of medicine consists on the one hand in storing up in the mind an enormous number of facts, which are simply memorized without any real knowledge of their foundations, and on the other hand in learning practical skills, which have to be acquired on the principle "Don't think, act!" Thus it is that, of all the professionals, the medical man has the least opportunity of developing the function of *thinking.* So it is no wonder that even psychologically trained doctors have the greatest difficulty in following my reflections, if they follow them at all. They have habituated themselves to handing out prescriptions and mechanically applying methods which they have not thought out themselves. This tendency is the most unsuitable that can be imagined for the

> practice of medical psychology, for it clings to the skirts of authoritarian theories and techniques and hinders the development of individual thought.[1]

Anyone who has been through medical school well understands the powerfully transformative nature of that experience. One's whole being is altered as one is shaped into a doctor.

As a result of my relationship to Tom, I changed direction and took up psychiatry as a specialty. I read a great deal of Jung's *Collected Works* in my years of psychiatric and then Jungian analytic education, but I found that I could grasp only fragments of his ideas and retain little of its content. I always felt that I was chasing after Jung in my mind, badgering him to say more or to elaborate more fully his pithy observations on human nature and the structure and function of the psyche. His seemingly digressive amplifications neither delighted nor informed me. On the contrary, they interfered with my learning! My intellect demanded the satisfaction of comprehending Jung and particularly of understanding how he created such difficulty for me, when he seemed to be so clear to others. My difficulty was compounded by the fact that my (by now) husband's sense of himself had been formed under the influence of Jung's ideas by his analyst parents, James and Hilde Kirsch. In Chapter 11, "A Lifelong Reading of Jung", Tom Kirsch gives an account of his early independent study of the powerful figure whose work dominated his childhood and adolescence. It is my experience that years of reading and rereading Jung and living and working in the context of a Jungian professional culture actually does re-form one's mind. The reformation of my mind was a rough and lengthy process.

While appreciating that the work of the Jungian analyst, like that of the physician, is as much art as science, I still expected to be able to acquire knowledge of analytical psychology in somewhat the same way I had learned biochemistry and pharmacology – that is, by approaching each new subject with the confidence that it could be learned through diligent attention to its fundamentals and progressively building upon the basics. I could not understand why this body of knowledge resisted my efforts. My difficulty is clarified by George Hogenson's comment that most of Jung's work is "pre-theoretical". Also, he recognized that scientific advances in Jung's lifetime fell short of producing adequate models with which he could frame his developing ideas about the psyche and its transformation.[2] As he reiterates in Chapter 9 of the present work,

> Jung presents a set of observations and hypotheses that are all too often taken to be final statements in a theory. This characteristic of Jung's work can be both intensely frustrating and intensely provocative at the same time, but I would suggest that it represents a continuation of Jung's attitude toward psychological research.

Despite my fairly good comprehension of the essence of Jung's psychology after a while and my growing ability to translate his ideas into terms that are relevant to the analytic process, I still had an unsatisfied and nagging question: what was it about Jung's writing that generated my continuing difficulty with following and retaining his texts? After many years of living with this dilemma, it happened that by chance I was asked to review Susan Rowland's book *Jung as a Writer*, and, since for this I would be entering a field that was brand new to me, I spent the next year reading and studying all her published work in order to understand more fully her perspective as a feminist writer of literary criticism.[3] Reading Rowland clarified much in Jung that had baffled me. For example, her explication of the way he constructs his arguments and the way she analyses his rhetorical style made sense of Jung's sudden reversals and abrupt pivots in his process of setting forth the evidence for his hypotheses. In her interpretation, Jung constructs his text as a net to hold and develop his ideas and intuitions rather than making a linear argument.[4] With Susan as my guide, I could take delight in Jung's creative genius. But above all, her thesis on the nature of Jung's overall goal – namely, to undermine the one-sided rationality of the Enlightenment and to restore the contemporary psyche to a state of balance between the rational and the nonrational, materialism and spirituality, consciousness and unconsciousness – became my touchstone in reading Jung. Now that this has been pointed out to me, I see it everywhere in his works. Having this perspective also clarifies why I have had so much difficulty reading Jung, given the enduring stamp of my earlier education in science and medicine, unmodified as it was by my too-brief acquaintance with the humanities.

My experience of reading Rowland was a major discovery. A non-analyst, someone not initiated into the art of containing the analytic process for another, could cast a totally new light on what I had been reading for decades and make Jung comprehensible, as none of my earlier teachers had done! Just as, in shaping my Jungian analytic practice, I had needed to be open to the theory and methods developed by contemporary psychoanalysts, I now find that Jungian scholars, whose primary focus is scholarly, not clinical, add a dimension to my perspective on Jung. Simultaneously, my curiosity about what draws us to Jung and how each of us reads him was piqued.

Murray Stein has recommended that Jung's recently published work, *The Red Book*, should be read deeply, in the manner described by Harold Bloom in *How to Read and Why*.[5] I found that idea intriguing and so looked at Bloom's work to orient my thinking about the essays we received for this book. Bloom's prologue offers a concise description of what he means by deep reading.[6] His first recommendation, borrowed from his own ideal reader, Dr Samuel Johnson, is to "clear your mind of can't", which he describes as "the peculiar vocabulary of a sect or coven".[7] Can Jung's psychological writing perhaps help us to follow this dictum, to clear our minds of cant? David Tacey makes a case for this. In Chapter 10, "Jung: Respect for the Non-literal", he passionately objects to the form of cant that was pressed upon him by his early religious upbringing and shows how reading biblical passages in the light of Jung's ideas gave him room to develop, spiritually, as a young man. Shiuya Liuh does something similar in Chapter 8, "Chinese Modernity and the Way of Return", in comparing Jung's inventive reading of *The Secret of the Golden Flower* to the original Chinese text, whose language (cant) she has found to be dead and restrictive. Bloom's second principle, "Do not attempt to improve your neighbor or your neighborhood by what or how you read",[8] definitely finds application within a movement that endorses individuation, which can, however, be misread and imposed upon one's neighbour as a moral good. In Chapter 7, we find Betsy Cohen "Tangled Up in Blue" and taking issue with the way some Jungian analysts have misused Jung's concept of the complexes to categorize the Other in their efforts to improve the neighbourhood.

Ralph Waldo Emerson is the source of Bloom's third principle: "A scholar is a candle which the love and desire of all men light".[9] Jungians have increasingly embraced the scholar and serious scholarship in recent decades. In Chapter 9, "Philosophy, the Thinking Function, and the Reading of Jung", George Hogenson shares his intellectual journey toward analytic training, giving us a deeper appreciation of the diversity and richness of experience that he brings to the field. Jungian literature added the potential for greater breadth and depth in 2001 with the founding of the International Association for Jungian Studies, a group that is open to analysts, academicians, and all interested people. This increasingly influential sector of Jung scholarship is well represented in this book by the contributions of Paul Bishop, Susan Rowland, and David Tacey, all non-analysts. In Chapter 4, "On Reading Jung in German: Jung's Significance for *Germanistik*", Bishop shows Jung writing in the noble tradition of German literary analysis and discussion. The influence of academic Jung studies also shows up in Craig Stephenson's Chapter 6, "Reading Frye Reading Jung", in which he gives us an account of Jung's influence upon the famous Canadian literary critic. Bloom's fourth principle is most liberating: "One must be an inventor to read well."[10] Bloom's long experience with reading and teaching has convinced him that "inventive reading" leads to self-trust, which "is not an endowment, but is the Second Birth of the mind". Fine examples of this principle are Susan Rowland's inventive reading/writing in Chapter 5, "Reading Jung for Magic: 'Active Imagination' for/as 'Close Reading' ", with her visions of Jung's nets and magic, giving us new windows to frame Jung's textual landscape. Chapter 3, "Jung and Alchemy: a Daimonic Reading", Stanton Marlan's essay in this collection, showing the way to a daimonic reading of Jung's alchemical texts, is an example of inventive reading. Also, in Chapter 2, "A Lecture for the End of Time – 'Concerning Rebirth' ", Murray Stein gives us a careful rereading of one of Jung's less-known essays and demonstrates the timelessness of Jung's apperceptions. Finally, I would adapt Bloom's fifth and perhaps most important principle, "the recovery of the ironic", to the purpose of reading Jung with *an appreciation for ambiguity.*[11] Ambiguity is the warp in the fabric of Jung's writing, and attention to this quality is essential to reading him in depth. Mark Saban has demonstrated this feature in Chapter 1, "Ambiguating Jung". Like irony, ambiguating Jung "demands a certain attention span and the ability to sustain antithetical ideas, even when they collide with one another".[12]

Why does Jung continue to engage the lives of so many intelligent and creative people in a lifelong study of his works? And how do they read him? These are the questions that came to me, and so I decided to ask these questions of others and find out where they led. This book represents a sampling of the strongest contemporary writers among Jungian readers. No single author here can teach *the* way to read Jung, but among them one may find clues that can suggest possible readings of Jung and lead to discovering one's own way.

Notes

1 C. G. Jung, "General aspects of dream psychology", in *The Structure and Function of the Psyche*, *The Collected Works of C. G. Jung*, vol. 8, Princeton, NJ, Princeton University Press, 1960, p. 526.

2 George Hogenson, "Archetypes: emergence and the psyche's deep structure", in J. Cambray and L. Carter (eds.), *Analytical Psychology: Contemporary Perspectives in Jungian Analysis*, pp. 32–55, Hove and New York, Brunner-Routledge, 2004.

3 Jean Kirsch, "Reading Jung with Susan Rowland", *Jung Journal*, 2007, vol. 1, nos. 1 and 2, pp. 13–48.

4 Susan Rowland, *Jung as a Writer*, London and New York, Routledge, 2005, p. 92.

5 Murray Stein in his televised seminar on Jung's *The Red Book* through Ashville Seminars, May 2010.

6 Harold Bloom, *How to Read and Why*, New York, Touchstone, pp. 21–9.

7 Ibid., p. 23.

8 Ibid., p. 24.

9 Ibid.

10 Ibid., p. 25.

11 Ibid.

12 Ibid., p. 27.

1

AMBIGUATING JUNG

Mark Saban

Mark Saban reads Memories, Dreams, Reflections with the same openness that one brings to a big dream or an active imagination. He captures the enthusiasm Jung brought to rediscovering, remembering, and mythologizing the most important moments of his life, while also noting Jung's ambivalence toward the "so-called autobiography", which Saban relates to a parallel tendency in Jung's psychology to undermine the univocality of the self. He suggests that the importance of this posthumously published text, which stands outside Jung's official body of writing, derives from Jung's willingness to reconfigure in this book the deeper meanings and ambiguities of his life's work.

J. K.

One of the few undisputed facts about the text we know as *Memories, Dreams, Reflections* (henceforth *MDR*)[1] is that, thanks to the groundbreaking work of Sonu Shamdasani[2] and Alan Elms,[3] we can no longer read it "naively" as Jung's autobiography. However, it would not be an overstatement to suggest that, in the wake of Freud and Jung, it has become difficult to persist in a naive reading of *any* text, if we mean by this the passive reception of what presents itself uncomplicatedly as univocal and unidirectional truth. This is not to suggest that all reading must be shadowed by a hermeneutics of suspicion, but rather that the very process of reading is subject to an inevitably reciprocal movement of meaning. For example, if analytical psychology itself is built on the idea that we do not read the world literally – as an object "out there" – but are already imaginatively intertwined with it, then how can our reading of any text, even one published in Jung's name, remain immune from such a notion? In other words, if to read a dream is to approach it through a motion of close attunement, opening us gradually and gently to the rich and ambiguous specificity of its very rhythms and images, so that eventually, *deo concedente*, an inner reverberation of meaning is attained, one that inhabits a paradoxical place of complexity and simplicity in which objective is seen through subjective and vice versa, why would we not bring such a notion of reading to the very texts that have brought us to this understanding, such as *MDR*?

A reading of this kind, which requires from the reader a certain willing vulnerability, a proneness to be affected by the alterity of the text, should be understood as quite different from a personalistic or pathologizing reading, one designed to reduce the text to a catalogue of "unconscious motivations" or "complex indicators". A reading of this prophylactic kind is evidently designed to protect the reader from contamination by the text. What, for example, saves Winnicott's famous review of *MDR*[4] from being reductive in this way, is that, despite an insistence upon diagnosing Jung as suffering from childhood schizophrenia, his reading of the text has transformed his attitude not only towards Jung, but also, more importantly, towards himself. Those who have gone on to dismiss Jung by parroting Winnicott's diagnoses, but without undergoing the transformative nature of his reading, have failed to enter the space in which true reading can occur.

It is quite clear from Jung's writings on the transference, among others, that he is quite aware of the impossibility of engaging psyche in depth without opening oneself to the potentially destabilizing experience of radical ambiguity. He asserts his commitment to the equivocal nature of psychological life in a 1952 letter to Zvi Zerblowsky:

> The language I speak must be ambiguous, must have two meanings, in order to do justice to the dual aspect of our psychic nature. I strive consciously and deliberately for ambiguity of expression, because it is superior to unequivocalness and reflects the nature of life.[5]

It is impossible to differentiate the ambiguities of reading from the ambiguities of self. They occur in the same place and derive from the same source. Jung's writings never stop circling the intricacies and paradoxes of subjectivity. Often Jung seeks to dismember us, pointing at our infinite dissociability, revealing the enlightenment subject as no more than a chimera, or, rather, a shoal of chimeras, an alchemical ocean of fishes' eyes, each with its own consciousness offering its own perspective. In such a sea, most of the old metaphysical self simply dissolves, and what survives bobs – tiny, uncertain, and unstable – on the vast surface of the deep. No longer impermeable and unitary, this is a self that no longer knows itself and is obscurely aware that it *can* no longer know itself in full. Once the master of language, now inextricably caught in the linguistic net, it has lost both confident agency and authoritative sovereignty.

But in uneasy tension with this centrifugal *solutio* comes the *coagulatio* of individuation, the mandala, the Self – a teleology that dictates an endless spiralling toward an (inevitably virtual) centre and a perpetual straining toward an (ultimately ineffable) meaning. Jung is read most fruitfully as a difficult place of tension and torsion – always holding the strain between impossible alternatives.

Nowhere is this more evident – because, as we shall see, it is not just stated but performed – than in the "so-called autobiography" as Jung insisted on calling what eventually saw print as the posthumous *Memories, Dreams, Reflections.* One reason why this text is a *locus classicus* for the enactment of ambiguity in Jung is because, as I shall attempt to show, it succeeds in achieving indeterminacy on several different, though related, levels.

Autobiography

As recently as the early 1970s, the field of autobiography seemed relatively secure as a bastion of the unitary self. James Olney writes in *Metaphors of the Self*:

> What is ... of particular interest to us in a consideration of the creative achievements of individual men [*sic*] and the relationship of those achievements to a life lived, on the one hand, and an autobiography of that life on the other is ... the isolate unique-ness that nearly everyone agrees to be the primary quality and condition of the individual and his experience.[6]

Olney offers an essentialist view of individuality, which, rising above social, political, or historical factors, achieves apotheosis in autobiography. This is a portrait of the enlightenment self, flourishing in its proper element: unified, univocal, unique.[7]

But even as Olney wrote in 1972, this notion of autobiography was beginning to suffer a profound internal destabilization. Battered for more than a century by antagonists as diverse as Marx, Nietzsche, and Freud, the concept of unitary selfhood was in the process of undergoing radical dismemberment by energies we can summarize under the names of Barthes, Lacan, and Derrida. Under such an attack, the genre of autobiography found itself deconstructed from within. Latent ambiguities of the self now began to be manifested, paradoxically in the very place that had hitherto provided for self-identity: autobiography itself.

The "essential core of selfhood", constituted in and by our self-narratives, appeared suddenly all-too-fragile. In this new light, the deeper and closer we read the autobiographical text, the more the all-important *I* seems to split: *I* as narrator, *I* as narratee, *I* as he or she who re-members, *I* who is re-membered in fiction.

Eventually, distinguishing the autobiographical text from any other text becomes hard. For Paul de Man, for example, autobiography consists of two persons constructing their own identities through reading each other, a process that establishes a "specular structure" within the text. The author reads him- or herself in autobiography, the subject of his or her own knowledge, and the writing *I* gets substituted for the written *I*. But, de Man goes on, this structure is merely a special case of what happens in any text that claims to be "by" someone: "any book with a readable title page is, to some extent, autobiographical".[8]

The so-called autobiography

As I have suggested, psychoanalysis constituted one of the primary threats to the unitary self and, therefore, to the very possibility of writing (or reading) the self as unitary. This is partly the case because to think of self as naively self-identical becomes impossible once one has recognized the potentially destabilizing factor of the unconscious psyche, whether characterized as id and superego or as anima and shadow. But with regard to life stories, what is equally important is the complex way in which psychoanalytic work simultaneously weaves together and tears apart the fabric of our self-narratives.

We can catch the ambivalent nature of this process at the very birth of psychoanalysis. In his first case histories, Freud wants to tell us the story of the patient, to offer us the meaning behind it, and to show us how he, Freud, has uncovered the truth. In effect, what we eventually read is a dialogue (and not infrequently a competition) between Freud's version of the story and that of the patient. And all this occurs within a therapy that has the stated goal of enabling the patient to achieve full possession of her own story.

These narratives also serve to weave Freud's life closely into the development of his theory. The early case studies are at least as much the story of a man called Freud discovering a new science, as they are the story of the patient. As the secret lives of the patients are revealed, so are the secrets of the new science of psychoanalysis. With *The Interpretation of Dreams*,[9] the autobiographical element becomes more disguised, but even more central: the dreams interpreted are Freud's own dreams, the analysis his own self-analysis.

In his own *An Autobiographical Study*, Freud makes an attempt to disentangle the personal from the theoretical: "The Autobiographical Study shows how psychoanalysis came to be the whole content of my life and rightly assumes that no personal experiences of mine are of any interest in comparison to my relations to that science."[10] As Linda Anderson comments, "Oddly ... for someone uniquely aware of the decisive influence of the hidden aspects of the psyche on the public self, Freud pushes his own private and affective life to the margins of his autobiographical text."[11] It is as if the overtly autobiographical nature of the early case histories has become superfluous for Freud, as his writings on psychoanalysis, he realizes, constitute and are constituted by all that matters in his life.

In the case of *An Autobiographical Study* then, such a sketchy and blatantly unsatisfactory ("no personal experiences of mine are of any interest") enterprise is, in effect, inviting the reader to fill in the gaps and, like a psychoanalyst, explore the very ambiguities that Freud is attempting to erase. But Freud's insistence that "psychoanalysis came to be the whole content of my life", can, of course, also be read to mean that Freud's life came to be the whole content of psychoanalysis. Such a claim lends support to a fundamental and oft-repeated belief of Jung's, that "every psychology – my own included – has the character of a subjective confession".[12] When Jung playfully said, "Thank God I am Jung and not a Jungian", he was making a serious point about the paradoxes that spring up around a psychology that purports to offer to all a more or less clear map of the territory of "individuation", even though the map is itself closely modelled upon Jung's own personal and peculiar psychic development. It would sometimes seem that individuation is all about doing it your way, so long as you do it Jung's way.

By the time he had celebrated his 80th birthday, Jung had made it very clear that, not only was it *theoretically* necessary for his psychology to be his alone, but also, in fact, it had emerged out of his own inner and outer experiences. What, then, beyond a kind of tautological embroidery, could the project of an autobiography have to offer him or his reading public? Replying in 1952 to an enquiry about the possibility of a biography, he offered two related reasons for avoiding it:

> As long as people don't understand what I have done with psychology there is little use for a biography. My psychology and my life are interwoven to such an extent that one cannot make my biography readable without telling people at the same time about the things I have found out about the unconscious.[13]

Nor did he see how it could be done. How could anyone manage to "disentangle this monstrous Gordian knot of fatality, denseness and aspirations and what-not!"?[14]

Jung's other stated reason for disliking biography in general was that it was seldom *true:* "I know too many autobiographies, with their self-deceptions and downright lies, and I know too much about the impossibility of self-portrayal, to want to venture on any such attempt."[15] This question of truth and fictionality is one that haunts recent writing on biography and particularly autobiography. As Jung implies, the project of writing a life, and especially one's own life, is problematic because it tends to reveal "the impossibility of its own dream: what begins in the presumption of self-knowledge ends in the creation of a fiction that covers over the premises of its construction".[16]

By 1957, however, under pressure from Kurt Wolff of Pantheon Press, Jung had suspended his reluctance sufficiently to allow some kind of bio/autobiographical project to begin. His continuing ambivalence about the enterprise found expression in his insistence on referring to it as "my so-called autobiography" and "Aniela Jaffé's project". R. F. C. Hull even reported a suggestion of Jung's that the book should be entitled "Fragments from an Unintentional Autobiography".[17] Jung also obdurately refused to let it be published in his lifetime or to allow it into *The Collected Works.* The principal agents in the creation of the book may have hoped that Jung's initial ambivalence would resolve as the project moved forward, but as Jaffé put it, "To the day of his death the conflict between affirmation and rejection was never entirely settled".[18]

Jung did, however, manage to find certain characteristic ways to overcome some of his objections to the autobiographical form. With regard to the question of truth, the published text of *MDR* is unabashed in its ingenious solution to this issue; on the first page, it simply states: "Whether or not the stories are 'true' is not the problem."[19] Here, then, Jung cuts the Gordian knot. He achieves this sleight of hand by remaining loyal to the logic of his own psychology. That psychology has always been more interested in psychic reality than in reality as such. Psychoanalysis was born at the moment when Freud came to the realization that what mattered psychologically was not the literal truth of the "memories" that his patients were recounting, but rather their symbolic meaning. From the very beginning "truth" became bracketed and suspended within depth psychology. It was made ambiguous: a psychological truth can be, in a sense, true and also not true.

Now Jung applies this fundamental insight to his own memories, his own stories. To do so, he takes a step further than he had done before. The reason, Jung says, that truth is not the problem is that what he is undertaking in this text is the telling of a myth. As everyone knows, true/false criteria do not apply to myths. But this is not a myth you have heard before, he continues, it is "my personal myth", it is "my fable, my truth".[20]

The fully paradoxical nature of what Jung is conveying here should be noted. In *The Collected Works*, Jung regards myth as a collective phenomenon, made up of traditional stories whose origins are lost in the mists of time but which contain a wealth of archetypal motifs and symbols that modern man can recognize as comparable to those spontaneously produced by the individual psyche in dream, fantasy, and psychosis. When he refers, as here, to a "personal myth", there is a jarring clash of incompatible associations: how can the personal be mythic; how can myth be personal? "Personal myth", if it means anything, implies an impossible collision between the individual and the collective, the timeless and the time-specific, the general and the particular. What Jung has in mind is illuminated by a passage a page later: "In the end the only events in my life worth telling are those when the imperishable world irrupted into this transitory one."[21]

This also helps us see how Jung manages to find a way around one of his other objections to autobiography: "My psychology and my life are interwoven to such an extent that one cannot make my biography readable without telling people at the same time about the things I have found out about the unconscious."[22] Jung's solution is to invert the autobiographical project radically by producing a text for which the primary goal is the remembering of "the things [he has] found out about the unconscious" through the recounting of those very moments "when the imperishable world irrupted into this transitory one".

Jung had shied away from traditional autobiography partly because he recognized its problematic tendency to collude in the monumentalizing of a (fictional) ego identity, but having now discovered a way to re-vision it as a true Self-writing, a writing from the Self, he could begin to allow the text to begin to shape itself.

The early title for the autobiography, "Improvised Memories", nicely captures the quality of spontaneity that characterizes the early chapters of *MDR*. Jung starts with this avowal: "Thus it is that I have now undertaken, in my eighty-third year, to tell my personal myth."[23] His emphasis on the precise year of the undertaking is intended to mark the *contemporary* nature of what he was attempting: this is new, fresh work, he says, that could only have been accomplished now, at *this* moment. Analytic work concerned with memories of past childhood events often finds its transformative meaning in the momentous and spontaneous *present event* of that very work, rather than in some supposed literal past, and particularly in the patient's appreciation that freedom and choice are to be found only in this momentous and spontaneous present. So it is that Jung's three chapters on his early life achieve their freshness of meaning in the evident excitement that accompanies Jung's re-membering, a re-membering that enables him to connect, re-vision, and discover meanings that are taking form *for the very first time*, both for him as writer and for us as readers. The sense of immediacy but also of psychic necessity that accompanied Jung's breakthrough as he started to write those early chapters is palpable: "[T]his 'autobiography' is now taking a direction quite different from what I had imagined at the beginning", Jung wrote at the time:

> It has become a necessity for me to write down my early memories. If I neglect to do so for a single day, unpleasant physical symptoms immediately follow. As soon as I set to work they vanish and my head feels perfectly clear.[24]

As this new phase began, Jaffé wrote to Wolff, "[S]omething so wonderful and meaningful happened … Jung himself is writing his autobiography all over again … so much had become clear to [Jung] and especially the meaning of his life which he had apparently not seen to its full extent."[25] According to Jung, "the demon and the creative force" needed to run their course, and that this would only occur once he had established "the connection to [his] scientific work". What needs emphasizing here is that the writing Jung was doing was seen by him as of the utmost importance *to his psychology*.

Anima ventriloquy

Before venturing into a close reading of just what it was in the first three chapters that seemed so significant to Jung, it is worth noting what a strikingly ambiguous text *MDR* is. As noted previously, the autobiographical form per se has proved as unstable and heterogeneous as its apparent subject – the self. In this particular "autobiography", this instability is magnified by virtue of its dual authorship. It is apparently Jung's autobiography, but it is also authored by Jaffé. Some of the text was written by Jung alone, some by Jaffé alone, and some was the product of conversations between the two. This process was what both Jung and Jaffé had signed up for, and it was reflected in the terms of the original contract, which divided profits equally between Jung's family and Jaffé. Crucially, it also enabled Jung to maintain his ambivalent attitude to the book and retain a critical detachment from what he tended to refer to as Jaffé's project. But even this attempt at distancing was complicated by the fact that Jaffé, the "ghostwriter", was already practised at assuming Jung's voice. Not only was she Jung's secretary, but also, in the aftermath of Emma Jung's death, when Jung did not feel up to writing letters, she even answered his correspondence for him, subject to Jung's minor corrections.[26]

As both secretary and erstwhile analysand of the great man, Jaffé was thoroughly saturated in Jung. When we hear, therefore, that she wrote some of Jung's letters for him, or that she "composed" whole tranches of *MDR*, this is perhaps not as shocking as it at first sounds. One might even suggest that the real question for Jaffé was less whether she was capable of writing as Jung than whether she was capable of writing as Jaffé. Arguably, Jung's animation of Jaffé had enabled her, in return, to animate Jung. In other words, if any ventriloquism was going on, it is far from clear who was the dummy and who the ventriloquist. One interesting irony of the situation was that the chapter of *MDR* in which Jung discovers and allows himself to be ventriloquized by the anima – "I reflected that the 'woman within me' did not have the speech centers I had. And so I suggested that she use mine"[27] – was one of the chapters composed by Jaffé, mostly from the 1925 seminar notes.[28] I need not labour the complexities of a situation in which the story of Jung discovering and giving voice to his inner feminine (through the voice of an ex-patient) is here written by Jaffé (a woman ex-patient), though in the voice of Jung.

To complicate the picture even more, we should remember that this piece of writing has emerged partly from a process in which Jung explicitly urged Jaffé, as he reports in a letter to Kurt Wolff to "[a]sk critical or curious questions interfering with my propositions. This could loosen up my explanations as well as liven them up, if done skilfully."[29] If the anima is, as Susan Rowland puts it, "a textual anarchist" who "refuses to be consistent, defined, corralled into concepts, and stable truths",[30] then Jung is, in effect, consciously attempting to achieve an anima effect in the writing of *MDR* when he asks Jaffé to function in this way – an incitement of the anima to haunt his writing into disruption.

MDR turns out to have been ghostwritten in more ways than one. Rowland has drawn attention to the ways in which, within the text, "gender as the inner other arrives in the company of ghosts".[31] Moreover, the erasure or absence from the text of all the most significant women in Jung's life, with the exception of his mother, tends, for the modern reader, to make their haunting of the text that much more glaring.[32] However one regards it, this is certainly a text with a very curious relation to the feminine.

As Rowland, after Charet, points out, anima has, for Jung, much in common with the figure of the medium.[33] Just as the spirit world makes its presence felt through the vessel of the medium, so, for Jung, the individual makes contact with the world of the archetypes through the anima, the doorway to the unconscious. Jung's refusal in *MDR* to give space to the feminine, in the shape of the various important women in his life, has been read as a symptom of profound unrelatedness, or as a masculine resistance to the threatening destabilization of ego that the encounter with the anima inevitably brings about. I suspect that a more interesting approach would be to attempt to do justice to the ambivalence that the text presents by allowing it to be heard as an expression of profound ambiguity.

Two souls alas...

I now want to pursue the ways in which this emerging motif of the necessary and productive friction between incompatible elements of the psyche is developed in *MDR* and how the elaboration of such themes may not only feed back reflexively into our reading of *MDR* itself, but also enable us to revisit *The Collected Works* from a fundamentally and productively equivocal perspective. I shall begin by looking closely at those important passages that persistently, almost obsessively, revisit images and ideas of divided identity in the early chapters of *MDR*.

Jung's clearest thematization of the motif of doubleness occurs when he discusses his two personalities, No. 1 and No. 2.:

> Somewhere deep in the background I always knew that I was two persons. One was the son of my parents, who went to school and was less intelligent, attentive, hard-working, decent, and clean than many other boys. The other was grown up old, in fact skeptical, mistrustful, remote from the world of men, but close to nature, the earth, the sun, the moon, the weather, all living creatures, and above all close to the night, to dreams, and to whatever "God" worked directly in him.[34]

Before addressing the two personalities in *MDR*, however, it is first necessary to take note of the context out of which they emerge. This means examining those earliest experiences of Jung's that he describes as providing him with a mysterious sense of otherness and that burdened him with a secret that could not be told. First, however, we must remind ourselves of Jung's parents and the tension that both held and separated them, as this too played a part in the gradual formation of his abiding internal division.

The parental binary

Jung's description of his parents in *MDR* may, of course, be taken simply on the level of autobiographical fact, but, for the purposes of this chapter, I intend to approach the parental dyad on a more symbolic level. The theme of Jung's relation to his father and mother runs throughout the entire book; his dreams about them are still occurring in the late 1940s when he is writing *Mysterium Coniunctionis*. By then, the parental figures have long since become abstracted into "contradictory principles". But even in Jung's personal/factual description of them in the early chapters of *MDR*, a sense of a necessary opposition gets conveyed that prefigures and underlies the state of disunity that he later elaborates. This is explicitly thematized in the passages in which he relates both parents (and the tension between them) to the ongoing strain between his two personalities.

Jung's personality No. 2 is overtly linked to his mother, especially in her own No. 2 guise, which is described as "uncanny", "unexpected and frightening", "archaic and ruthless; ruthless as truth and nature", "the embodiment of ... the 'natural' mind".[35] The mother's "nighttime" personality is also described as closely connected to the occult and to madness. Jung's personality No. 1 is directly associated by him with what he calls the "paternal tradition".[36] Not only does this refer to the specific fact of Paul Jung's inability (as Jung saw it) to break out of a conventional and dogmatic approach to religion and touch the living numinosity of the Other, but also it encompasses the much broader field of the patriarchal intellectual/cultural hegemony of Western modernity before the First World War. For Jung, the masculine is "dead" because it fails to acknowledge that "Other", which, in an autobiographical context, shows up in Jung's early life as "the secret", becomes associated with the uncanny mother, and then becomes identified as personality No. 2. More broadly, this version of the masculine takes the form of a materialistic and positivistic scientific tradition that refuses to find a place for the "Other", thereby exiling it to marginal fields such as the occult, the primitive, the insane, and so on.

Jung's parents' failed marriage also symbolizes the sterility of a dead masculine (father) existing completely out of relation to the living feminine (uncanny mother), such that neither is able to help the other towards transformation. It is a failed *coniunctio* that leaves Jung, as its inheritor, with his life's task: "Something had remained unfinished and was still with my parents; that is to say, it was still latent in the unconscious and hence reserved for the future."[37] This task becomes apparent to Jung in later life when he dreams of the house with two rooms: one of which is his father's laboratory and the other that is his mother's – a haunted meeting place for "ghostly married couples".[38] Jung's task was not only to find a way to enable the two revenants, father and mother, to be in fruitful relation, a problem set him in the form of the difficult tension between his own personalities No. 1

and No. 2, but also to create a psychology that would enable others too to find a way to do justice to this "play and counterplay" within them, which "is played out in every individual".

When Jung became "crown prince" of the psychoanalytic movement, he was able to project onto Freud all the numinosity of the life-giving Father, but as that sense of potential ebbed away, Freud was revealed as the old dead father in a new guise: Jung realized with growing dismay that, like Paul Jung, Freud was desperately hanging on to his faith and was unable to brook doubts, though in Freud's case the faith was invested in the sexual basis of neurosis.

Jung needed to break with Freud, not because of any specific theoretical differences between them (though such differences did exist), and not because Freud was intolerant of dissent (although he was), but primarily because for Jung psychoanalysis had become associated with the dead hand of the father, no longer functioning as either a vessel that could contain, or as a matrix that could birth, the conflicting energies that are represented in *MDR* as personalities No. 1 and No. 2. He finally came to realize that he would have to fashion his own vessel/matrix for that purpose.

The secret

The word *secret* recurs again and again in *MDR*. In the first three chapters alone, it appears at least 27 times. Jung says that the possession of an "inviolable secret which must never be betrayed" was "the essential factor of [his] boyhood".[39] It was initially applied to the phallus dream, which Jung describes as initiating him into "the secrets of the earth" and as his "first great secret".[40] The secret subsequently achieved solidity in the shapes of the little mannikin and the stone, his "secret treasure" in the attic.[41] Renos Papadopoulos has drawn attention to the fact that each of these various secret objects and experiences relates to "an other in Jung's own personality", and that, later, when Jung came to identify his personality No. 2, it was directly linked with these "secrets" in that it "had all the qualities of the previous Others".[42]

The experience that pointed most clearly to later developments and that Jung describes as a "feeling of curious and fascinating darkness", was of sitting on the stone and wondering if he were sitting on the stone or if he was the stone on which he sat.[43] This mysterious sense of doubleness seems to have been the first conscious opening of a division between Jung as normal time-bound boy and Jung as eternal "it". Thirty years later, Jung, now a busy professional psychiatrist and married with children, stood again in the presence of the stone and was frightened by the "pull of that other world", which made even his vivid and engrossing life as No. 1 seem distant and unreal.[44] The "secret" behind these experiences possessed no positive content as such, that is to say, there was no actual secret that could be told;

its mysterious sense of significance derived from its ability to point to what was to develop into personality No. 2. Jung increasingly felt that possession of the secret marked him out in some way as different and constituted a "powerful formative influence".[45]

Split?

One of the most striking aspects of Jung's discussion of the two personalities in *MDR* is his refusal to conceptualize them according to the system we find throughout his mature psychological writings. He never, for example, applies the term *shadow*, or *Self*, to either. Nor does he parallel the two personalities with conscious and unconscious. We can regard this refusal as being in accord with his decision both to keep *MDR* out of the officially recognized body of *The Collected Works* and to find a different translator for it as well. Jung seems to have wanted *MDR* to offer a perspective upon his psychology that differed from everything that he had written so far.

Nowhere in *The Collected Works* is the emphasis upon the dual nature of the human personality so powerfully expressed as in the first three chapters of *MDR*. Jung is adamant that this interior division is not to be understood as a pathological condition:

> The play and counterplay between personalities No. 1 and No. 2, which has run through my whole life, has nothing to do with a "split" or dissociation in the ordinary medical sense. On the contrary, it is played out in every individual.[46]

This claim is a very strong one, unparalleled elsewhere in his writings. Jung seems to want us to see this divided nature as a psychological given, a fundamental of existence, shared by all, even if "perceived by the very few". By this account, what marks Jung out from an early age is his fateful awareness that, as well as his normal everyday identity, he also has access to a very different identity. It is this awareness that "two souls, alas, are lodged within [his] breast" that, although it opens up a world of difficulty for him, also grants him access to great psychological depths.

Anyone acquainted with Jung's psychology must surely harbour an expectation on first reading *MDR* that Jung's early divided state will, at some point in the narrative, be outgrown: that he will eventually integrate the two parts into a more homogeneous whole. Nothing in *MDR* supports such an idea. On the contrary, Jung is quite clear about this:

> The opposites and the contradictions between them do not vanish ... even when for a moment they yield before the impulse to action. They constantly threaten the unity of the personality, and entangle life again and again in their dichotomies.[47]

There is also an abiding temptation to adapt Jung's statements about the two personalities into a more familiar Jungian narrative. For example, Marie-Louise von Franz, in *C. G. Jung: His Myth in Our Time*, identifies personality No. 1 with Jung's ego and No. 2 with the unconscious.[48] She puts a great deal of stress upon Jung's storm lantern dream, which she interprets as a crucial turning point at which Jung understood that No. 1 was his ego and that No. 2 was the unconscious and from that point on ceased to identify with No. 2.[49] It is not, from the classical Jungian perspective, that such an interpretation is *wrong*, but that it remains unsatisfying because it does not seem to do justice to the particular way Jung articulates the split in *MDR*, especially his insistence that his engagement with these two aspects was a *lifelong* activity and was never outgrown: "the play and counterplay" between the two personalities, Jung insists, "has run through my whole life". Moreover, one cannot help feeling that if Jung had wanted to slot his discussion of the two personalities into his own ready-made categories, then he would have done so. The closest he gets to doing so is when he describes No. 1 and No. 2 as "two contradictory aspects" of his ego, which is not saying much more than that he felt a split between them.[50]

Early on, Jung's No. 1 is the personality through which he functions as an ordinary boy, "less intelligent, attentive, hard-working, decent, and clean than many other boys".[51] It is characterized by conventional character faults, conventional reading habits, and conventional ambitions for the future. Later it becomes more closely aligned with school-learned knowledge and the systematic pursuit of "questions ... consciously framed".[52] In the realm of school and university, it leads eventually to an identification of personality No. 1 with the world of science. In the realm of "ordinary life", it means the active decision "to go forward into study, moneymaking, responsibilities, entanglements, confusions, errors, submissions, defeats",[53] that is, the usual stuff of the first half of life.

The common factor to all these highly varied expressions of personality No. 1 is not so much their *conventional* nature as the emphasis upon *limitation* that tends to accompany these conventional aspects of life. With regard to Jung's father, the limitation took the form of an inability or unwillingness to break through to a more numinous spirituality. It takes its most abstract form in the embrace of a scientific *Weltanshauung* that is reliant upon various ideas of finitude: measurability, predictability, and the ability to conceptualize logically.

Paradoxically, personality No. 2 felt for Jung both deeply personal (it was his "true self"),[54] but also deeply other. It extends to infinitude in space and time (future and past), and it breaks all scientific and logical boundaries by being imperishable, irrational, unquantifiable, and impossible to conceptualize. Inevitably, perhaps, its definition becomes caught up with the idea of totality and God, but even there, it is the God of negative theology. What all these varied aspects of personality No. 2 have in common is the motif of boundlessness. Personality No. 2 is thus, in every sense, however trivial and however profound, Other to personality No. 1.

We can begin to see how Jung's remark at the beginning of *MDR*, "In the end the only events in my life worth telling are those when the imperishable world irrupted into this transitory one", gets subsequently expanded and fleshed out in his account of the conflict between personality No. 1 and personality No. 2. He is making the important statement that the history of these irruptions is the (secret) history of his life and that, as such, it has conditioned the shape and *telos* of his work. Moreover, the place of the irruption is the place where the mythic and the personal become intertwined.

His transitory life, with all its limitations, is, of course, his place of dwelling, but Jung insists that it is an essential characteristic of that life that it is perennially haunted by in-breaks of (mythic) otherness. That otherness is not a *relative* otherness, one that can be erased through a reduction into sameness,[55] but it is nonetheless an alterity that is experienced as very personal. In the form of personality No. 2, it can never be integrated into or contained by personality No. 1. Evidently, what is without limit can never be included in what is limited. The two are not balanced polar opposites, but radically unsymmetrical. They do not inhabit the same category; indeed personality No. 2 is defined by its inaccessibility to categorization. And yet No. 1's awareness that the world of personality No. 2 is "out there/in there" makes all the difference to the way "ordinary" life is lived. In Jung's early life, the two personalities problematize each other. Jung could not quite just get on with being an ordinary schoolboy because he was too aware of that other personality who lurked just out of sight: this was the burden of the unspeakable secret. Yet the necessity and forward movement of Jung's conventional goals and ambitions could never allow him to be simply absorbed into the timelessness of "God's world".

It is the sheer incommensurability between the two realms as described in Jung's account of his life that presents us with an important new perspective upon his psychology. Analytical psychology in its classical form, as presented in *The Collected Works*, is strongly characterized by a dynamic model of psyche animated by multiple polar tensions within the psyche: Jung's typology hangs on the traction of multiple opposites (extra/introversion, rational/irrational, feeling/thinking, intuition/sensation); archetypal theory constantly emphasizes polarity and syzygy (for instance, anima/animus and puer/senex) and stresses the movement of psychic enantidromia. This model also locates opposites within opposites (unconscious within conscious and vice versa, senex within puer and vice versa). Individuation is characterized as an ongoing process of integration, enabled by compensation, and culminating in the paradoxical *coniunctio oppositorum*.

Thus Jung's psychology, as articulated in *The Collected Works*, carefully positions the dynamics of the psyche outside the rules of classical logic, such as the law of noncontradiction, which have no force within the Jungian psychic economy. However, by emphasizing the symmetrical nature of the opposites, he enables us to think of them as, in a sense, dependent upon each other and, therefore, ultimately as a possible unity. In other words, however violent the strife, however painful the tension between the opposites, there comes a point at which, if they have been sufficiently "held", they can always be resolved or "transcended". Although Jung's model of the transforming psyche allows for, in Goethe's words, "formation, transformation, the Eternal Mind's eternal re-creation"[56] and possesses a capacity for huge heterogeneity and multiplicity within itself, its *telos* is always resolution; its goal is always oneness. However, what gets introduced in *MDR* with the two personalities is what seems to be a radically different approach to those tensions, contradictions, and aporias that characterize psychic life. Because the two personalities are, according to *MDR*, radically incompatible, they do not lend themselves to any attempt to conjoin them into wholeness. Hence, Jung's insistence that the tension between them is never resolved but lasts the whole life.

Ambiguating Jung

What is apparent, even from this cursory survey, is that *MDR* is profoundly haunted by ambiguity, particularly when it comes to the Self: I have drawn attention to the issues of self-destabilization introduced by the autobiographical genre itself; I have noted the indeterminacy of authorship that characterized the composition of *MDR* as auto/biography, and finally, I have identified a persistent theme of instability in the region of Self and Other as experienced in the two personalities.

How, then, as readers, should we approach a work as anomalous as *MDR*? My argument has been that Jung's insistence on keeping *MDR* out of *The Collected Works* and his refusal to allow it to be attached to "C. G. Jung" (qua author of *The Collected Works*) should be seen as a (more or less) conscious attempt to offer a final (posthumous) perspective upon the "official" body of analytical psychology. Without being overtly critical or undermining, *MDR* offers a subtle destabilization of all the sedimented dogma that has accumulated around "C. G. Jung" and thus effectively counters the tendency toward the univocal and monolithic, which bedevils any long-standing theoretical framework.

What then are the implications of *MDR* for our reading of Jung's psychology? Jung offers us a psyche that is made up of two, equally necessary, but entirely incompatible, "personalities": one of which binds us to this life, this body, this limited set of possibilities, this limited range of conceptual expression; and the other, through its radical alterity, that challenges those limits, dissolves those boundaries, and situates itself outside of accepted conceptual expression. *Neither can be reduced to the other; neither is more "real" nor more fundamental than the other.*

I need to note again that the attempt to articulate this state of affairs immediately constellates a pressure to fall into classical Jungian terminology, to refer, for example, to personality No. 1 as ego and personality No. 2 as Self. Given that Jung himself chooses *not* to express himself in this way when discussing the two personalities, such a pressure must be strongly resisted. Were we to fall into describing them as ego and Self, we would immediately reintroduce a whole set of hierarchical assumptions – precisely those assumptions that are being put into question. For example, the classical assumption that ego is ultimately in the service of the Self immediately places the two personalities into a similar relation. We need to be reminded that Jung does not characterize personality No. 1 as in any way inferior or subservient to personality No. 2, or vice versa. What he does imply is that when he attempted to live exclusively in the realm of either No. 1 or No. 2, he did not flourish as a human being. To the extent that Jung eventually achieved a mature attitude toward this state of affairs, that attitude consisted in an acceptance of the interminable nature of the play and counterplay between the two personalities. For Jung, it became not a question of either/or, but rather of both/and. This is a strong suggestion that, ultimately incompatible though they are, both personalities need to be lived. Jung concretely exemplified this in his decision to live simultaneously in two houses, Küsnacht and Bollingen.

If we translate this insight into our further reading of Jung, we gain a deeper understanding of his emphasis in the letter to Zerblowsky (quoted previously) on the importance of ambiguity. His reference there to the "dual aspect of our psychic nature" indicates a recognition that the psyche dwells in two contradictory realms and that psychic life consists of the difficult negotiation of that fact. Given that clarity and univocality are qualities identified with personality No. 1, any clear, univocal statement about psyche must inevitably function as a betrayal of the realm of qualities identified with personality No. 2 and can, therefore, only ever function as a partial, and inaccurate, statement about psyche.

My suggestion is that Jung invites us to do some difficult psychological work when we read his writings: the work of ambiguation. To ambiguate Jung means to read his texts as ambiguous, even when the statements they contain appear superficially unambiguous. The task is to keep awake to the voice of whichever personality is *not* most audibly present at any one time: to try to catch, behind the voice that is most overt in the text, that trace of the Other that haunts it like a harmonic overtone. According to von Franz, Jung once said, "Everything I have written has a double bottom".[57]

An ambiguated reading is particularly necessary in those texts in which Jung first attempts to differentiate, clarify, and systematize the "stream of lava" that burst into his "confrontation with the unconscious":

> I saw that so much fantasy needed firm ground underfoot, and that I must first return wholly to reality. For me, reality meant scientific comprehension. I had to draw concrete conclusions from the insights the unconscious had given me and that task was to become a life

> work.... My science was the only way I had of extricating myself from that chaos ... I took great care to try to understand every single image, every item of my psychic inventory, and to classify them scientifically so far as this was possible and, above all, to realize them in actual life.[58]

We may understand those parts of *The Collected Works* written in the years immediately after the events he describes here as Jung's attempts to fashion consciously, and to translate into the language of No. 1, this overwhelming in-break of No. 2. Jung's motives for undertaking such a project were, as he admits, at least partly defensive. He needed to "extricate [him]self from that chaos" that "threatened to trap him in its thicket" and strangle him "like jungle creepers".[59] By utilizing the language of No. 1 – "*rigorous* ... understanding", "scientific comprehension",[60] he was attempting to bind the pandemonium into a psychological system. That Jung was in many ways successful in such an attempt is a remarkable achievement, but it is my contention that the system created in this way nonetheless stifled the development of what had the potential to become a more flexible and ambiguous psychology. We should remember, however, that Jung never regarded analytical psychology as a closed structure: he continued to embellish and amplify his core insights until his death.

The texts written in the immediate aftermath of the shattering "confrontation with the unconscious" seem to be trying so hard to keep the disruptive power of No. 2 under control that they sometimes fail to allow its Otherness to be fully present. Jung acknowledges in *MDR* that "it was only after some twenty years ... that I reached some degree of understanding of my fantasies".[61] For all the insights these works possess, they seem to function, on the manifest level at least, as textual mandalas – magic circles offering systematic polarities and complementarities that keep No. 1 safe and contained. Those texts of Jung's in which both No. 1 and No. 2 are somehow co-present are truer to the psyche and, therefore, more psychologically successful.

The manifest reason for Jung's enthusiastic embrace of the literature and visual world of alchemy, an enthusiasm that grew only more intense during the last 35 years of his life, was his intuition that it functioned as a parallel to what he had described as the individuation process. The extraordinary fertility of this hugely heterogeneous set of texts and pictures made them invaluable to Jung, who was all too aware that no single case history could hope to be remotely representative of a process that varied in almost every way from person to person. However, it is no coincidence that the alchemical texts Jung seized upon are also rich seams of ambiguity: it is not an exaggeration to say there is hardly a term in alchemy that is not open to multiple, often contradictory, interpretations.

By employing such radical polysemy, and by avoiding the attempt to conceptualize prematurely what was, by its nature, beyond containment, Jung is enabled to write a psychology that did justice to the dual nature of the psyche. The language he used thus manages to be simultaneously concrete and ambiguous, reflecting the duality that his beloved alchemy itself acknowledged in its double exhortation: *ora et labora*.

Conclusion

There are striking, though not surprising, parallels between the work of reading, as I have been attempting to describe it, and the work of psychotherapy, a work that Jung never ceased to pursue, even in the depths of his confrontation with the unconscious. In the consulting room, the therapist reads the patient reading the therapist. This work, too, is made up of a highly developed reciprocal dance involving an ongoing movement of intertwined pattern and chaos. Points of certainty and limitation in both patient and therapist require constant dissolution, and places of vagueness and confusion need to be constantly congealed: *solve et coagula*, as the alchemists put it. The transformative nature of the process requires mutuality, though it would be naïve and unrealistic to assume that it is perfectly symmetrical.[62] Behind these dynamics is the unsymmetrical play of same and Other that occurs between and within both therapist and patient, the very same play that Jung describes in his description of the two personalities in *MDR*.

This chapter has been concerned with the reading of a particular book, but conclusions may be drawn from it that perhaps apply not only to the reading of all Jung's writings but also to reading in a wider sense. Jung shows us in *MDR* how the coexistence of two personalities throughout his life and work, and the resulting oscillation between them, enabled his eventual recognition of the psyche as a region of irreducible ambiguity, an ambiguity reflected not just in the content of *MDR* but also in its form and origin. In the light of this, we, his readers, are implicitly encouraged to return to the 20 volumes of his *Collected Works*, and reambiguate those aspects of his writing that, for various reasons, have undergone a kind of sedimentation into singleness of meaning and rigidity of structure.[63] In order to accomplish such a reading, we need to remain open to the difficulties and possibilities inherent in our divided natures and allow, in our turn, the "play and counterplay" to be sustained even within that double-reading. This is what is difficult about this task, this attempt to revive and re-vision the complex and irregular interweaving of Jung's personality No. 1 with No. 2. This re-vision cannot be achieved at a distance, but only through a further interweaving, whereby we entwine our own doubleness into Jung's and hence become accomplices in his opus, which necessarily becomes our own.

Notes

1 C. G. Jung, *Memories, Dreams, Reflections* (rev. edn), New York, Pantheon Books, 1973.
2 S. Shamdasani, "Memories, dreams, omissions", in P. Bishop (ed.), *Jung in Contexts: A Reader*, pp. 33–50, London and New York, Routledge, 1999.
3 A. C. Elms, *Uncovering Lives: The Uneasy Alliance of Biography and Psychology*, New York and Oxford, Oxford University Press, 1994.
4 D. W. Winnicott, "Review of *Memories, Dreams, Reflections* by C. G. Jung", *International Journal of Psychoanalysis*, 1964, vol. 45, pp. 450–5.
5 C. G. Jung, *Letters*, vol. 2, *1951–1961*, ed. G. Adler, Princeton, NJ, Princeton University Press, 1973, pp. 69–70.
6 J. Olney, *Metaphors of Self: The Meaning of Autobiography*, Princeton, NJ, Princeton University Press, 1972, pp. 20–1.
7 Olney devotes a chapter of his book to Jung's "autobiography".
8 P. de Man, *The Rhetoric of Romanticism*, New York, Columbia University Press, 1984, p. 70.
9 S. Freud, *The Interpretation of Dreams*, London, G. Allen & Unwin, 1954.
10 S. Freud and J. Strachey, *An Autobiographical Study*, London, Hogarth Press and the Institute of Psycho-Analysis, 1935, p. 131.
11 L. R. Anderson, *Autobiography*, London and New York, Routledge, 2001, p. 67.
12 C. G. Jung, "Freud and Jung: contrasts", in *Freud and Psychoanalysis*, *The Collected Works of C. G. Jung*, vol. 4, London, Routledge & Kegan Paul, 1929/1961, p. 774.
13 Jung, *Letters*, p. 38.
14 Ibid., pp. 38–9.
15 Jung, *MDR*, p. viii.
16 S. Benstock, *The Private Self: Theory and Practice of Women's Autobiographical Writings*, Chapel Hill, University of North Carolina Press, 1988, pp. 11–12.
17 S. Shamdasani, *Jung Stripped Bare by His Biographers, Even*, London and New York, Karnac, 2005, note 92.
18 Jung, *MDR*, p. ix.
19 Ibid., p. 3.
20 Ibid.
21 Ibid., p. 4.
22 Jung, *Letters*, p. 38.
23 Jung, *MDR*, p. 3.
24 Ibid., p. vi.
25 D. Bair, *Jung: A Biography*, London, Little, Brown, 2004, p. 595.
26 Shamdasani, "Memories", p. 38.
27 Jung, *MDR*, p. 186.
28 C. G. Jung and W. McGuire, *Analytical Psychology: Notes of the Seminar Given in 1925 by C. G. Jung*, London, Routledge, 1990.
29 Bair, *Jung*, p. 602.
30 S. Rowland, *Jung as a Writer*, London and New York, Routledge, 2005, p. 54.
31 Ibid., p. 52.
32 Helly Preiswerk, Jung's cousin, who, as medium, facilitated his entrée into the world of the spirits and of the unconscious, is reduced in *MDR* to an anonymous "young girl of fifteen and a half". Sabina Spielrein – who, until 1980, existed only as a footnote in accounts of the beginnings of Jungian and Freudian psychology, but over the last 25 years has been brought back to vivid life in books, plays, and films as a crucial presence in the development of both analytical psychology and psychoanalysis – is never mentioned. The "talented psychopath" whose voice becomes the inaugural voice of the anima for Jung in *MDR* is given no name. Most surprisingly for readers at the time of publication, Toni Wolff, who, above all others and for the longest time, embodied the anima for Jung, has

no place in the published *MDR.* Even Jung's own wife, Emma, receives barely a mention. These latter erasures can, for different reasons, be plausibly attributed to the influence of the Jung family, though it seems naïve to assume that Jung did not to some extent collude in that influence.

33 F. X. Charet, *Spiritualism and the Foundations of C. G. Jung's Psychology*, Albany, State University of New York Press, 1993; S. Rowland, *C. G. Jung and Literary Theory: The Challenge from Fiction*, Basingstoke, Macmillan, 1999, p. 44.

34 Jung, *MDR*, p. 44.

35 Ibid., pp. 48–50.

36 Ibid., p. 91.

37 Ibid., p. 214.

38 Ibid., pp. 213–14.

39 Ibid., p. 22.

40 Ibid., p. 15.

41 Ibid., p. 26.

42 R. Papadopoulos, "Jung and the Concept of the Other", in R. Papadopoulos and G. Saayman (eds.), *Jung in Modern Perspective*, pp. 54–88, Bridport, Prism, 1991, p. 58.

43 Ibid., p. 20.

44 Ibid.

45 Ibid., p. 22.

46 Ibid., p. 45.

47 Ibid., p. 346.

48 M.-L. von Franz, *C. G. Jung: His Myth in Our Time*, New York, Putnam for the C. G. Jung Foundation for Analytical Psychology, 1975, p. 9.

49 Ibid., p. 38ff.

50 Jung, *MDR*, p. 57.

51 Ibid., p. 44.

52 Ibid., p. 68.

53 Ibid., p. 88.

54 Ibid., p. 45.

55 M. Saban, "Entertaining the stranger", *Journal of Analytical Psychology*, 2011, vol. 56, pp. 92–108.

56 J. W. v. Goethe, W. Arndt, and C. Hamlin, *Faust: A Tragedy: Backgrounds and Sources, the Author on the Drama, Contemporary Reactions, Modern Criticism* (1st edn), New York, Norton, 1976, pp. 287–8.

57 Von Franz, *C. G. Jung*, p. 4.

58 Jung, *MDR*, p. 188.

59 Ibid., p. 192.

60 Ibid., p. 188.

61 Ibid., p. 200.

62 Such symmetricality, whether within the consulting room or the individual psyche, would lead to stasis; conflicting dynamics would have balanced themselves to a halt. This is not, as I read it, the goal, if it can be described as such, of the living engagement in the endless ambiguous movement of the psyche, which Jung calls individuation.

63 In a sense, this project parallels Lacan's "return to Freud" in that it is an attempt to read Jung against Jung. The difference is that Jung's psychology implicitly sanctions such a reading.

2

A LECTURE FOR THE END OF TIME – "CONCERNING REBIRTH"

Murray Stein

"Those are not books. That is bread."[1]

With the clarity that only an experienced scholar can bring to a deep reading of Jung, Murray Stein opens up a rather neglected and unfamiliar essay from *The Collected Works*, one that is as timely today as it was at its inception in 1939 when Jung first presented the raw material for his later masterful work, "Concerning Rebirth". Stein brings to life the political tensions that charged the atmosphere of the Eranos Conference that summer as Jung delivered to the scholars gathered at Ascona an impromptu address built around a rebirth mystery story told in the 18th Sura of the Koran.

J. K.

Preface

My teacher of choice for enhancing the experience of reading continues to be the masterful, indeed canonical to some, American literary critic, Harold Bloom. His *How to Read and Why* pleads for us, though without great hope of success in this most nonliterary of ages, to pursue the "more difficult pleasures" offered by "deep reading" of the great works of imaginative literature. His advice to those who would do so is essential: "find what comes near to you that can be put to the use of weighing and considering, and that addresses you as though you share the one nature, free of time's tyranny".[2] Such "nearness" to an author's thoughts and the feelings of sharing "the one nature" and becoming "free of time's tyranny", which Bloom advocates and so convincingly demonstrates in his superb commentaries on the plays of Shakespeare and the poems of Walt Whitman, is what I find almost invariably to be the case when I read Jung's works and particularly his late books and essays. Even though Jung's writing would not, with perhaps the exception of *The Red Book*, be classified as "imaginative literature", the principles espoused by Bloom for deep reading still apply. This type of reading is not, it should be said, "critical" in the sense that much contemporary commentary is, which sets itself against the text with an attitude of superior insight and wisdom in a contest for intellectual (or political) supremacy. It is rather an attempt to understand a text and to enter deeply into an intimate dialogue with it and with the mind of its author. One could say that it is a receptive, rather than a combative, approach to reading.

If one accepts Bloom's guidance into deep reading, the path leads directly to what Jung, drawing on Rutland's *Lexicon alchemiae*, writes of as *meditatio* (inner dialogue), or even to the stronger *imaginatio* (opening up an "intermediate space" with active imagination).[3] Deep reading can become a meditative or imaginative engagement with figures, images, and ideas that effectively transform one's mind. It is a kind of alchemical process involving exploration of the inner world that brings intense stimulation and nourishment to soul and spirit, even therapeutic healing as Bloom testifies autobiographically. In fact, it initiates the reader into an experience of "rebirth" of the kind Jung describes in the essay I introduce here. Most practised readers will immediately recognize the difference that Bloom draws between reading for easy pleasure or information and this kind of full immersion in a text, which results in an intimate dialogue with it and oneself. Reading Jung in this way certainly yields the "more difficult pleasures" spoken of by Bloom, but even more than bringing one exquisite and subtle enjoyment, such reading affects the reader at levels beyond the aesthetic and cognitive and often introduces the themes consciously meditated upon and reimagined into the dreams of the night. A deep reading of Jung's writings, especially of his later works, opens an astonishing window to the most profound features of the soul, its movements and figures, and its potential for transformation.

With the following commentary on the essay, "Concerning Rebirth", I would like to offer an invitation to consider this short but essential text of Jung's for such deep reading. In the course of the exposition, I trust it will become clear why this essay deserves this type of attention, and how it can assist one to understand Jung's whole *oeuvre* more completely and instill a more capacious sense of what is possible for individuation in the Jungian sense of the word.

"Concerning Rebirth" is not as frequently cited by commentators and scholars as some other of Jung's essays on similarly overt religious or spiritual themes, like the magnificent trinity, "Commentary on 'The Secret of the Golden Flower'", "A Psychological Approach to the Dogma of the Trinity", and "Transformation Symbolism in the Mass".[4] In fact, "Concerning Rebirth" can be regarded as an orphan offspring, overlooked and sadly neglected. Perhaps this is because it features an obscure (to Western eyes, at least) Koranic text, the 18th Sura, which, on its own, may well strike one as disjointed and enigmatic. Moreover this essay does not reveal its treasures to view as openly as those other works. Its psychological insights lie quietly concealed behind a rough outer shell of encyclopedia-like prose. It is like a coconut with a hard, dry cover that protects a small but sweet and meaty interior. "Concerning Rebirth" requires patience of the reader (that is, deep reading) in order to penetrate the husk before tasting and savouring its ripe interior fruit. Admittedly, it is not as strong and developed an essay as the other three just mentioned, but its core is nuclear and deals a mighty impact to the mind if fully realized. It may prove also to be highly instructive for the work of the Jungian psychoanalyst.

Sitz im Leben: Eranos *Tagung* 1939 – time, place, speakers

For full appreciation of this essay, it is helpful to know something about the context in which it originated, about its *Sitz im Leben*, as German scholars refer to the historical functions and purposes of a particular biblical book or passage. How and when did it come into being? Who was the audience? What was the occasion? This background places the text in life as lived physically and socially as well as mentally.

"Concerning Rebirth" began as an extemporaneous pair of lectures at the annual Eranos Conference of 1939. The setting of the conference was, as always, the Casa Eranos, which is one of the three cottages that lie on the beautiful lakeside grounds of the Eranos Foundation in Moscia, near Ascona (Switzerland). The cottage contains a small auditorium (with a capacity of around 25 persons) that was occupied annually for a week during August from 1933 until 1952 by C. G. Jung and an invited group of scholars of world religions. The aim of the Eranos Conferences was to place a specific theme under the spotlight of a spectrum of religious traditions as well as under the beam of Jung's modern analytical psychology. The topic for each year was selected after the previous year's conference and was meant to carry the discussion another step forward. In this way, the Eranos Conferences became a continuous long conversation among notable European scholars on a variety of cultural and spiritual themes. It was not, strictly speaking, an academic conference focused on or by specialist scholarship, but rather an occasion for high-level intellectual exchange and conversation. The intention of the conferences was to cross-fertilize the invited lecturers' thinking through a sustained dialogue. The occasion was also usually quite festive: The name Eranos means "banquet" in ancient Greek, and the symbol of the conference was the round table that served as the locus for spirited conversations over lunch. The conference of 1939 proved to be an extraordinarily rich and multifaceted banquet.

During the previous year's conference, "the Great Mother" had occupied centre stage thematically, which yielded Jung's essay "Psychological Aspects of the Mother Archetype". The logic of the 1938 conference had led the conveners to settle on the theme, "The Symbolism of Rebirth in the Religious Conception of all Times and Peoples", for 1939. For this discussion, ten brilliant and well-known intellectuals were invited, hailing from five European countries, nine of whom attended and one who was unable to come for political reasons.[5] In the *Eranos-Jahrbuch 1939*, Jung's contribution appears at the end of the book. Because he had not intended to speak at this conference, he took the podium last, and his two lectures brought it to a close.[6] The lecture occcured just before the end of time at Ascona that year.

For Jung, the spring and summer of 1939 had already been full and demanding. After a trip to England where he addressed the Royal Society of Medicine ("On the Psychogenesis of Schizophrenia") and the Guild for Pastoral Psychology ("The Symbolic Life") in April, he had, in his role as president of the Internationale Allgemeine Ärztliche Gesellschaft für Psychotherapie [International General Medical Society for Psychotherapy] (IAÄGP), presided over a meeting of the delegates in Zurich in July, where he insisted on resigning his position as president, a post he had held since 1933.[7] For Jung, this was a painful and difficult meeting of the IAÄGP, and by the time he finally arrived at the Eranos Conference he must have been tired and on edge. He had not planned to give any lectures, only to listen and participate in the discussions. He was 64 years old on 26 July of that year.

"The tension in Europe was almost unbearable that summer", writes Barbara Hannah, who drove the Jungs to Eranos in her car.[8] The conference took place on 4–12 August amid terrible weather conditions and frightening political turmoil. Jung himself summarized the atmosphere by saying that there was "a feeling of the Last Judgment in the air".[9] It must have seemed like the end of time to Jung and the participants. This would be the last Eranos Conference before the onset of the Second World War, during which the gatherings were greatly attenuated due to restrictions on travel.[10]

The personal, cultural, and political context in which Jung composed "Concerning Rebirth", therefore, consisted of endings, crises, and high anxiety about the future. Nevertheless the essay still shows faith in an archetypal process that will, in the course of time, lead through death to new life, perhaps on another level of consciousness and not without great suffering. The essay concerns transformation and, therefore, death and rebirth, mostly on the individual level but also on the collective, and speaks to people who face deep questions of meaning. In my view, this makes it exceptionally relevant to analytic work, which so often takes place during anxious and trying times of transition in a person's life.

The first lecture – "we are that pair of Dioscuri"

Jung's first lecture at the conference was divided into two sections: (a) a summary of several traditional religious views on rebirth, and (b) a list of eight psychological aspects of rebirth, which concludes with a trenchant description of the individuation process, that is, of "rebirth" in the psychological sense rather than in the traditional religious sense of a spiritual experience. In the published version, these are named "Forms of Rebirth" and "The Psychology of Rebirth".

In itself, Jung recognizes, *rebirth* is an ambiguous term within the context of the world's religions and is subject to a variety of meanings. Literally, it means "born more than once", but this can take quite a few different forms. It might refer to the idea of *metempsychosis*, a long series of births in which karma, carried over from one lifetime into another in a multitude of incarnations, may form a basis for some degree of continuity. Or it might designate the idea of *reincarnation*, which implies a strong notion of the soul's continuity in a series of human forms and even continuous memory from one lifetime to another. Alternatively, it might refer to *resurrection*, the transformation from one type of body and existence into another, like that of the resurrected Christ who could pass through solid material but still handle bread and fish.[11] Or the word can refer to an inner change of the personality that would not necessarily be perceived by others, a spiritual *renewal* such as was suggested by Jesus to the Pharisee, Nicodemus, who came to him by night for instruction and was told "Ye must be born again".[12] Or, says Jung finally before taking up his real theme as a psychologist, the term may refer to the effect on an individual who participates in a *collective process* like the Mass,[13] where strong believers undergo a spiritual transformation in alignment with the mystery of the transsubstantiation of the bread and the wine. Any one of these versions of rebirth could easily inspire an entire essay or book on its own, but after a brief rendition of these traditional religious understandings (this constitutes the dry outer husk of the essay), Jung moves on to "the psychology of rebirth", his special area of interest and expertise, and ours too as psychoanalysts.

Turning to the psychological meaning of the rebirth notion and experience, Jung opens his argument by affirming the psychic reality of the phenomenon. Since the idea of rebirth is ancient, primordial, and universal, it is archetypal and, therefore, possesses psychic reality:

> The mere fact that people talk about rebirth, and that there is such a concept at all, means that a store of psychic experiences designated by that term must actually exist.... Rebirth is an affirmation that must be counted among the primordial affirmations of mankind. These primordial affirmations are based on what I call archetypes.[14]

Jung goes on to build his further reflections upon this premise: the notion of rebirth is grounded in the archetypal psyche and, therefore, expresses a fact of life, psychically real and true. He proceeds by first considering briefly the common experience of "a moment of eternity in time".[15] This experience, which he would often refer to as *numinous*, using the term borrowed from Rudolf Otto, may take place within a collective context, such as a religious or cultic ritual, or it may befall an individual as a mystical experience in solitude. He mentions Zarathustra's "Noontide Vision"[16] as "a classic example of this [second] kind"[17] (Jung, a lifelong "deep reader" of Nietzsche, had become fully immersed in *Thus Spoke Zarathustra* while conducting a long series of seminars[18] on this work, which had concluded only several months before the Eranos Conference of 1939). Whether individual or collective, such experiences of transcendence bear a close resemblance to each other because all are grounded in the archetypal level of psyche where psyche and world merge in an *unus mundus*. The question of whether such numinous experiences of "eternity in time" bring a transformational effect to the individual and result in "a change of one's nature" is, for now, left open. They may be merely aesthetic and of only passing significance, writes Jung, or they may instigate "rebirth". In and of themselves, experiences of transcendence are not the critical issue. They are generally available to everyone, but not all are changed by them.

Following this introductory passage, Jung delves more deeply into the consideration of psychological transformation. What is possible? The premise of an archetypal basis for rebirth has been stated, and the possibility of experiencing transcendence that may result in personality transformation has been recognized. There remains the question of different types of "subjective transformation". Here, Jung the psychiatrist and psychoanalyst takes over as he considers the options:

a *Abaissement du niveau mental* is one possible outcome. It refers to a transformation into lesser ego functioning, perhaps through trauma or shock, and "has a restrictive influence on the personality as a whole", resulting in the "development of an essentially negative personality"[19] if it continues for an extended period of time. It is a morbid transformation, a birth into a personality with a reduced level of conscious functioning.

b *Enlargement of the personality* is a second possible outcome, the contrary of the first. It takes place when the ego relates strongly to, or even completely identifies with, an emergent archetypal figure. Again, Jung references Nietzsche as an example, whose encounter with Zarathustra turned him into "a tragic poet and a prophet".[20] In this case, a greater spiritual personality took over the lesser ego personality, or at least greatly inflated it. Other such examples cited by Jung are St Paul and Christ ("Christ himself is the perfect symbol of the hidden immortal within the mortal man"[21]). Jung is now approaching what is the heart of his reflection in "Concerning Rebirth": the dual nature of the personality, which consists of a pair, one the lesser part (the ego) and the other the greater (the archetypal self). Moses and Khidr, as a pair of symbolic figures interacting with each other, represent this duality. They are the focus of the comments in the second lecture. Here, we receive only a slight foretaste of what is to come. For now, in the first lecture, however, Jung is careful to attest to the pathological possibilities of this encounter between lesser and greater personalities. Generally, this enlargement of the personality applies to "any case where the recognition of a greater personality seems to burst an iron ring round the heart".[22] It is a dangerous moment, psychologically speaking, but a necessary one for individuation.

c *Change of internal structure*, the third option that Jung mentions, includes a number of possible variants: possession by the "inferior functions", which brings into play the shadow and a Jekyll-and-Hyde type of alternating transformation of personality; possession by the anima or animus, which results in gender identity modifications; confusions or states of emotional or ideological possession; or possession by archaic features of the personality, such as a specific "ancestral soul" or forebear. These transformations have to do with change in psychic structure, whether temporary or more permanent, into a psychically alien personality type. This is not a particularly to-be-desired "rebirth".

d *Identification with a group*, where the individual's identity becomes fused with a collective identity, and forms the basis of "mob psychology". The individual is transformed into a representative of the mass and forfeits uniqueness. Jung takes the opportunity here to offer some comments on the current political situation, which saw large numbers of people, indeed whole nations, falling under the sway of charismatic "leaders" (Stalin, Il Duce, the Führer) and one-sided fanatical ideologies (Communism, Fascism, National Socialism).[23] This is a change that in the individual does not last long: "On the contrary, you must have continual recourse to mass intoxication in order to consolidate the experience ... But as soon as you are removed from the crowd, you are a different person again."[24] This "rebirth" is based on *participation mystique* – an unconscious identification with the "other", in this case, the crowd. Much more than "conformity" to collective standards, which involves normal adaptation and persona formation, this is a total and possessed state of mind.

e *Identification with a cult-hero*, which also requires repeated acts of identification but, in this instance, with an ideal figure held up by a group. This type of rebirth usually occurs in religious mysteries where "the individual undergoes an indirect transformation through his participation in the fate of the god".[25] Thus, one would gradually develop a sense of, for instance, an identification with the life of Jesus as presented in the New Testament and featured in dramatic re-enactments in the religious context of Christian worship.

f *Magical procedures*, which rely on techniques such as rituals that symbolize passing through a symbolic death and rising miraculously as a semi-divine being, may bring about inner transformations. Jung cites baptism as a magical procedure.

g *Technical transformation* takes place through the use of less magical procedures, such as meditation or spiritual exercises, which are "designed to induce the transformation by imitating"[26] a sequence of events. In the fall semester 1939, Jung lectured at the ETH-Zurich on the *Ignatian Exercises*, which exemplify this form of inducing "rebirth".

h *Natural transformation (individuation)*, in contrast to the magical or technical methods just mentioned, comes about through the use of dreams and active imagination, in other words, by using the methods we see Jung himself employing in *The Red Book*. Jung had previously shown this method in operation with analytic patients and described the results in two previous Eranos lectures.[27] In this essay, he gives only a very abbreviated account. The basic notion is that the rebirth process may be fully symbolized in dreams over a period of time, which detail the process of individuation as "a long-drawn-out process of inner transformation and rebirth into another being. This 'other being' is the other person in ourselves – that larger and greater personality maturing within us, whom we have already met as the inner friend of the soul."[28] This "larger personality maturing within us" occupies Jung in the remainder of his essay.

Jung now begins to hit his heightened rhetorical stride. When he calls out to the members of this audience, "We are that pair of Dioscuri, one of whom is mortal and the other immortal",[29] I imagine him as charged up with passion and also addressing us, his readers, directly. His audience at Eranos would, of course, have been immediately familiar with the mythological twin children of Leda – Castor and Pollux, the one mortal and the other divine. Individuation (that is, natural rebirth) entails bringing these two figures together, as psychic processes "strive to approximate them to one another, but our consciousness is aware of resistances".[30] Jung tells us of how a struggle naturally ensues as these two parts encounter one another, leading perhaps to a stand-off, suspicion, or doubt. All of what Jung speaks about generally and abstractly in these paragraphs is vividly depicted in *The Red Book*, where the protagonist (Jung's ego-surrogate) engages in prolonged confrontations and tense dialogues with such figures as Elijah, Soul, and Philemon.[31] "We should prefer to be always 'I' and nothing else", he confesses, speaking for us all. "But we are confronted with that inner friend or foe, and whether he is our friend or our foe depends on ourselves."[32] His challenge to us is this: How this story turns out depends on us, for we are free to turn away and ignore the puzzling and maybe threatening greater personality within, but it will be to our later regret, or even tragic detriment, if we do; or we can enter into a dialogue through the use of active imagination and try to work out a relationship. The choice is ours.

Immersed at this time, too, in alchemical studies, Jung cannot resist reaching for images from alchemy to illustrate the resulting transformation process that ensues from a confrontation with the inner other, the "immortal one". What the alchemists described in their perplexing texts was mainly the transformation of material substances, but Jung adds:

> [S]ome were clever enough to know, "It is my own transformation – not a personal transformation, but the transformation of what is mortal in me into what is immortal. It shakes off the mortal husk that I am and awakens to a life of its own; it mounts the sun-barge and may take me with it."[33]

Ultimately, psychological transformation (rebirth) results in the enthronement of the immortal within the mortal, the archetypal within the historical, the hugely complex and multifaceted self (the "soul" as *imago Dei*) within human consciousness.

The first lecture ends on this exciting note, with a promise of more to come in the next.

The second lecture – "How the immortality-bringing rebirth comes about"

After a break, Jung continues. He wants now to present an example of rebirth as a psychological phenomenon that, he says, will tie in with "the outstanding lecture you have heard by Prof. Massignon. I have chosen this example because I can connect to something with which you are already familiar."[34] Jung had come late to Eranos and missed Massignon's lecture that year, but he was familiar with the French scholar's work and his great love of the Sura that he had placed at the centre of his reflections on the topic for the year. The famous Islamist's lectures were concentrated on the 18th Sura of the Koran, "The Cave", with its images of the Seven Sleepers and the angelic figure, Khidr. This text was a "favorite theme of Louis Massignon".[35] "This entire Sura", Jung states categorically, "is taken up with a rebirth mystery."[36] Whereas Massignon's two lectures had focused on the theme of resurrection in Sufism and Islam from a more traditional history of religions perspective, Jung turns to the text with his eye on the symbolic meaning from a psychological angle and renders the Sura as a statement about the individuation process:

> The cave is the place of rebirth, the secret cavity in which one is shut up in order to be incubated and renewed ...
>
> Anyone who gets into that cave, that is to say into the cave which everyone has in himself, or into the darkness that lies behind consciousness, will find himself involved in an – at first – unconscious process of transformation. By penetrating into the unconscious, he makes a connection with his unconscious contents. This may result in a momentous change of personality.[37]

In *The Red Book*, we see that Jung's own journey into and through the underworld, that is, his own individuation process, began with entry into a cave.[38]

In these remarks on the Koranic cave is an implicit reference, therefore, back to his own experience.

While the transformative experience of rebirth is taking place in the cave where the Sleepers remain for 309 years and are occasionally turned over by an angel, the Sura continues with a fascinating story about a meeting between Moses and Khidr, "the Verdant One", an angel and stand-in for Allah. It tells of a highly instructive journey undertaken by a human and a divine personality, and of Moses' subsequent message to his people derived from this experience but delivered in the form of a mystery legend. In his interpetation of this mysterious and disjointed religious narrative, Jung stakes out the absolute centre of gravity in his essay. Although brief, this section of "Concerning Rebirth", which bears the unassuming title "A Typical Set of Symbols Illustrating the Process of Transformation", touches on the boiling political issues of the day in which the essay was composed, but beyond that it speaks of the timeless experience of individuation. In Jung's interpretation, the 18th Sura of the Koran offers us an instructive description of what it means to walk with the creator of destiny and to view our personal life history from a transcendent perspective. Additionally, it also makes a strong argument for the necessity to create a defence of the self against its destructive enemies, and (further) it gives us very practical advice about how to talk about all of this.

The story unfolds like this:

> Moses undertakes a journey with a servant to "the place where the two seas meet" (the "centre"), and for nourishment along the way they take a fish. They succeed in arriving at their destination and then journey on, but the servant forgets the fish and leaves it behind. Only later when Moses gets hungry do they realize the fish is missing. They retrace their steps back to the "centre" and look for the fish.

This initial and important phase of the individuation process, Jung states, first goes well enough and seems to attain its goal, that is, arrival at "the centre", but is followed by a "loss of soul" (the fish symbolizes contact with the unconscious) and by a consequent state of mind that the alchemists referred to as *nigredo*, or spiritual death. This is the first major crisis of this individuation process. For himself, Jung could think back to the moment some 25 years earlier when he realized that he had lost his soul and called out, "My soul, where are you? Do you hear me?"[39] at the beginning of *The Red Book.* Filled with despair, he recognized his emptiness and inner deadness. In his autobiography, he recounts how at this time in his life (he was 37 years old) he had to hearken back to childhood and take up playing in the garden with stones and sticks and water as he tried to find his way again to the lost world of the soul, a timeless space filled with archetypal energy.[40]

He realized, in other words, that he had lost the living contact with the unconscious (the "fish", in the Koranic narrative) and needed to retrace his steps. Such a realization of loss of soul is, Jung says, a typical moment in the individuation process, which does not follow a direct line onward and upward but circumambulates the "centre" and also involves resistance and retreat as well as forward motion. Since the meeting of the two seas can also be taken as a metaphor for the confrontation of the lesser with the greater personalities, one should always expect turbulence.

> When Moses and his servant retrace their steps, however, the fish is not to be found. It has disappeared into the waters, but in its place they come upon "one of Our servants, whom We had endowed with Our grace and Our wisdom",[41] an Angel of Allah named Khidr by tradition. Moses asks to follow him but is at first refused because Khidr says he will not understand what he sees and will ask foolish questions. Moses promises to keep silent, so finally Khidr relents and they proceed on a journey together.

Jung says that Khidr is the fish as transformed in the darkness of *nigredo*, for in alchemy from "the *nigredo* issues the Stone, the symbol of the immortal self".[42] Khidr is such a symbol and represents "a higher consciousness" that brings with it "the feeling of immortality".[43] The ego has now come into full contact with the self. The transformation of the fish into Khidr is a key insight into the process of individuation, because it "shows how the immortality-bringing rebirth comes about ... The immortal being issues from something humble and forgotten",[44] that is, from the often overlooked and underrated unconscious. This being emerges from the place where the fish was lost and disappeared into the water; now it comes forth as a figure who "symbolizes not only the higher wisdom but also a way of acting which is in accord with this wisdom and transcends reason".[45] This was precisely Jung's experience during his "confrontation with the unconscious", as we can see so clearly in *The Red Book*: Out of his descent into the "cave" and the subsequent quest for the unconscious emerged his encounter with Philemon, who, for him, functioned as the equivalent of Khidr to Moses in the Koranic text. The parallel is dramatic and striking, and Jung must have felt totally at home with this Sura.

> Moses follows Khidr and observes three actions that confound him: Khidr bores a hole in the bottom of a poor man's boat and sinks it; he kills a young man; and he props up a wall that is about to collapse. Each time Moses fails the test to keep silent and asks for an explanation. Khidr refuses angrily and threatens to dismiss Moses. Finally, after the third incident, Khidr has had enough of Moses' prying questions, but before sending him on his way, he explains

> the rationale for each of his actions. In the first instance, his purpose was to save the fisherman's life since he was being pursued by pirates; in the second, it was to kill a bad son so that a better one could take his place and make the parents happy; and in the third, it was to preserve a buried treasure for later retrieval by the heirs. Each action, though inexplicable on the surface, served to further the good in the future. Moses is astonished at the meanings revealed by Khidr.

Oddly, Jung comments not at all on this portion of the Sura. He could have said so much, but perhaps he thought the text was self-evident enough as a parable teaching us about the ego's limited knowledge and the greater perspective of the transcendent self. We can recognize that much in the course of history, whether personal or collective, cannot be fathomed at the moment, but in retrospect can be seen as the working out of a pattern woven by a hidden hand with unexpected meaning. The Koranic narrative testifies to "the left hand of God" working His Will in history in what looks to our narrow consciousness like tragedy, mishap, catastrophe, or surprise, which at one moment threatens our very lives and at another offers an astonishing reprieve or windfall. Given the political situation in Europe at the time, Jung may have felt it wiser to remain silent about this perspective.

Barbara Hannah reports that after the Eranos Conference Jung had a nightmare:

> We were all home again and Jung was at Bollingen when the news of the unholy alliance of Germany with Russia burst upon a horrified Europe [23 August]. Jung was further disturbed by a most indigestible dream which he had immediately afterward. He dreamed that Hitler was "the devil's Christ", the Anti-Christ, but that nevertheless, as such, he was the instrument of God. He told me it took him a long time and much effort before he was able to accept this idea.[46]

Something like this shocking dream-thought must have kept Jung from commenting on this section of the Koranic text, which takes a similar view on how the Divine Will moves history in dark and inscrutable ways. It is akin to the dire theological implications of the biblical Book of Job, which Jung found so irritating and also difficult to accept as attested in his later angry outburst, *Answer to Job.* The strong message is that we as humans cannot know the Divine Will, which is hidden behind life's tragedies and windfalls, except in retrospect or perhaps through messages sent from the self in the form of dreams and visions or intuitions, some of which are shocking in the extreme and may be terribly offensive to our sense of morality and ethics. In later writings, Jung would give a lot of attention to the dark side of God, an intuition that haunted him throughout his life and is recurrent in *The Red Book*. Here, in "Concerning Rebirth", he passes over the issue in silence. My feeling is that it was too hot to handle at this moment in history when the world was teetering on the brink of the abyss. Like Job, he put his hand over his mouth as he gazed into a mystery beyond his understanding.

> Moses is now told that he will be asked to report back to his people on his experiences with Khidr, and he is instructed by Khidr to do so in a disguised and indirect fashion. He is to tell the story as though he were not himself involved, but rather the pair Dhulquarnein (aka Alexander the Great) and Khidr. The story now proceeds as an adventure undertaken by Khidr and Dhulquarnein who go forth together, traveling to the East where the sun rises. Later they erect a great rampart to protect the people from Gog and Magog. There is a prophesy of the later destruction of this rampart by the Lord and the ensuing Last Judgement when "Hell shall be laid bare before the unbelievers".[47]

Jung's commentary on this opaque passage in the Sura displays his brilliant hermeneutical gifts in a highly imaginative but also very self-revealing interpretation of the text. Moses, he says, has had "a profoundly moving experience of the self, which brought unconscious processes before his eyes with overwhelming clarity",[48] but when he reports on this to his own people – the Jews – he is instructed to cast his account in the form of a legend, but to leave himself entirely out of the account and to substitute Dhulquarnein in his place. Khidr and Dhulquarnein are to be reported as the ones who experience rebirth, not Moses. By placing the narrative in the third person and leaving himself out of it, Moses (the ego) affirms that the transformation is happening to a non-ego aspect of the personality. This aspect is crucial to avoid the devastating psychological inflation that would threaten should the ego identify with the transformation and itself claim to be the one "reborn". Here, again, Jung references Nietzsche, whom he views as a cautionary example in this regard and as a victim of precisely this catastrophe. For his own part, Jung used this strategy in employing alchemy and other symbol systems to speak about what he had personally experienced in his "confrontation with the unconscious" and recorded in *The Red Book*. In this essay, he uses the Koran's 18th Sura for the identical purpose. The transformations are spoken of as taking place "out there" in a traditional text, and the reference to subjective experience on the author's part remains unspoken. The teaching is also that the transcendent and the reborn figures remain in the unconscious as points of orientation but do not become ego-syntonic.

At this point in the essay, Jung brings the European Dioscuri pair, Faust and Mephistopheles, into the discussion:

> The Faustian hybris is already the first step towards madness. The fact that the unimpressive beginning of the transformation in *Faust* is a dog and not an edible fish, and that the transformed figure is the devil and not a wise friend ... might, I am inclined to think, offer a key to our understanding of the highly enigmatic German soul.[49]

The German soul, as a psychic collective, seems to have drawn forth from the self its negative and destructive potential in the transcendent figure of Mephistopheles and was now in 1939–40 following him on a sure course to perdition. Jung had been thinking about this possibility at least since his statement about "the blond beast" in the German psyche in 1918,[50] following up on this theme of a destructive archetypal constellation in his 1936 article "Wotan". Here, in "Concerning Rebirth", he places Mephistopheles in contrast to the much more evolved spiritual symbol of the transcendent self in the Koranic figure of Khidr. It is a blunt indictment of what was going on in Germany.

Jung sees the building of the rampart against Gog and Magog as a repetition of the wall-building scene from the previous section of the Sura where Khidr props up an old wall that is falling down. Here, it becomes a project on a gigantic scale, extending between two mountains. Gog and Magog symbolize "the featureless, hostile masses" and "envious collective forces" that threaten anyone who attempts to follow the mandates of individuation, since "individuation is an *opus contra naturam*, which creates a *horror vacui* in the collective layer [of the individual psyche or of the general surrounding population] and is only too likely to collapse under the impact of the collective forces of the psyche".[51] Against this threat, Dhulquarnein builds a defence in order to protect the one "who has found the jewel on his quest".[52] Jung is referring to the psychological defence needed to protect the integrity of the person who dares to individuate, whether against a threat from within the psyche (from harsh inner persecutors) or from others in the surrounding environment who become hypercritical out of envy toward the individuating personality and the prospect of change. Every psychotherapist will immediately recognize the project of building such a rampart with clients who begin to individuate and have to face the hostility of their families and acquaintances or equally violent attacks from within. These persecutory forces are the primitive elements represented by Gog and Magog in the Koranic text.

The Sura ends with the scene of the Last Judgement: "On that day We will let them come in tumultuous throngs. The Trumpet shall be sounded and We will gather them all together."[53] The rampart built earlier by Dhulquarnein to protect the reborn is now dissolved, and the opposites are permanently divided. This signifies the moment "when individual consciousness is extinguished in the waters of darkness ... when consciousness sinks back into the darkness from which it originally emerged ... the moment of death".[54] The story of psychological transformation, that is, rebirth, is now complete, and the "timeless state of permanence sets in which ... is nevertheless one of supreme tension and therefore corresponds to the improbable initial state".[55] This is a *Götterdämmerung* that Jung also felt hanging over the Eranos Conference and the entire world in August 1939.

Conclusion

What one comes away with from reading this highly engaging essay again and again is an awareness of the supreme importance that Jung, especially in his later works, placed on contacting the spirit of the unconscious and creating an ongoing exchange with its symbolic images and persons. In meditating on this work and letting it engage my imagination, I find myself pondering similar experiences of transcendence and dialogues with imaginal figures as they have emerged in dreams and active imagination over the years. Jung's essay draws one back to the self in a movement toward renewal and a more lively contact with the unconscious, in other words, to a kind of rebirth experience similar to what is described so vividly in the text. At the very least, one is called to reflect again on the mysteries of lived experience, outer and inner, from an extra-ego perspective.

For Jung, imagination is the key to rebirth and transformation in that it generates and secures an "intermediate realm" wherein the encounter with transcendence and mystery can take place and be accepted as valid and real. In *The Red Book*, we find a detailed account of how this looks and plays out over the course of years. The Khidr figure there is variously named and described as "the spirit of the depths", the couple Elijah and Salome, Soul, Philemon, and so forth. The emphasis that Jung places so firmly on the critical importance of working with the figures of the unconscious has been continued, at least in some measure, by later Jungian psychoanalysts who follow the dream series seriously and foster intense engagement with inner figures through the practice of active imagination. In some cases, this creates such a level of profound change in the depths of the psyche that one can speak of rebirth into "Dioscuri awareness". In nearly all analytic cases that go deep, the result is an abiding awareness of the inner "other", a link to feelings of eternity and the timeless dimension of the soul. This experience is the much sought after "treasure hard to attain". More than anything else, what Jungian analysis at its best has to offer is such an experience of the self.

If Jung has one big idea around which he circles incessantly in his abundant writings, it is the notion of individuation. Reading and studying Jung's writings over the course of more than 40 years, I am impressed by the timeless numinosity of this theme. Its symbols forever fascinate and lure one into even deeper reading and consideration. My conclusion is that such transformation as Jung writes of is the great mysterium of life. Variously described as psychological development over the lifecycle, structural transformation, progressive integration of the self, or the mystical experience itself, it can also be named, as in this essay, rebirth. As a consequence of a conscious "re-entry into the cave" (introversion) and prolonged incubation there, whereby the mysteries of the unconscious psyche are revealed and contemplated, the reborn person emerges with "Dioscuri awareness", a realization of onself as one part human-all-too-human (ego identity) and one part transcendent and divine (archetypal self). Holding the tension between these two persons and creating a balanced and continuous dialogue between them is, as Jung argues in this essay, the crux of individuation.

For me, reading Jung has itself been an essential part of this journey because of the ways his writings evoke the very processes spoken of in the texts. When read deeply, they guide one into a journey through the soul's depths and offer brilliant hints for how to unveil its mysteries.[56]

Notes

1

> Two or three years ago, when Jung was attending an art exhibit in Zurich, a woman introduced herself to him and expressed her gratitude for what he had done for her. Dr Jung asked her if this had come about through reading his books. Her reply was: "Those are not books. That is bread."
>
> F. McCormick, *Carl Gustav Jung, 1875–1961, A Memorial Meeting*, New York, The Analytical Psychology Club, 1962, p. 16.

2 H. Bloom, *How to Read and Why*, New York, Simon & Schuster, 2000, p. 22. Bloom's works are far too abundant to mention here. Of particular significance, however, I would cite his latest and perhaps his final major work, since he is now in his 80s, *The Anatomy of Influence: Literature as a Way of Life*, New Haven, CT, and London, Yale University Press, 2011. This work sums up his views on literature, his prejudices and preferences, and his strong arguments against recent trends in literary dismemberment in what he calls "the long Age of Resentment" (p. 17). He was my teacher at Yale in the early 1960s, and I still find his voice strong and his sense of humour outlandish and resonant. His passion for literature remains unabated and his brilliance untarnished by the ravages of time. His cautionary advice to his readers and students, "confront only the writers who are capable of giving you a sense of something ever more about to be" (p. 18), is pertinent here since of all psychological writers I know Jung has the most to offer in this regard. After Bloom, I have found Alberto Manguel to be a most stimulating and friendly guide for reading deeply and well. His delectable book, *A History of Reading*, is a fascinating trip through the world's libraries and literatures (London, Penguin Books, 1996).

3 C. G. Jung, *Psychology and Alchemy*, *The Collected Works of C. G. Jung* (hereafter *CW*), vol. 12, Princeton, NJ, Princeton University Press, 1970, pp. 390–400. Jung says here that imagination is the key to alchemy. Equally one must say that imagination is the key to Jung. Jung shares with the authors of great imaginative literature a key to the poetic frequencies of the mind.

4 C. G. Jung, "Commentary on 'The Secret of the Golden Flower'", in *Alchemical Studies*, *CW* 13, Princeton, NJ, Princeton University Press, 1929/1967; "A psychological approach to the dogma of the Trinity", in *Psychology and Religion: West and East*, *CW* 11, Princeton, NJ, Princeton University Press, 1948/1969.

5 The conference speakers in the order in which their lectures appear in the *Eranos-Jahrbuch 1939*, which is also presumably the order of their presentations at the conference, are as follows: Louis Massignon (1883–1962), Chair of Muslim Sociology and Sociography at the Collège de France in Paris ("an electrifying speaker", according to William McGuire, and according to Patrick Laude "among the great spiritual figures of the twentieth century"), on "Resurrection in Sufi initiations" and "Resurrection in Islam"; Charles Virolleaud (1879–1968), French archaeologist, on rebirth in Phoenecian culture ("The classical Adonis legend" and "The god Baal in the poems of Ras-Shamra"); Paul Pelliot (1878–1945), French Sinologist and professor at the Collège de France, on Chinese views of the afterlife; Walter F. Otto (1874–1958), German professor of classical philology at the University in Königsberg, Prussia, on "The meaning of the Eleusinian Mysteries"; Charles Allberry (1911–43), English Egyptologist and Coptic scholar, fellow of Christ's College, Cambridge, on symbols of death and rebirth in Manichaeism; Hans Leisegang (1890–1951), German philosopher and specialist in Gnosticism, who, though not allowed to travel to Switzerland, contributed two papers, "The mysterium of the serpent" and "A contribution to the research on the Greek mystery cult and its continuation in the Christian world", which were included in the *Eranos-Jahrbuch 1939*; Heinrich Zimmer (1890–1943), German Indologist and historian of South Asian art, on ideas of death and rebirth in India; Ernesto Buonaiuti (1881–1946), Italian historian and philosopher of religion, on rebirth, immortality, and resurrection in early Christianity; Richard Thurnwald (1869–1954), German anthropologist and professor at the University of Berlin, on initiations and rebirth rituals among "natural peoples" [*Naturvölker*], especially the Aranda of Australia; C. G. Jung (1875–1961), who gave two extemporaneous and unplanned-for lectures on "Several different aspects of rebirth: forms of rebirth and the psychology of rebirth" and "An example of a symbol series that illustrates the transformation process"; W. McGuire, *Bollingen: An Adventure in Collecting the Past,* Princeton, NJ, Princeton University Press, 1982; P. Laude, *Louis Massignon: The Vow and the Oath*, London, The Matheson Trust, 2011.

6 The Eranos scholars did not necessarily come to the conferences with finished papers but rather often spoke freely or from notes. Their talks were later reworked for publication in the following year in the *Eranos-Jahrbuch*, which was edited and introduced by Olga Fröbe-Kapetyn, the official convener of the Eranos Conferences. Massignon's published text in the *Eranos-Jahrbuch 1939* is not a finished work due to the interruption of the war, only a rather meagre version of his talk as taken from a transcript prepared from his orally delivered remarks (O. Fröbe-Kapteyn (ed.), *Eranos-Jahrbuch 1939*, Zurich, Rhein-Verlag, 1940, p. 11, n. 1). Jung's work as published in the *Eranos-Jahrbuch 1939* is also based on stenographic notes taken during his extemporaneous presentations, which he later consulted and extensively reworked for the *Jahrbuch*. The same essay was published with a few minor revisions, including the title, as *Über Wiedergeburt*, in 1950 (*Gestaltungen des Unbewussten*, Zurich, Rascher Verlag); and that version was then translated into English by R. F. C. Hull for *The Collected Works* (1959) under the title "Concerning rebirth" (*Archetypes of the Collective Unconscious*, *CW* 9/i, Princeton, NJ, Princeton University Press, 1950/1971).

7 For a brief analysis of Jung's presidency, see G. Sorge, "Jung's presidency of the International General Medical Society of Psychotherapy: new insights", *Jung Journal*, 2012, vol. 6, no. 4, pp. 31–53. Since another president could not be immediately found, Jung remained in this position as honorary president while a solution was sought. By 26 October 1940, the decision to resign was finalized and accepted (see Jung's letter to J. H. van der Hoop, 26 October 1940, in C. G. Jung, *Letters*, vol. 1, *1906–1950*, ed. G. Adler, Princeton, NJ, Princeton University Press, 1973, pp. 286–8). He had tried to step down from this politically complicated and onerous job several times during the preceding years but was unable to do so for various reasons. Finally, his tumultuous pres-

idency, begun shortly after Hitler's appointment to the position of Reich's Chancellor of Germany, was coming to an end. For a further account of Jung's struggles in resigning the presidency, see D. Bair, *Jung, A Biography*, New York, Little, Brown & Company, 2003, pp. 460–2.

8 B. Hannah, *Jung: His Life and Work. A Biographical Memoir*, Wilmette, IL, Chiron Publications, 2000, p. 261. In her memoir of Jung, she tells many stories of driving the Jungs in her car around Switzerland and elsewhere. Later, Fowler McCormick would drive Jung about Switzerland after he was no longer able to drive for himself. By all accounts, these were companionable journeys with much conversation.

9 Ibid., p. 263. On 23 August 1939, Russia and Germany signed a "Non-Aggression Pact". Europe was horrified because this would allow Germany freely to attack the West. On 1 September, Germany invaded Poland, setting off declarations of a state of war on the parts of England and France. Poland was partitioned between Russia and Germany and quickly crushed. A grim nightsea journey had begun for the whole world. On 2 September, Jung wrote to his British colleague and friend, Hugh Crichton-Miller: "Hitler is reaching his climax and with him the German psychosis" (Jung, *Letters*, p. 276).

10 Writing her introduction for the *Eranos-Jahrbuch* at Easter, 1940, Fröbe-Kapteyn directly addressed the political situation:

> The theme of the *Tagung* 1939 ... was thoroughly suited to the times, since we are standing under the sign of a great death, in the puzzling and terrible passage from one world epoch to another, which is meant to bring us a rebirth of culture and a new order. The inner situation of the European person today is devoid of any sort of stability. But those who can place themselves into a relationship with the tested features of cultural history can find support in them and within these greater forces can also find balance. The foundation of every culture is religious. We need a historical and religious orientation, an overview of the essence and form of religious experience from the past. Without this overview, we do not have a connection with the people of the past, and without this connection our own problematic in the midst of an ending culture is not understandable
>
> (Fröbe-Kapteyn, *Eranos-Jahrbuch 39*, p. 6. Translations from the *Jahrbuch* are mine.)

A month later, on 10 May 1940, Germany invaded France and the Netherlands, and the Second World War was fully ignited. The world was set aflame. Switzerland, surrounded by the Axis powers, expected an invasion at any moment. This would not be an *Anschluss*, as in the case of Austria; it would be all-out war. On 19 June 1940, Jung wrote to Mary Mellon: "I think the night has descended upon Europe. Heaven knows if and when and under which conditions we shall meet again. There is only one certainty – nothing can put out the light within" (Jung, *Letters*, p. 284). In the fall of the same year, Jung left his home in Küsnacht with his family for the mountains, as invasion by Germany again appeared immanent, and he had been warned by Swiss authorities that his life was in danger should the Germans capture him. (See Barbara Hannah's graphic firsthand account, *Jung: His Life and Work*, pp. 267–70.)

11 John 9:13.

12 John 3:7.

13 Jung would greatly elaborate on this topic in his Eranos lecture of 1941, "Transformation Symbolism in the Mass", an essay that Fr Victor White, OP, would later find very attractive because it gives the strong impression that Jung is not a typical Reformed Protestant with a lack of sensitivity for the mystery of the Mass (*Psychology and Religion: West and East*, *CW* 11, Princeton, NJ, Princeton University Press, 1954/1969).

14 Jung, "Concerning rebirth", *CW* 9/i, pp. 206–7).

15 Ibid., p. 209.

16 F. Nietzsche, *Thus Spoke Zarathustra*, Cambridge, Cambridge University Press, 2006, Chapter 70. One senses the background presence of Nietzsche in much of this essay.
17 Jung, "Concerning rebirth", *CW* 9/i, p. 210.
18 The record of this seminar is published in two volumes as edited by James L. Jarrett, *Nietzsche's Zarathustra: Notes of the Seminar Given in 1934–1939 by C. G. Jung*, Princeton, NJ, Princeton University Press, 1988.
19 Jung, "Concerning rebirth", *CW* 9/i, p. 214.
20 Ibid., p. 216.
21 Ibid., p. 218.
22 Ibid., p. 219.
23 Barbara Hannah writes that Jung told her shortly after the outbreak of war, "It is no use saying you are not at war with the German people, you are; they are all possessed like Hitler and absolutely unapproachable" (*Jung: His Life and Work*, p. 263). Similarly, Jung had spoken of such a collective possession taking hold of the German nation in his 1936 essay, "Wotan" (*Civilization in Transition, CW* 10, Princeton, NJ, Princeton University Press, 1936/1961).
24 Jung, "Concerning rebirth", *CW* 9/i, p. 226.
25 Ibid., p. 230.
26 Ibid., p. 232.
27 "A study in the process of individuation" in *Eranos-Jahrbuch 1933* and "Dream symbols of the individuation process" in *Eranos-Jahrbuch 1935*.
28 Jung, "Concerning rebirth", *CW* 9/i, p. 235.
29 Ibid.
30 Ibid.
31 C. G. Jung, *The Red Book: Liber Novus*, ed. Sonu Shamdasani, New York, W. W. Norton & Co., 2009.
32 Jung, "Concerning rebirth", *CW* 9/i, p. 235.
33 Ibid., p. 238.
34 Fröbe-Kapteyn, *Eranos-Jahrbuch 1939*, p. 430.
35 McGuire, *Bollingen*, p. 31. Massignon's name and reputation are not widely known or appreciated in the English-speaking world. For an account of his significance, two studies by Patrick Laude can be recommended: *Pathways to an Inner Islam*, Albany, State University of New York Press, 2010; and *Louis Massignon: The Vow and the Oath* (see note 5). Mary-Louis Gude has written a biography titled *Louis Massignon: The Crucible of Compassion*, Notre Dame, IN, University of Notre Dame Press, 1997. Massignon may well have influenced Jung much more strongly than has been recognized so far.
36 Jung, "Concerning rebirth", *CW* 9/i, p. 240.
37 Ibid., pp. 240–1.
38 Jung, *The Red Book*, pp. 237 ff.
39 Ibid., p. 232.
40 C. G. Jung, *Memories, Dreams, Reflections*, New York, Vintage Books, 1961/1989, pp. 173–5. In a seminar he gave in 1925, he said:

> I remembered that when I was a boy I used to delight in building houses of stone, all sorts of fantastic castles, churches, and towns. "For Heaven's sake", I said to myself, "is it possible that I have to get into this nonsense for the sake of animating the unconscious?" That year I did all sorts of idiotic things like this, and enjoyed them like a fool.
>
> (S. Shamdasani (ed.), *Introduction to Jungian Psychology: Notes of the Seminar on Analytical Psychology Given in 1925 by C. G. Jung*, Princeton, NJ, Princeton University Press, 2012, pp. 43–4.)

41 Jung, "Concerning rebirth", *CW* 9/i, p. 243.

42 Ibid., p. 246.
43 Ibid., p. 248.
44 Ibid.
45 Ibid., p. 247.
46 Hannah, *Jung: His Life and Work*, pp. 264–5.
47 Jung, "Concerning rebirth", *CW* 9/i, p. 252.
48 Ibid., p. 253.
49 Ibid., p. 254.
50 C. G. Jung, "The role of the unconscious", in *Civilization in Transition*, *CW* 10, Princeton, NJ, Princeton University Press, 1918/1964, p. 17.
51 Jung, "Concerning rebirth", *CW* 9/i, p. 256. Here, too, there is a personal reference. This is precisely the issue Jung speaks of in his lecture, "Adaptation, Individuation, Collectivity", given at the Psychological Club in 1916, the year of its founding, when he was in the midst of his own deepest inner work (*The Symbolic Life*, *CW* 18, Princeton, NJ, Princeton University Press, 1916/1976.)
52 Ibid.
53 Ibid., p. 252.
54 Ibid., p. 257.
55 Ibid.
56 With gratitude to my in-house deep reader, Jan Stein.

3

JUNG AND ALCHEMY

A Daimonic Reading

Stanton Marlan

Pray, Read, Read, Read.
Read again, Work and
you shall find.
Mutus Liber

One book opens another.
Rhazes

You read as much into
a book as out of it.
C. G. Jung, *Liber Novus*

After examining the various ways earlier scholars read Jung's alchemical writing, Stanton Marlan offers his own way to approach it, which he calls a *daimonic* reading. Meditating on the flow of alchemical images gathered by Jung, he opens himself to an inner voice, one that is at once personal and "other", to discover their hidden depths. We are allowed a rare glimpse into the laboratory of Marlan's mind and soul, where he follows his lifelong passion for these old alchemical writings.

J. K.

I am grateful to the editors, Jean Kirsch and Murray Stein, for the invitation to reflect on my reading of Jung's alchemy and, particularly, for the opportunity to do so in a personal and subjective way as opposed to a strictly academic one. For me, this is not an easy distinction. I find it difficult to separate personal and academic work in any absolute way. Jung once wrote, "My life is what I have done, my scientific work; the one is inseparable from the other."[1] Again, in his "Late Thoughts", he elaborated: "making 'theory' … is as much a part of me, as vital a function of mine, as eating and drinking".[2] Likewise, I find that to whatever extent my academic work has become meaningful and integrated into my life, the apparent categories of personal and academic no longer sit strictly outside one another.

The editors have posed a few questions to guide contributors to this book, which aims to consider why we still read Jung and how, as well as how to do so deeply and well. Reading Jung's alchemical work is no easy task, and alchemical texts are themselves even more difficult. Von Franz has noted:

> As soon as we get into the [alchemical] texts you will understand ... how alchemy came to be forgotten, and why still, even in Jungian circles ... when it comes to alchemy, they give up, and either do not read, or grumble while reading his books on the subject.[3]

She goes on to say that "[t]his is because alchemy, in itself, is tremendously dark and complex".[4] Likewise, Edward Edinger recognized how difficult alchemy was to understand: "We encounter a wild, luxuriant, tangled mass of overlapping images that is maddening to the order-seeking conscious mind."[5] Hillman, too, has commented that "the phenomena of alchemy present a chaos".[6] He quotes Bonus of Ferrara:

> [T]he only method that prevails is that of chaos ... all the writers seem to begin ... with that which is quite strange and unknown ... The consequence is that one seems to flounder along through these works, with only here and there a glimmering of light.[7]

Jung had a similar first reaction. His early attempt to understand alchemy left him with the feeling that "[t]his stuff is impossible to understand ... blatant non-sense".[8] And yet it continued to intrigue and fascinate him and eventually became a major part of his life's work. In fact, Jung's interpretation of alchemy came "as a breath of fresh air ... while historians had been struggling against a sense of futility, JUNG seemed to have found the key that could 'make sense' of alchemy, and even endow it with meaning and significance for modern man".[9]

Some of Jung's closest followers were aware that Jung's writings on alchemy were difficult to read, and so it is not surprising that some of them dedicated themselves to helping readers gain access to his primary works. A number of these analysts and scholars have been essential to my own reading, especially Marie-Louise von Franz, Edward Edinger, James Hillman, and Wolfgang Giegerich.

For von Franz and Edinger, Jung's works were authoritative, so they did not criticize Jung or offer any fundamentally different approach. They tended to see their own work basically as a bridge to Jung's, but their evaluation does not represent the extent to which their own contributions have extended both our understanding of Jung and alchemy, and the field of analytical psychology as a whole.

For me, von Franz's uncanny symbolic sensitivity, her appreciation of the "dark feminine", her work on alchemical history and active imagination, and her exploration of psyche and matter – to say nothing of her work on the

Aurora consurgens – have been important companions to my reading. The work of Edinger has also affected me deeply. His book, *Anatomy of the Psyche*, organizes the typical operations and stages of the alchemical process and, in so doing, brings order to the chaos of alchemy. Perhaps even more directly than von Franz, Edinger lays out guiding principles for how to read Jung.[10] Like von Franz, he held Jung in the highest esteem, if not in a profound idealization. His first principle for how to read Jung is to recognize Jung's magnitude:

> realize that JUNG's consciousness vastly surpasses your own.... If you make the assumption that you know better than he does and you start out with a critical attitude, don't bother. The book isn't for you. JUNG's depth and breadth are absolutely awesome. We're all Lilliputians by comparison.[11]

I read such statements with ambivalence and draw back from what appears to be Edinger's god-like projection onto Jung. Yet, I too hold Jung's work in the highest esteem, and I deeply respect Edinger's integrity. Nevertheless, Edinger's seeming foreclosure of a critical attitude appears to my taste as too literal. For me, the best way to read Edinger is to accept the importance of approaching Jung with an open attitude and initially suspend judgement in order to remain open to what we do not understand. Edinger is keenly aware of the temptation to criticize as a defence against the anxiety of not knowing. In Zen Buddhism, only the empty vessel can receive, and, by being empty, we become teachable. In the face of the difficult challenge of Jung's alchemical work and with respect for the laborious process he went through to gain insight into this field, an initial bracketing of one's criticism is a reasonable approach. For me, it is not hard to idealize Jung's work in alchemy. Perhaps it is the case, as Harold Bloom has noted, that "[w]e read, frequently if unknowingly, in quest of a mind much more original than our own".[12]

Edinger's second principle for how to read Jung is to appreciate that Jung presents "psychic facts", rather than "theories about facts". From my perspective, however, the separation between theories and facts is a bit problematic in that it takes for granted a vision of *reality* based on a clear subject–object perspective that may not do justice to the complexity of the relationship between thought and reality. Still, my critical reading of Edinger may not do justice to his vision since, by "psychic fact", I believe he means something beyond psyche as a literal "object" of consciousness. Based on Jung's views of amplification, he developed a method of *cluster thinking* that is more like a phenomenology of images that gives one a variegated, dynamic, and mosaic-like view of the psyche.

The third principle is what Edinger calls "the 'fruit cake' principle".[13] By this, he means that "you must read Jung the way you eat fruit cake – very slowly. The reading is exceedingly rich, exceedingly delicious, because it is the richness of psyche itself."[14] Jung gives us "kernels ... rich pieces of nut and heavy fruit which have to be masticated and digested slowly in order to be appreciated".[15] For Edinger, you cannot read Jung's alchemical work the way you read an ordinary book. Each kernel, each image, has to be unpacked "the way one works on a dream".[16] One has to have the capacity to enter into the unknown and to stay open, to "disidentify from the ego sufficiently" in order to go on in the work. For me, Edinger's recommendations about keeping an open mind, thinking in images, "cluster thinking", reading slowly, patiently, diligently, while disidentifying from the ego are all good advice when reading Jung's alchemy. Edinger's personal depth and profound introversion, as well as the integrity of his order-seeking mind, make him a compelling reader of Jung.

Nevertheless, in spite of my positive regard for both von Franz and Edinger, they, at times, too easily translate alchemy into a conceptually taken for granted framework of Jung's psychology, and such a reading sets the stage for the criticism and alternate readings of James Hillman and Wolfgang Giegerich. Hillman's approach to reading alchemy resists translating its images and language into the structures of any conceptual rationalism that leaves the image behind. He gives these examples:

> White Queen and Red King have become feminine and masculine principles; their incestuous sexual intercourse has become the union of opposites; the freakish hermaphrodite and uniped, the golden head ... have all become paradoxical representations of the goal, examples of androgyny symbols of the Self.[17]

For him, these are a move from "precision into generality".[18] Hillman challenges us to imagine the process of reading alchemy differently. For him, sticking to the image recovers the point of the ancient Greek maxim "save the phenomena", and allows us to speak imaginatively and to dream the dream onward. Hillman is not simply suggesting that we replace our concepts with "the archaic neologisms of alchemy"[19] or take alchemical language literally as substitutions for our own concepts. It is not the literal return to alchemy that he proposes, but rather a "restoration of the alchemical mode of imagining".[20] For Hillman, this means the move from a psychology of alchemy to an alchemical psychology rooted in the fundamental principle of the imagination and not in reified fixed structures of theoretical abstractions.

If Hillman moves from conceptual rationalism to image and imagination, and from a psychology of alchemy to an alchemical psychology, Giegerich moves from image and imagination to a radically revised notion of "the concept". For Giegerich, the conceptual is something not to move beyond, but to arrive at, as a furthering of dialectical thinking beyond imagination. One might characterize this move as one from an imaginal and alchemical psychology to an animus psychology not interested in "saving the phenomena", but rather in following the path of thinking out of the imaginal to the logical life of the soul. Reading alchemy from this perspective leads Giegerich to note that while, for Jung, "medieval alchemy was the historical link between the ancient past (mythology, Gnosticism, Neoplatonism) and the present", for Giegerich "it is also the link between the imagination and dialectical logic",[21] as well as a link to his revisioned notion of psychology.

In addition to these analysts, a number of historians also have influenced my reading: Sonu Shamdasani, Adam McLean, Lawrence Principe, William Newman, Hereward Tilton, Wouter Hanegraaff, Hayden White, Ruth Meyer, and others – all have contributed perspectives on how I read Jung and his alchemy. Within the limits of this paper, I cannot elaborate the complexity of all these positions. In general, many of them share a conviction that there are problems in our reading of Jung due to a tendency to project speculative theories onto Jung's life and his reading of alchemy. Shamdasani has demonstrated the value of historical criticism through his correction and revisioning of what he has called the "Jungian legend".[22] In a similar way, McLean has criticized interpreters of alchemy for projecting their theoretical fantasies onto what alchemists *actually said*. For him, both psychological and esoteric interpretations of alchemy, including Jung's, have fallen prey to this problem. Like Shamdasani, he has worked diligently to make unknown texts available to modern readers and has taught courses on how to read alchemy. He describes his way of approaching alchemical texts as a forensic reading.[23] Like McLean, Principe and Newman have been highly critical of Jung for what they consider his a-historical and over-generalized reading and "for effectively writing laboratory alchemy out of the picture".[24] They reject the idea of a psychological or spiritual interpretation of alchemy. On the other hand, other historians such as Tilton and Hanegraaff have shown the limitations and problems with Principe's and Newman's readings, including their not well-researched criticisms of Jung.[25]

If there is any shadow to the historical readings of Jung and alchemy, it is a tendency to view historical reading as getting it "right", getting to the "real" Jung or "real" alchemy. Nevertheless, setting criticisms aside, classical amplification and active imagination (von Franz), cluster thinking (Edinger), sticking with the image (Hillman), following the logical life of the soul (Giegerich), historical rectification of the Jung legend (Shamdasani), and the forensic reading (McLean) continue to influence me. These are all strong and persuasive readings, and I read with them, through them, as well as against them – stepping back and reading Jung again and again, trying to find my own perspective. Harold Bloom has noted, "Reading well is best pursued as an implicit discipline; finally there is no method but yourself, when your self has been fully molded."[26] In a resonant voice, Giegerich has written: "every potential reader has to try for himself to lift JUNG's work and see what happens. No other person can do it for him."[27] Reading Jung's alchemy is heavy lifting.

If I step back from Jung in my academic reading, it is less a stepping back from Jung than from the shadow of certain essentialist readings. By this, I mean readings that place emphasis on fixed and unchanging structures and static views of the archetypes that have minimized individual, cultural, and historical differences and that reify a centralizing tendency and concept of the centre. The latter is an understandable temptation since the process of centring became, for Jung, the touchstone for the recognition of the self and for the individuation process. He represented the centre and centring process in mandala-like forms such as the "Window on Eternity", the golden castle mandala, and in an impressive geometric rendering of the philosopher's stone. Although I find such images beautiful and profound, they can easily become encrusted, rock-hard representations of a dynamic psychic reality difficult to describe in abstract form. These images came to Jung as a compensation to the chaos of the unconscious, and he created them in his effort to gain stability in the midst of this turmoil. Thus Jung was able to see the potency of the self and the healing value of the centring process. Images representing this stabilizing function capture the "archetype of orientation and meaning",[28] but it is important to remember that the self is also a destabilizing power that continues to deconstruct the ego's effort to represent reality in any kind of static hypostasis that obscures the self's reality. I have attempted to read Jung with this concern in mind and have valued a postmodern sensibility, perhaps best characterized by Jacques Derrida, who has been credited "with the achievement of finding a solution to the fundamental logical task of the postmodern situation: switching from stability through centering and solid foundations to stability through greater flexibility and decentering".[29]

In many places, Jung likewise resists Cartesian clarity and values a dynamic reading. In "Paracelsus as a Spiritual Phenomenon", he writes about our "understandable desire" for unambiguous clarity:

> but we are apt to forget that in psychic matters we are dealing with processes of experience, that is, with transformations which should never be given hard and fast names if their living movement is not to petrify into something static. The protean mythologem and the shimmering symbol express the process of the psyche far more trenchantly and, in the end, far more clearly than the clearest concept; for the symbol not only conveys a visualization of the process but – and this is perhaps just as important – it also brings a re-experiencing of it, of that twilight which we can learn to understand only through inoffensive empathy, but which too much clarity only dispels.[30]

Reading Jung in a way that conjures up that twilight draws the reader closer to what lies within it. This twilight is a softer light and, by it, the ego's brightness is diminished. This reading gives room to the unconscious, to dreams and visions, and allows for the unknown to play an important role. I call such a reading a daimonic one.

I have been reading Jung and his alchemical work for most of my adult life and continue to do so. There is something about the arcane and impenetrable quality of alchemy and Jung's passionate reading of it that continues to draw me back into its mad obscurities, its dark matter, and its fantastic images. My basic laboratory is the analyst's consulting room and the library, with its old texts and tomes. "Pray, Read, Read, and Read again, Work and you shall find" says the *Mutus Liber*, an old alchemical text aimed at the production of the Philosophers' Stone.[31] And yet, my love of alchemy draws me down to the basement, from library to lab, from texts to textures, from weighty tomes to the weight of lead – to the al-chemistry of the soul, to its fire and heat, to anthor and alembic, holding and cooking, combustion, distillation, cooling, sublimating, transformation, multiplication, and refinement – to what comes alive in the work.

I remain passionate about alchemy and am deeply drawn to its images and objects, to its smells and colours, to its aesthetics, art, and artistry, to its graphics and symbolic designs, and to its hermetic vision of the transformation of matter – to what matters to the soul and to Jung's reading of it. For me, alchemy is a madness, a journey into the unknown and unimagined. Its *nigredo* is poisonous, a "blacker than black" darkness. But if one has the skill, good luck, or divine favour, it may be a *pharmacon*, a poison that also heals, and in the healing, one can find a light that shines in the midst of darkness and is said to reveal a miracle that Jung called the Self and the alchemists, the Stone.

Jung found such an image in his now famous Liverpool dream. At the core of the dream is the following:

> While everything round about was obscured by rain, fog, smoke, and dimly lit darkness, the little island blazed with sunlight. On it stood a single tree, a magnolia, in a shower of reddish blossoms. It was as though the tree stood in the sunlight and were at the same time the source of light.[32]

Jung commented that the "dream represented my situation at the time.... Everything was extremely unpleasant, black and opaque – just as I felt then. But I had had a vision of unearthly beauty, and that was why I was able to live at all."[33] In the midst of darkness, Jung experienced a self-generating source of light and noted, "This dream brought with it a sense of finality"[34] and a vision of the goal. "Through this dream", Jung wrote, he "understood that the self is the principle and archetype of orientation and meaning ... its healing function."[35]

Later, in *Alchemical Studies*, Jung wrote about the relationship between the lapis and the tree. In the "Consilium coniugii", Senior said:

> Thus the stone is perfected of and in itself. For it is the tree whose branches, leaves, flowers, and fruits come from it and through it and for it, and it is itself whole or the whole [*tota vel totum*] and nothing else.[36]

The stone refers to taking "wisdom with all thy power, for from it thou shalt drink eternal life, until thy [stone] is congealed and thy sluggishness depart, for thence cometh life".[37] These alchemical comments could well be understood as an amplification of Jung's Liverpool dream.

Between 1918 and 1920, Jung writes that he began to understand the individuation process and the Self as the goal of psychological development and to represent it in mandala-like form. One of the beautiful mandalas he drew around this time he identified as a representation of the Philosophers' Stone. Shamdasani has noted that, "[i]n a manner of speaking, Jung had found the philosopher's stone before he had come to his psychological understanding of alchemy".[38]

The Ariadne-like thread that led to Jung's serious reading of alchemy is dramatically portrayed in *Memories, Dreams, Reflections*, a text I consider to be one of the best descriptions of Jung's encounter with alchemy and the subsequent unfolding of his ideas. *MDR* is a rich weave of events, inner and outer, that reads like a complex mystery story, a page turner that I return to again and again. I continue to do so with the knowledge that *MDR* is a complex text that contains many omissions and other problems noted in Jungian scholarship over the years.[39] I will refrain from reiterating the now well-known issues that make *MDR* a less than historically accurate "autobiography" or "biography". Clearly, the Jung portrayed in *MDR* is at least in part a "fiction", but I would claim that these fictional elements are just as important for reading Jung's biography as they are for the psychological reading of his alchemy.

On the other hand, Shamdasani has pointed out the dangers of the divide between fantasies of Jung and his historical actuality. He is alarmed by the fact that even "professional Jungians are not immune to this":[40]

> Jung's dreams and fantasies, all too often, have functioned like Rorschach ink blots, and attracted all manner of fantasies, and … the boundary line between novels and plays about Jung and non-fictional works has not always been as sharp as it could be.[41]

Yet, I remain sceptical that any absolute line can be drawn between the fictional Jung and the historical figure. Although historical scholarship can help correct the worst biases, the fantasy that we can or should completely purge the fictive elements of our reading and arrive at the "correct" perception of the way things really are adds another fiction to our misreadings of Jung.

The master words "interpretation" and "reading" are themselves debatable.[42] Hayden White, a historian by training and an important figure in debates about practices of historical and literary interpretation, argues there is always a fictional dimension to what some perceive as historical fact. For him, historical narratives are always also fictions that "have more in common with their counterparts in literature than they have with those in the sciences".[43] In this way, White links mythic and historical consciousness and challenges the radical oppositions between history, fiction, fact, and fantasy. He insists on the fictive elements in all historical narrative. For White, "history as a discipline is in bad shape today because it has lost sight of its origins in the literary imagination ... [i]n the interest of *appearing* scientific and objective".[44] For White, this does

> not mean the degradation of historiography to the status of ideology or propaganda. In fact, this recognition [of "the fictive element"] would serve as a potent antidote to the tendency of historians to become captive of ideological preconceptions which they do not recognize as such but honor as the "correct" perception of "the way things *really* are".[45]

For White, "history has served as a kind of archetype of the 'realist' pole of representation",[46] but historical realism should never be read "as unambiguous signs of the events they report, but rather as symbolic structures, extended metaphors".[47] A good professional historian consistently "reminds his readers of the purely provisional nature of his characterizations of events, agents, and agencies found in the always incomplete historical record".[48] Just what is meant by the "fictive element", "symbolic structures", and "extended metaphors" needs continued reflection and refinement. If one way of reading Jung reflects the "realist" pole of representation, perhaps White's insight gives room for a "fictive" pole, leaning toward the contributions of a psychological, subjective, and daimonic element in all readings?

This perspective has been richly elaborated by Ruth Meyer in her book *Cleo's Circle: Entering the Imaginal World of Historians*,[49] where she shows that "being an historian is in part an imaginal activity"[50] and "that dreams, visions, and altered states form an unacknowledged and misunderstood part of the historian's creative process".[51] Perhaps a mysterious intertwining of the fictive and real is the ideal goal of any historian, psychologist, or general reader, but it is easy to err in either direction, subjective or objective, and perhaps a one-sided reading may be impossible to avoid. I have no doubt my reading is an errant one, and while I applaud and remain excited about the ongoing scholarship that will no doubt give us a more comprehensive and perhaps more "accurate" picture of Jung, I think it is also important to realize that our understanding of Jung is always dependent on interpretation. No matter what materials we have before us, interpretation is the key factor; that is, the Jung we come to know personally and collectively is never simply the real or literal Jung, but a figure known through individual and collective fantasies and transferences as well as historical "evidence". Perhaps it is even the case, as literary critic Harold Bloom has argued, that every reading is also a misreading.

As noted, Shamdasani has demonstrated the value of his approach to historical criticism. However, I would hold with White and Meyer that history must always be interpreted and that we live in an historical and psychological world in which imagination and fiction both play an essential role. To believe that we will ever get to the "real" Jung is a limiting fantasy since the "real" Jung is always a Jung-for-us. He is always a figure immersed in a fabric of relationships and contexts of psyche and world. He is an inner figure and a collective one – a figure that has, and will continue to have, many faces.

Shamdasani begins his book *Jung and the Making of Modern Psychology* by noting that Jung has been seen as an "Occultist, Scientist, Prophet, Charlatan, Philosopher, Racist, Guru, Anti-Semite ... Polygamist, Healer, Poet, Con-Artist, Psychiatrist, and Anti-Psychiatrist".[52] As he notes, "what has Jung not been called?" and "the very proliferation of 'Jungs'" drive Shamdasani to wonder "whether everyone could possibly be talking about the same figure" and to recognize that Jung "has become a figure upon whom an endless succession of myths, legends, fantasies, and fictions continues to be draped. Travesties, distortions, and caricatures have become the norm. The process shows no signs of abating."[53] After decades of myth making, Shamdasani notes, "one question becomes more insistent: who was C. G. Jung?"[54] He quotes Jung's remark, "Don't make a legend of me."[55] While careful scholarship can help us correct the worst biases of the Jungian legend, I do not think we can ever escape the truth of mythos, and we must, by necessity, "dream the dream onward". Perhaps it is the case that Jung is all of this and more.

Even prior to current scholarship, both Jung and Jaffé had acknowledged the many problems with *MDR* that make it less than an accurate, scientific, or objective account of Jung's life and work. In Jung's own words, what he has written uses an "improvisation ... born of the moment",[56] a passionate retrospective and brief sketch. Jaffé notes that it was "written in response to a special occasion" and, therefore, one should "not expect it to be comprehensive".[57] For Jung, accurate, literal, and historical events were of little importance. They had, in his words, become "phantasms ... barely recollect[ed]".[58] They were events that he had "no desire to reconstruct" since they no longer "stirred his imagination".[59] What was important to Jung were his inner experiences. They were what remained vibrant and alive and which over the years had "grown all the more vivid and colorful".[60] It is precisely these experiences that continue to draw me to this text and make *MDR* not simply less, but also more, than an ordinary autobiography or biography. I do not read *MDR* for a factual account of Jung's life, but rather because his description of his inner world opens onto a larger view of psychic reality. I consider *MDR* a document of the soul that recounts important *fictions* – archetypal moments that reach out beyond Jung's personal life and toward a vision of the objective psyche. *MDR* is replete with such moments, which include fantasies, dreams, visions, and synchronistic experiences.

Jung's openness to the power of the unconscious is vividly described in *MDR* as "hitting upon a stream of lava", a fiery magma that burst forth from the unconscious and provided "the *prima materia* for a lifetime's work".[61] It was "like fiery liquid basalt; out of [which] crystallized the stone that I could work".[62] For Jung, these experiences were the heated fires that reshaped his life. Like the figure of Faust in Goethe's classic epic, Jung opened himself to the unconscious out of which a new way of seeing emerged. With Goethe's words he proclaims: "Now let me dare to open wide the gate / Past which men's steps have ever flinching trod."[63]

The visions that came did not always come benignly, and his descent into the unconscious initiated Jung into a period of great uncertainty and isolation. At one point, he regarded his work on alchemy as a sign of his inner relationship to Goethe. Jung felt Goethe's secret was that he was in the grip of a process of archetypal transformation that has continued through the centuries. If Jung's engagement with the unconscious was a kind of madness, as some have claimed, it was also the beginning of his *opus magnum* or *divinum*[64] – a divine madness and, at the same time, a growing sense of archetypal reality.

I imagine the "madness" Jung experienced to be the kind described by Plato and Aristotle. For Plato, poetic inspiration was a form of divine madness, and Aristotle likewise noted that great genius was always mixed with insanity. Plato and Aristotle, both champions of the rational, show a deep ambivalence about insanity, an ambivalence that Plato helps to differentiate in the *Phaedrus*, one of his great dialogues on love. Socrates comments on two kinds of madness, "one produced by human infirmity, the other a divine release of the soul from the yoke of custom and convention".[65] If Jung at times came close to the first kind, his strength of character brought him forward to a liberating vision. Ultimately, Jung experienced his "inner madness" as "a suprapersonal process of the mundus archetypus (archetypal world)" that "was alive and active . . . a living substance"[66] in both Goethe's creative process and his own. He confesses that these experiences haunted him and, in Goethe's case, led to the production of a classic work of literature, whereas Jung was single-mindedly driven to the mysteries of the personality and to the development of a new vision of psychology. The struggle to work his way through this difficult process and come to terms with the unconscious required that Jung abandon the idea of the ego's superordinate position. He felt compelled to let himself be carried along by the current of his experiences without knowing where it would lead.

Like Jung, I find myself gripped by Jung's story of his descent into the unconscious and his fateful encounter with alchemy. I find something infectious about this story. I read it over and over again, and identify with Jung's experience as a symbolic "as if", an inflation – part transference, part fetish, part *participation mystique*, and part poetic inspiration. What feels like an autonomous process draws me into a phantasmagoria of alchemical fiction, one that has become an important part of my life and study.

In the preface to James Hillman's book *Healing Fiction*, the poet George Quasha quotes Wallace Stevens as saying, "The final belief is to believe in a fiction, which you know to be a fiction, there being nothing else. The exquisite truth is to know that it is a fiction and that you believe in it willingly."[67] Quasha contends that our reality is created through our fictions; to be conscious of these fictions is to gain creative access to and participate in the poetics of soul making. My own reading of Jung is filled with such "fictions" in Quasha's sense. Harold Bloom quotes Virginia Woolf's advice about reading, that "there is always a demon in us who whispers, 'I hate, I love', and we cannot silence him".[68] Like Bloom, "I cannot silence my demon" who loves alchemy and identifies with Jung's mad passion. According to Shoshana Felman, Gérard de Nerval also hints at the daimonic quality of this passion:

> Every reading, says Nerval, is a kind of madness since it is based on illusion and induces us to identify with imaginary heroes. Madness is nothing other than an intoxicating reading: a madman is one who is drawn into the dizzying whirl of his own reading.[69]

I do not read Jung for history, but for his-story. While I am interested in Jung's history, I am not a historian and have little to contribute to the objective facts of Jung's life. Jung once wrote, "You read as much into a book as out of it",[70] and my reading of Jung is an errant one insofar as his-story has also become a my-story. For me, reading Jung daimonically has meant a bracketing of my academic ego and letting myself be carried by fictions and gripped by an archetypal passion, a kind of madness that opens onto the scene of a magical adventure requiring an engagement not only with Jung and alchemy, but also with my own psychic depths.

One captivating moment of my identification with Jung's story was his report of a series of dreams that he felt prefigured his discovery of alchemy:

> Beside my house stood another, that is to say, another wing or annex, which was strange to me. Each time I would wonder in my dream why I did not know this house, although it had apparently always been there. Finally came a dream in which I reached the

> other wing. I discovered there a wonderful library, dating largely from the sixteenth and seventeenth centuries. Large, fat folio volumes, bound in pigskin, stood along the walls. Among them were a number of books embellished with copper engravings of a strange character, and illustrations containing curious symbols such as I had never seen before.[71]

At the time, Jung reports, he did not realize that the images in these dreams represented alchemical symbols. He was only aware that these images fascinated him. He thought the unknown wing of the house represented something unconscious in himself and that the dream referred to alchemy, which at the time he knew little about, but which he "was soon to study".[72] Many years later, he had acquired a collection of alchemical books very much like the library in his dreams.

One of the most compelling parts of his story is the idea that somehow behind such dreams is the working of the objective psyche, leading the way to Jung's discoveries as if following a teleological thread or seeing a fate prefigured and meant to be. The images of Jung's library and of ancient alchemical books activated in me a passion to see Jung's library, as if it were possible to enter his dream and to make it my own, to hold in my hands the texts that he found so essential for his work and that were progressively becoming important for my own. One summer while I was teaching in Zurich, my wife Jan and I had the good fortune to visit Jung's library and to examine and study his alchemical books. I was able to hold in my hands Jung's copy of the *Artis Auriferae* and the *Rosarium Philosophorum* (Figures 3.1 and 3.2), an experience as real as it was dreamlike.

The story of a dream leading to alchemical books and their mysteries is not unique to Jung. One example is from a story about the famous alchemist Nicolas Flamel (1330–1418). (The extraordinary events of his life have been popularized in J. K. Rowling's *Harry Potter and the Philosopher's Stone*.) According to legend, Flamel had a vision of a mysterious book. Later, in a Paris bookstall, he discovered what he imagined to be the book from his dream. It was entitled *The Book of Abraham the Jew*.[73] It was replete with mysterious images, and legend has it that it contained the secret of the Philosophers' Stone. I had often fantasized about this book, although I could never find it. After visiting Jung's library, I was in Basel at an old bookshop and asked the dealer if he had any old alchemical books. He said he had a very rare one, which turned out to be a copy of *The Book of Abraham the Jew* (see Figures 3.3 and 3.4). Such experiences stir my imagination.

Another strange coincidence concerned John Dee (1527–1608), an English magus and alchemist. I have felt a special connection to Dee because of a powerful dream I had earlier in my life.

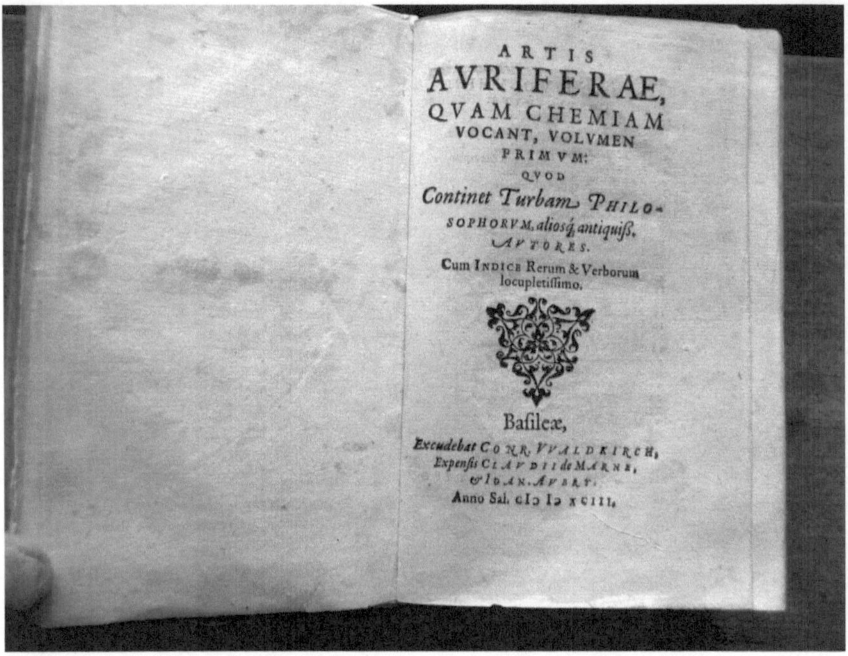

Figure 3.1 Artis Auriferae (1593) (photo courtesy of the author and Jan Marlan).

Figure 3.2 Rosarium Philosophorum (photo courtesy of author and Jan Marlan).

Figure 3.3 *Uraltes Chymisches Werck* by Abraham Eleazar (1735) (photo courtesy of the author and Jan Marlan).

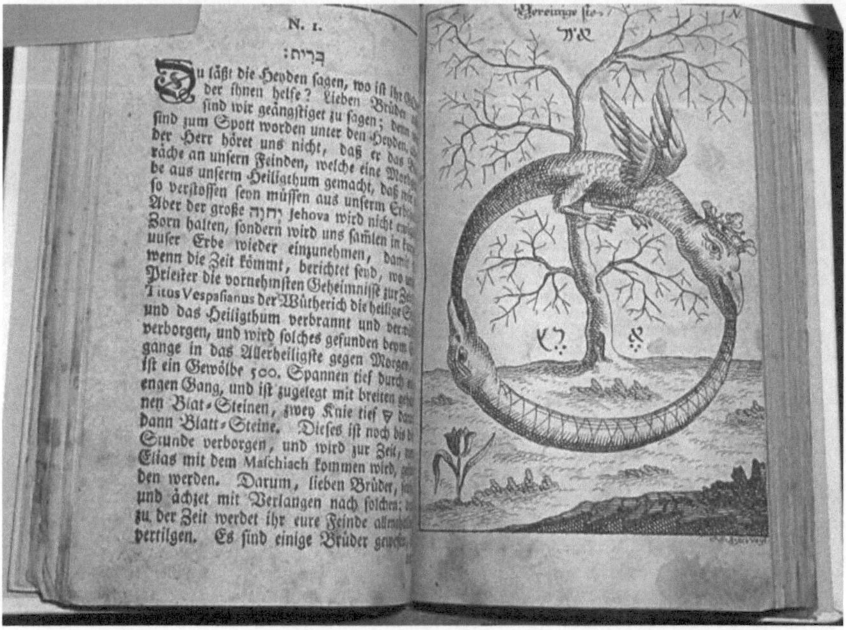

Figure 3.4 The unification of air and earth, from Eleazar's *Uraltes Chymisches Werck* (photo courtesy of the author and Jan Marlan).

> I am in some kind of underground cavern; I think Egyptian. I feel something in my chest start to fly up and out of my body to an opening. It is a cat being resurrected. It is a numinous feeling, powerful and real. Organ music is starting to play deep and resonant, and a voice says, "Who is John Dee?"

At the time, I had never heard of John Dee and puzzled over my dream. When I discovered who Dee was, it gave me the chills and the dream has stayed with me throughout my life. Is it possible that such a dream has any relationship to John Dee, the Elizabethan alchemist who collected one of Europe's great alchemical libraries? During his lifetime, Dee was also noted for his ability to converse with spirits. Is it possible that his spirit and my dream truly reach beyond the subjectivity of time and place – and reflect a connection to the archetypal world? Is it possible that my dream was already connecting me to a transpersonal reality that was to become important in my future? Perhaps this is another mad fantasy, a wild inflation, but dreams have convinced me that they speak to a world beyond the ego.

Many years after the John Dee dream, another dream experience reawakened such questions. I dreamt that two small rabbits had fallen into a window well in front of my house. When I awoke, the dream bothered me, and I began to think of it subjectively: What had fallen into a hole or trap? Was I stuck somewhere or depressed? Nothing I worked on seemed to reveal the dream's meaning. A few days later, while out in the garden, the memory of the dream returned. I suddenly decided to look in the window well – and there I found two small dead rabbits. I was deeply saddened and wondered: If I had looked right after I had the dream, perhaps I could have saved them? Is it possible that the souls of these rabbits were calling out for help? Is it possible that my dream was connecting me to the objective psyche? Whatever the case, the existential impact of this experience led me to recognize the importance of not simply and automatically reducing dreams to a personal level.

I am aware that such "fictions" are a slippery slope: illusion, intoxication, inflation, and daimonic passion. Such a state destabilizes our sense of the factual, the real, and the line between fiction and truth. It is a challenge to our everyday sensibilities. Perhaps it is the madness of the daimon that says "I love". A daimonic reading can be perilous, but I believe that opening the gates to the unconscious is important, and I have come to see that the corrections to these inflations can be found within the fictions themselves. An example of this is found in the following story.

On my first trip to Zurich many years ago, I saw Jung's house for the first time. I walked up the driveway, very excited to be close to Jung's spirit. I wanted to carry home some of this feeling, something more substantial than a memory I knew would fade. I wanted an object, a material thing associated with Jung – even a stone to put on my desk to hold this spirit firm.

I collected a few rocks from the ground and took them with me. I placed one on my desk and the others in a glass vessel. At times I would give one to a good friend on a special occasion. Through the stone, I felt I had a special connection to Jung, a *participation mystique*, a rock-hard alchemy. When I touched these stones and looked at them, the feeling of connection was reinforced – Jung and I were one in stone, a gift from psyche. Eric Neumann would call this oneness an ego-Self identity that calls for an ego-Self separation.[74] This deflation came in the form of a dream:

> I am at the side door of Jung's house. I desperately want something of Jung's to take home with me. I knock and Emma Jung comes to the door. I explain who I am and tell her how important her husband is to me and ask her if there is anything of his she could give me. She says "I'll be right back" and goes into the house. She returns and on the ground before me she places a pair of Jung's shoes. With excitement, I step into them – only to discover they are far too big.

My first reaction to this humorous dream was the deflation it brought in its wake, but as time went on, the gift I took home with me was that Jung's shoes were not for me. This recognition led me to understand the problem of the *imitatio* of Jung: that simply identifying with Jung was not the way to follow what his spirit opened in my soul. With this recognition, I was able to relate to Jung's work in a more differentiated way. There was movement in my archetypal transference and a response to it, and my small feet were a catalyst to a further development of my soul.

Through experiences like the ones I have recorded here, it became clear to me that dreams, synchronicities, and living in an archetypal fiction have sustained my lifelong interest in reading Jung and alchemy. For me, it was and is important to live in the fire of imagination, to find the lava flow that participates in shaping one's life journey. Such "fictions" are essential components in my reading of Jung, and I believe this is the way Jung read his own life. It requires following the promptings of the unconscious "as if" they contain a meaningful *telos* that can shape one's life.

But living in such fantasies and so close to the fire can lead to getting burnt. Opening to the unconscious is only part of the story, though I would claim it is an essential one. One must also turn towards the unconscious and engage it. Alchemical texts are filled with descriptions of how to work with this fire, and Hillman has noted, "The alchemist must be able to fight fire with fire, using his own fire to operate upon the fires with which he is operating. Working the fire by means of fire."[75] I believe this is the passion Jung brought to his lava, and it is what prepared him to study alchemy and sustained him in the process of doing so.

I have allowed myself for the purpose of this reflection to draw apart the personal and academic to a greater extent than has been my custom. When I reflect upon what draws me to read Jung, it is a passion that continues to stir my imagination, to follow a mythos that carries me along in a fictional "as if" that suggests a mysterious *telos*. I have called this way of reading Jung a daimonic one because it is open to the unconscious and to enacting its promptings in a way that gives them substance in daily life. I consider this a living extension of active imagination and a gesture of respect to Jung's work and to the psychic reality it invokes. Like every responsible active imagination, it also requires an ongoing engagement with one's fictions, and a living dialogue with otherness and with our reading. "Reading well", says Bloom, "is one of the great pleasures that solitude can afford you, because it is, at least in my experience, the most healing of pleasures. It returns you to otherness."[76] Such a process often draws me down into my depths and out beyond them and to the limits of my understanding. It relativizes my point of view and, in so doing, continues to open new horizons and to broaden my vision. It gives meaning to what originally appeared as nonsense and helps to deconstruct the fixity of stale meanings. It opens a fertile abyss and connects me with the larger world. Reading Jung's alchemy is ponderous and difficult, but ultimately it enlivens me with a sense of richness and substance. It is both inflating and deflating. Following Jung's insights into alchemy is by no means a benign quest. It is a *massa confusa* filled with impasses and dead ends, with shadows and suffering. But, for me, it is also an entrance to the treasure house of the soul.

Notes

1 C. G. Jung, *Memories, Dreams, Reflections*, recorded and edited by Aniela Jaffé, trans. Richard and Clara Winston, New York, Pantheon, 1963, p. 222 (*MDR*).

2 Ibid., p. 327.

3 M.-L. von Franz, *Alchemy: An Introduction to the Symbolism and the Psychology*, Toronto, Inner City, 1980, p. 13.

4 Ibid.

5 E. F. Edinger, *Anatomy of the Psyche: Alchemical Symbolism in Psychotherapy*, LaSalle, IL, Open Court, 1985, p. 14.

6 J. Hillman, *Alchemical Psychology*, Uniform Edition, vol. 5, Putnam, CT, Spring Publications, 2010, p. 7.

7 Ibid., p. 8.

8 Jung, *MDR*, p. 204.

9 W. J. Hanegraaff, *Esotericism and the Academy: Rejected Knowledge in Western Culture*, Cambridge, Cambridge University Press, 2012, pp. 293–4. (Quoting Walter Pagel, "Jung's views on alchemy", *Isis*, 1948, vol. 39, nos. 1–2, pp. 44–8, quote from p. 48.)

10 See "Preface", in Edward Edinger, *The Aion Lectures: Exploring the Self in C. G. Jung's* Aion, ed. Deborah A. Wesley, pp. 11–13, Toronto, Inner City Books, 1996; and Edward Edinger, *The Mysterium Lectures: A Journey Through C. G. Jung's* Mysterium Coniunctionis, ed. and trans. J. Dexter Blackmer, pp. 17–21, Toronto, Inner City Books, 1995.

11 Edinger, *Aion Lectures*, p. 11.

12 H. Bloom, *How to Read and Why*, New York, Simon and Schuster, 2000, p. 25.

13 Edinger, *Aion Lectures*, p. 12.

14 Ibid.
15 Ibid.
16 Edinger, *Mysterium Lectures*, p. 18.
17 Hillman, *Alchemical Psychology*, p. 15.
18 Ibid.
19 Ibid., p. 18.
20 Ibid.
21 W. Giegerich, *The Soul's Logical Life: Towards a Rigorous Notion of Psychology*, Berlin, Peter Lang Publishing, 1998, p. 134.
22 S. Shamdasani, *Jung Stripped Bare by His Biographers, Even*, London, Karnac, 2005, p. 3.
23 A. McLean, *Adam McLean's Study Course on Reading Alchemical Texts*, published privately, 2005–6, Lesson 24, p. 4.
24 Hanegraaff, *Esotericism*, p. 289.
25 Ibid., pp. 290–1.
26 Bloom, *How to Read and Why*, p. 19.
27 Giegerich, *The Soul's Logical Life*, p. 60.
28 Jung, *MDR*, p. 199.
29 P. Sloterdijk, *Derrida, An Egyptian: On the Problem of the Jewish Pyramid*, Cambridge, Polity Press, 2006, pp. 7–8.
30 C. G. Jung, *Alchemical Studies*, *The Collected Works of C. G. Jung*, vol. 13, Princeton, NJ, Princeton University Press, 1953/1968, p. 199.
31 See A. McLean, *A Commentary on the* Mutus Liber, Edinburgh, Magnum Opus Hermetic Sourceworks, 1982, p. 59.
32 Jung, *MDR*, p. 198.
33 Ibid.
34 Ibid.
35 Ibid., p. 199.
36 Jung, *Alchemical Studies*, *CW* 13, p. 423.
37 Ibid., p. 421.
38 S. Shamdasani, *C. G. Jung: A Biography in Books*, New York, W. W. Norton, p. 169.
39 See S. Shamdasani, "Memories, dreams, omissions", *Spring*, 1995, vol. 57, pp. 115–37; and *Jung Stripped Bare*.
40 Shamdasani, *Jung Stripped Bare*, pp. 2–3.
41 Ibid., p. 118.
42 Vincent B. Leitch (ed.), "Introduction", in *The Norton Anthology of Theory and Criticism*, New York, W. W. Norton, 2001, p. 3.
43 H. White, "The historical text as literary artifact", in Vincent B. Leitch (ed.), *The Norton Anthology of Theory and Criticism*, pp. 1712–29, New York, W. W. Norton, 2001, p. 1713.
44 Ibid., p. 1729.
45 Ibid., p. 1728.
46 Ibid., p. 1719.
47 Ibid., p. 1721.
48 Ibid., p. 1713.
49 Ruth Meyer, *Clio's Circle: Entering the Imaginal World of Historians*, New Orleans, Spring Journal Books, 2012.
50 M. Watkins, "Praise for *Clio's Circle*", Spring Journal & Spring Journal Books, www.springjournalandbooks.com/cgi-bin/ecommerce/ac/agora.cgi?cart_id=7095785.18039*le6YC4&p_id=03293&xm=on&ppinc=search2 (accessed 15 April 2012).
51 Ibid.
52 S. Shamdasani, *Jung and the Making of Modern Psychology: The Dream of a Science*, Cambridge, Cambridge University Press, 2003, p. 1.
53 Ibid.

54 Ibid., p. 2.
55 Ibid., p. 1.
56 Jung, *MDR*, p. 222.
57 A. Jaffé, "Introduction" in *MDR*, p. xiii.
58 Jung, *MDR*, p. ix.
59 Ibid.
60 Ibid.
61 Ibid., p. 199.
62 This is from an additional sentence in the German edition of *MDR*, as translated by Giegerich. Jung quoted in Giegerich, *The Soul's Logical Life*, p. 61.
63 *Faust*, Part 1; Goethe quoted by Jung in *MDR*, pp. 188–9.
64 Jung, *MDR*, p. 206.
65 B. Jowett, *The Dialogues of Plato: Phaedrus*, New York, Random House, 1937.
66 Jung, *MDR*, p. 206.
67 George Quasha, "Preface", in J. Hillman, *Healing Fiction*, pp. ix–xii, Barrytown, NY, Station Hill Press, 1983, p. ix.
68 Bloom, *How to Read and Why*, p. 20.
69 S. Felman, *Writing and Madness: Literature/Philosophy/Psychoanalysis*, Ithaca, NY, Cornell University Press, 1985, p. 64.
70 C. G. Jung, *The Red Book: Liber Novus*, ed. Sonu Shamdasani, London, W. W. Norton, 2009, "Liber Primus", p. 244, n. 145.
71 Jung, *MDR*, p. 202.
72 Jung, *MDR*, p. 202.
73 R. Patai, *The Jewish Alchemists*, Princeton, NJ, Princeton University Press, 1994, pp. 218–33.
74 E. Neumann, *The Origins and History of Consciousness*, London, Routledge & Kegan Paul, 1949.
75 Hillman, *Alchemical Psychology*, p. 22.
76 Bloom, *How to Read and Why*, p. 19.

4

ON READING JUNG IN GERMAN

Jung's Significance for *Germanistik*

Paul Bishop

Jung's well-known reticence to disclose the clinical details of his analytic practice led him to draw upon literature to demonstrate his hypotheses about the structure, nature, and function of the psyche. Thus Jung became, or so Paul Bishop maintains, a practitioner of literary criticism as well as a formulator of psychology, and he may fruitfully be read as both. More important, Bishop thinks our grasp of Jung will be enhanced by reading him as part of the German literary tradition, from Goethe's *Faust* and Hölderlin's *Hyperion* to Nietzsche's *Zarathustra*. Jung's analysis of the poet Hölderlin through his poetry is tracked in Bishop's contribution to this volume. For the psychotherapist, the narrative reveals the story of a young man whose development is arrested by a fateful longing for childhood's carefree and blissful unity with nature. But for the scholar of *Germanistik*, Jung is participating in a noble tradition of literary analysis and discussion. Bishop's contributions to the developing field of Jungian studies encourage dialogue between the Jungian analyst and the academic student of Jung.

J. K.

Despite the significant scholarly advances made in recent years and the increasing number of intellectual-historical approaches to Jung, he is still widely regarded by the academic establishment as an outsider and frequently dismissed with disdain, indeed, contempt. The sheer number of exclusion strategies to which Jung's work is routinely subjected has led one commentator to argue, not without good reason, that "the marginalization of Jungian literary and psychotherapeutic approaches in the academic context" is rooted in the same "eurocentric epistemological ideologies" that lead to the "trivialization and criticism" of feminist theories.[1] What are the reasons for this ongoing exclusion, or to put it another way: What *is* the problem with Jung?

There are a number of possible reasons for his continuing unpopularity within the academy (as opposed to his popularity with readers outside it, in the "real" world). First, there is the question of Jung's conservative political stance and the accusation that he showed himself to be a supporter of

National Socialism. Second, there is the question of Jung's attitude toward women; analytical psychology itself is often seen as "essentialist" (so the Anima and the Animus are frequently understood, not so much as archetypes, as stereotypes). Finally, there is the question of Jung's "madness", the episode – customarily, if euphemistically, referred to by Jungian commentators as his "confrontation with the unconscious" – that took place between around 1913 and 1918, a period to which the recently published *Red Book* bears witness as a document, albeit an aesthetically elaborated one, of his experiences.

Yet on all these counts Jung can be defended, or there are counterexamples where similar supposed defects do not exclude a thinker from academic discourse. The reasons for Jung's exclusion from the academy, I suspect, run deeper than these various reasons, taken singly or combined. These reasons have to do with Jung's style of thinking, and in order to appreciate his style of thinking, we have to consider his style of writing. In other words, we must follow the advice offered by the Homunculus in Goethe's *Faust*, Part 2: "Consider *what*, consider *how* still more" (*Das* Was *benenke, mehr bedenke* Wie) – a line that captures well the ambition expressed in the title of the present collection of essays.[2]

Of course, for many readers, Jung is not approached in his native German, but in translation, more specifically, in the English translations found in *The Collected Works of C. G. Jung*, prepared by R. F. C. Hull. The reason for Hull's selection as translator can be found in William McGuire's account of the Bollingen Foundation,[3] and Hull's achievement in translating the huge quantity of Jung's published writings should not be underestimated. Nevertheless, there are shortcomings in his translations, as Sonu Shamdasani has pointed out.[4] These shortcomings centre around what Shamdasani has described as the "conceptually rationalizing" version of Jung delivered by his translations,[5] and some of these shortcomings are bound up with the unsatisfactory editorial arrangements informing *The Collected Works*. Yet the issue of Jung's *style* transcends the question of the accuracy or appropriateness of Hull's translations.

Unlike Freud, who was awarded the Goethe Prize for his literary style, Jung has the reputation of being a bad writer. In his short introductory account of Jung's thought, Anthony Storr writes: "I know of no creative person who was more hamstrung by his inability to write." He goes on to make this "inability" to write responsible for the difficulty Jung's ideas have encountered in finding acceptance.[6] This is an astonishingly hostile charge from one of the most distinguished and, in other respects, sympathetic commentators on his work. Against this view is the stance of the sociologist Philip Rieff, who places Jung in the tradition of erudite writing: "Once the tradition of Protestant erudition has been carefully studied, Jung no longer seems such an eccentric figure."[7] Yet it turns out that, paradoxically enough, part of this tradition is precisely its unreadability: "That famous literary style, unreadability itself, is a hallmark of the Protestant erudite tradition." Jung himself "justified his style by declaring that it was not quite of his doing, rather a burden imposed upon him as the unwilling recipient of a revelational language of faith".[8] Even James Hillman noted that Jung's writing has been accused of most of Plutarch's faults – "bad philosophy, bad theology, bad history, and bad style" – while turning this critique into an acclamation of Jung's style as an exemplar of Renaissance rhetoric.[9]

More recently, attention on Jung's style has focused on his achievements *as a writer* – no more, no less – as Susan Rowland has put it.[10] According to Rowland, Jung "believed *and wrote as though he believed* that the thinking and discriminating mind – conventionally used to produce non-fictional argument – was situated within a sea of unconscious creativity", and this belief (and the concomitant reflection of this belief in his writing) has important consequences for understanding *how* Jung writes.[11] Although Rowland writes about Jung in translation without explicitly addressing the quality of those translations, she emphasizes the *performativity* of Jung's writing. Discussing Jung's lecture to the Lesezirkel Hottingen in 1930, subsequently published as "Archaic Man", Rowland argues that this text "*performs* its deepest achievement: it places the reader within its 'net of reflections', and it does so as an ethical act", inasmuch as "it works to undermine the sole supremacy of directed thinking in favour of re-*placing* it, changing its *place*, into a relationship, a net of reflections with the kind of 'otherness' that the term 'primitive' comes to represent in 'archaic' man's rhetoric".[12] The argument here, then, is that Jung's writing has a literary (or rhetorical) dimension that can be detected even through the medium of a translated version.

On one level, Jung's German is considerably less sophisticated than Freud's: it could even be described as, on occasion, unpolished; just as Jung cultivated the use of *Schwyzerdütsch*, the form of German spoken in Switzerland, so this exercised an influence on his written German. But equally, just as Jung was also capable of speaking in standard Swiss German, so his writing, on another level, is rich in cultural resonance and allusion. Nor is this cultural richness restricted to German: Jung, like Freud, was steeped in the classical heritage of educated Europeans. Ernest Jones, Freud's biographer, recalled how, at school, Freud had disliked classics and only read Xenophon, the New Testament, and Euripides' *Medea*, only to discover later that "it was certainly galling to have analytical friends in Vienna quoting Latin or Greek passages and being astonished at my blank response",[13] and similarly many, when first encountering members of analytical psychological circles, are struck by their knowledgeableness about mythology and symbolism.

When working with Jung's writings in translation, gaining a sense of Jung's own writing style is difficult but, even in translation, we can distinguish between a number of different writing styles he deploys. And not only is it possible, it is important to distinguish between them, just as it is to distinguish between the different kinds of audiences Jung saw himself as addressing. To begin with, there is the sober, scientific style he used for papers to medical or academic conferences, such as his inaugural lecture as lecturer in psychiatry in 1905,[14] his lecture to the Psycho-Medical Society in 1914,[15] his paper at the annual meeting of the British Medical Association in Aberdeen in 1914,[16] or his papers to the Royal Society of Medicine in London in 1919 and 1939.[17] Then again, there is his high literary mode, exemplified in those passages in *Transformations and Symbols of the Libido* where he talks about the "morning of life" when the individual tears himself loose from the mother and the domestic hearth,[18] or in "The Stages of Life" when he returns to the idea of the solar trajectory as an image of the human life.[19] By the same token, there is his *visionary* or *prophetic* mode, as we find deployed *in extenso* in *The Red Book*: "My soul, where are you? Do you hear me? I speak, I call you – are you there?"[20] Jung cries out, time and again, in the *Liber Novus*. In this sense, then, Jung's language could be called, as Susan Rowland does, "performative". And this performativity functions on another level: Jung makes his work classical by building in references and allusions to the great canonical texts of German literature. Part of the rhetorical performativity of Jung's writing, and an aspect that can be approached even in translation, lies in its persistent allusiveness.

There are numerous instances, for example, of Goethe's rhetorical presence in Jung's writings. In *Transformations and Symbols of the Libido*, for instance, he mentions Goethe's *Faust* on no fewer than 21 occasions. Allusions and references to *Faust* are subtly interwoven with Jung's interpretations of Miss Frank Miller's fantasies and with the general theory that he elaborates about the nature of the psyche. Another telling example can be found in *The Red Book*. In the second chapter of "Liber Primus", "Soul and God", which follows the first chapter with the programmatic title "Refinding the Soul", Jung wonders how he can attain "the knowledge of the heart".[21] As he pursues the answer – that "you can attain this knowledge only by living your life to the full" – he argues that "it appears as though you want to flee from yourself so as not to have to live what remains unlived until now. But", he continues, "you cannot flee from yourself" (*du kannst dir aber nicht entfliehen*),[22] citing directly from the opening stanza of Goethe's poem, "Primal Words. Orphic" (*Urworte. Orphisch*): *"So mußt du sein, dir kannst du nicht entfliehen"* (Thus you must be, you cannot flee yourself).[23]

If the central argument of *Transformations and Symbols of the Libido* is structured around Goethe's *Faust*, no less an important role is played by the poetry of Friedrich Hölderlin (1770–1834). Hölderlin is one of the greatest poets in the German lyric tradition, and in the twentieth century he exercised a fascination on a number of writers and thinkers, including the members of Stefan George's circle[24] and Martin Heidegger. Curiously, Jung's interest in Hölderlin has received very little attention, although Hölderlin is, along with Goethe and Wagner, one of the literary-cultural intertexts around which Jung organizes his argument.[25] In the third chapter of Part 2,

Jung constellates lines from the "Prologue in Heaven" from Goethe's *Faust*, Part 1, and from the opening scene of Part 2, as well as lines from the *Astronomica* of the first-century CE Roman poet and astrologer, Marcus Manilius, with the first stanza of Hölderlin's poem "Sunset" (*Sonnenuntergang*; 1798/1799).[26] All these texts demonstrate, so Jung argues, that "just as in archaic speech fire and the speech sounds (the mating call, music) appear as forms of emanation of the libido, thus light and sound entering the psyche [*in die Seele eintretend*] become one, become libido".[27] The basis for Jung's position here is an argument-by-analogy: as he puts it, citing the German philologist Hermann (or Heymann) Steinthal (1823–99) as his authority, "an absolutely overweening importance must be granted to the little phrase 'Gleich wie' (even as) in the history of the development of thought".[28] *Even as* or *just as*: Jung's central argument emerges in part from his engagement with Hölderlin's poetic texts, as I aim to show in the remainder of this essay. In so doing, I wish to illustrate how I *read Jung as a continuation and an extension of a set of ideas found in the German literary tradition.*

In his recent (and magisterial) account of German literature and ideas, *The German Genius*, Peter Watson cites Nicholas Boyle's judgement (based on correspondence between Caroline Herder and her husband) that, by the summer of 1788, Goethe had "discarded any belief in divine powers external to human life or determinant of it" and come to the view that "the purpose of life, when there is no god … is to *become*, to become much more than one was".[29] Or, as the scholar Hermann August Korff (1882–1963) put it in 1930, in his summary of Herder's outlook, "the ultimate meaning of our humanity" is to "develop that higher human being within ourselves, which emerges if we continually strengthen our truly human powers, and subjugate the inhumane".[30] What is described here as Goethe's project was Jung's too, and Jung expounded this project, not simply with reference to the great texts of German classicism and Romanticism, but using some of their central concepts.

In Part 2, Chapter 7, of *Transformations and Symbols of the Libido*, Jung turns again to Hölderlin's work to exemplify his thesis that "if the libido is not permitted to follow the progressive life [*ein vorwärtsstrebendes Leben*], which is willing to accept all dangers and all losses, then it follows the other road, sinking into its own depths, working down into the old intuition [*Ahnung*] regarding the immortality of all life, to the longing for rebirth".[31] Citing Hölderlin's poem "To a Rose" (*An eine Rose*; 1793) in full, Jung then provides a brief analysis of this text:

Ewig trägt im Mutterschoße,
Süße Königin der Flur!
Dich und mich die stille, große,
Allbelebende Natur;
Röschen! unser Schmuck veraltet,
Sturm' entblättern dich und mich,

Doch der ewge Keim entfaltet
Bald zu neuer Blüte sich.[32]

In the Mother-womb eternal
Sweetest queen of every lea,
Still the living and supernal
Nature carries thee and me.
Little rose, the storm's fierce power
Strips our leaves and alters us;
Yet the deathless germ will tower
To new blooms, miraculous.[33]

For Jung, the rose is a symbol of the beloved woman (as it is, he suggests, in Goethe's famous poem, "Rose on the Heath" (*Heidenröslein*),[34] but because it blooms in a rose-garden (although Hölderlin's poem does not actually say this), the rose represents, more specifically, the libido. For Jung, the image of the poetic speaker dreaming of being with the rose in nature's maternal womb can be understood, psychologically, as an image of the libido being with the mother (in an archetypal, not a literal, sense).

For Jung, there is a direct and unbroken (psychological) continuity between the motif of "eternal germination and renewal" found in a passage of the *Iliad* where Hera seduces Zeus,[35] Plutarch's account of the myth of Osiris,[36] and lines from the middle stanza of "Hyperion's Song of Fate" (*Hyperions Schicksalslied*; 1797/1798; pub. 1799):

Schicksallos, wie der schlafende
Säugling, atmen die Himmlischen;
Keusch bewahrt
In bescheidener Knospe,
Blühet ewig
Ihnen der Geist,
Und die seligen Augen
Blicken in stiller
Ewiger Klarheit.[37]

Fateless the Heavenly breathe
Like an unweaned infant asleep;
Chastely preserved
In modest bud
For ever in their minds
Are in flower
And their blissful eyes
Eternally tranquil gaze,
Eternally clear.[38]

In a passage such as this, Jung maintains, one finds nothing less than an expression of "heavenly bliss".[39] For in this text, one finds an intimation of the ancient (*altertümlich*) – indeed, "archaic" (*archaisch*) – motif of "the twins in the mother's womb", or of Isis and Osiris.[40] (To support this interpretation, Jung cites a legend presented by Leo Frobenius in *Das Zeitalter des Sonnengottes* (1904).[41]) But the recurrence of the image of being preserved "in modest bud" in Plutarch and Hölderlin alike clinches the issue for him.[42] (In a later paper, Jung uses the image of the unfolding bud in the context of the archetype of rebirth as experienced by Nietzsche.[43])

By contrast, in "Man" (*Der Mensch*; *c.* 1798; pub. 1826/1891), Jung's attention is caught by "the beginning of the discord between the poet and nature".[44] In particular, he focuses on the image of how "the boy ... wakes and ... as nurse he chooses / The holy vine" (*Der Knab' ... wacht und wählt ... die heil'ge Rebe / Zur Amme sich*).[45]

To this "Dionysian allusion" Jung finds analogues in the Jewish Bible,[46] in an emblem found on a Gnostic gem,[47] and in the Christian story of the miraculous conversion of water into wine. (Arguably, however, these intertexts add little to Jung's interpretation that the poem demonstrates how Hölderlin "begins to be estranged from reality, the natural actual existence".[48])

Two further poems, "To Nature" (*An die Natur*) (1795; pub. 1846)[49] and "Palinode" (*Palinodie*) (1799; pub. 1846),[50] are read by Jung in light of how "the separation from the blessedness of childhood, from youth even", robs nature of its "golden glamour" (*den goldenen Glanz*), leaving the future as "hopeless emptiness" (*hoffnungslose Leere*).[51] Central to Jung's reading is the idea of *effortlessness* or *spontaneity;* and, in an important footnote on a stanza in "To Nature", Jung glosses the lines

> Blessed be childhood's golden dreams, their power
> Hid from me Life's dismal poverty;
> ...
> In thy beauty and thy light, o Nature,
> Free from care and from compulsion free [*Ohne Müh' und Zwang*],
> Fruitful love attained a kingly stature[52]

as follows:

> In childhood everything was given to [the poet], and the man is unable to obtain it once more for himself, because it is won only through "care and compulsion" [*Mühe und Zwang*], even love costs trouble. In childhood the well of the libido gushed forth in bubbling fullness. In later life it involves hard work even to keep the stream flowing for the onward striving life, because with increasing age the stream has a growing inclination to flow back to its source,

> if effective mechanisms are not created to hinder this backward movement. In this regard there is the generally accepted preconception that love is something entirely spontaneous; only the infantile type of love is something absolutely spontaneous. The love of an adult human being allows itself to be purposefully directed. One could also say: "I want to love". The heights of culture are conditioned by the libido's capacity for displacement.[53]

Hölderlin's lyric verse shows, in Jung's view, that what "robs nature of its glamour, and life of its joy", is "the poison of the retrospective longing, which harks back, in order to sink into its own depths".[54] And the poem entitled "Empedocles" (*Empedokles*) (1797–1800; pub. 1800),[55] named after the great Presocratic philosopher, is said to betray "the secret longing for the maternal depths".[56]

But if – on this psychodynamic reading of Hölderlin's verse – the poet wishes to be "dissolved" like "rare pearls" in "wine", "sacrificing" (his wealth) in "the seething chalice" (that is, in what Jung calls the "krater" of rebirth), something holds him back: and what holds him back in the light of day is love. Earlier in *Transformations and Symbols of the Libido*, Jung had formulated the idea that "this world is empty to him alone who does not understand how to direct his libido towards objects, and to render them alive and beautiful for himself" (*leer ist diese Welt nur dem, der es nicht versteht, seine Libido auf die Dinge zu lenken und sie für ihn lebendig und schön zu machen*).[57] Harking back to this dictum, Jung now observes that "the libido still has an object, for the sake of which life is worth living", but if this object were to be "abandoned", then the libido "would sink back into the realm of the subterranean, the mother, who brings forth again",[58] as the unfinished poem entitled "Obituary" (*Nachruf*) (1800; pub. 1846) suggests.[59]

In the lines of this late text, Jung detects "a renunciation" (*ein Verzicht*), in the sense of "an envy of one's own youth", as "a time of 'effortlessness" – a "primitive" form of feeling life (*Gefühsleben*), be it archaic or infantile, associated with "an extreme inertia and spontaneity of production and non-production" – as opposed to "duty and endeavour" (*Pflichttätigkeit*) and "painstaking work for a long time and for a remote object" (*das mühevolle Arbeiten auf lange Frist und nach fernen Zielen*).[60] In the final stanza, and its final lines – "the eye will weep / For you each day, to look more keenly / Into the distance where you are staying" (*es weint um dich / das Auge, daß es heller wieder / Dort, wo du säumest, hinüberblicke*) – Jung senses an evil portent, a gazing towards something Other: "Love no longer holds the poet", he writes, "the bonds with the world are torn",[61] and, in the words of the poem called "Achilles" (*Achill*) (1798; pub. 1846),[62] he hears "a cry for help to the mother".[63]

For Jung, all these poems can be read in psychological terms as expressing "the gradual deep immersion into the maternal abyss of the individual being", or, in other words, "the persistent arrest and the constantly growing estrangement from life".[64] Over and against the psychological problem voiced in these texts, Jung juxtaposes as a reaction and response one of the greatest of Hölderlin's poems (and one of the best known in the canon of the German lyric tradition) – "Patmos" (*Patmos*) (1801/3; pub. 1807), a work that enters into Hölderlin's world, Jung notes, as "an uncanny guest" (*ein unheimlicher Gast*) "surrounded by the mists of the depths, the gathering 'clouds' [*Wolkenzügen*] of insanity, bred through the mother".[65] In this text, Jung writes, there bursts forth "the primitive thoughts of myth", namely "the symbol-clad intuition of the sun-like death and resurrection of life".[66]

> Near is
> And difficult to grasp, the God.
> But where danger threatens
> That which saves from it also grows.[67]

> *Nah ist*
> *Und schwer zu fassen der Gott.*
> *Wo aber Gefahr ist, wächst*
> *Das Rettende auch.*[68]

In these majestic lines, which also caught the attention of Heidegger,[69] Jung finds an expression of how "the libido has now sunk to the lowest depths".[70] In a remarkable act of textual conflation, Jung elides the lines from the Mothers Scene of *Faust*, Part 2, which talk of how "peril here is great" (*die Gefahr ist groß*),[71] with Hölderlin's statement that "near is ... the God".[72] The following lines –

> In gloomy places dwell
> The eagles, and fearless over
> The chasms walk the sons of the Alps
> On bridges lightly built.[73]

> *Im Finstern wohnen*
> *Die Adler und furchtlos gehn*
> *Die Söhne der Alpen über den Abgrund weg*
> *Auf leichtgebaueten Brücken.*[74]

– Jung reads as expressing how the individual may find within himself (or "hidden in the maternal womb, like the sun in the nighttime") what he calls "the inner sun, his own nature, sun-like and self-renewing"[75] (and, when he says this, it is hard not to think of *The Red Book*[76]). And in the subsequent lines –

Therefore, since round about
Are heaped the summits of Time
And the most loved live near, growing faint
On mountains most separate,
Give us innocent water,
O pinions give us, with minds most faithful
To cross over and to return.[77]

Drum, da gehäuft sind rings
Die Gipfel der Zeit, und die Liebsten
Nah wohnen, ermattend auf
Getrenntesten Bergen,
So gieb unschuldig Wasser,
O Fittige gib uns, treuesten Sinns
Hinüberzugehn und wiederzukehren.[78]

– Jung discovers a vestigial presence in the shape of those dwelling in the mountains, of those whom, in his "Song of Fate", Hyperion described as "walk[ing] above in the light" (*wandelt droben im Licht*);[79] and in the figure of the eagle flying over the depths, Jung detects the presence of the gods.

Now, although he is often dismissed as a literary critic,[80] Jung's analysis of the lines from "Patmos" is as precise as it is insistent: first, "a gloomy picture" of mountainous time, inspired by the passage of the sun; then, a sense of proximity, yet simultaneously a sense of separation between lovers (which reminds Jung of Odysseus' descent to Hades and his encounter with his mother),[81] a paradoxical experience of being "united with all that once was dear to him" and yet being unable to "enjoy the happiness of reunion, because it is all shadows and unreal and devoid of life".[82] Yet whoever descends to drink "the "innocent" (*unschuldig*) – or "childhood" (*kindlich*) – "waters, the drink of rejuvenation", will grow wings and, "winged, he may soar up again into life, like the winged sun".[83] (Again, one thinks of *The Red Book.*[84]) Following the "dark and obscure" words of this introduction (a description with which few are likely to disagree), the remainder of the poem enacts "the sun journey (the 'night sea-journey') towards the east, towards the ascent, towards the mystery of eternity and rebirth",[85] in which Hölderlin's writing reaches an ecstatic intensity that Jung rightly compares to Nietzsche's *Zarathustra* (and that was soon to be recaptured by Jung himself in *The Red Book*).

In the imagery of the third stanza – and in the Dionysian imagery (*beim Geheimnisse des Weinstocks* – "over the mystery of the vine")[86] of the sixth – Jung senses an apocalyptic resonance of the vision experienced on Patmos by St John the Divine and recorded in the Book of Revelation (a text to which, many decades later, at the end of his trajectory as a thinker, Jung would devote an insightful commentary in his *Answer to Job*). In the dense, but dazzling, lines of stanzas 7 and 8, Jung finds imagery that is at once religious – associated with "the sacrificial death and the resurrection of Christ" (and, in turn, with "the self-sacrifice of the sun, which voluntarily breaks its sceptre, the fructifying rays, in the certain hope of resurrection")[87] – and phallic. For Jung, the phallus is the pre-eminent symbol (in a sense completely different from how, say, Lacan understands the Symbolic Order): the phallus – like Thor's hammer, or the bull's shoulder held by Mithras, or the cloven hoof of the devil, or the ass's jaw-bone wielded by Samson (cf. Judges 15:17 ff.), or Hercules's club, or the key Mephisto gives Faust in the Mothers Scene (*Faust* II, lines 6259–93), or "the magic wand" in general – represents (indeed, *qua* symbol, it *is*) "the libido" that "springs from the mother, and with this weapon alone can the individual overcome death".[88]

Hence, the transition undertaken in Hölderlin's poem, moving from Asia, via Patmos, to the Christian mysteries, may appear to rest on a superficial connection, but in reality it is "a very ingenious train of thought" (*ein höchst sinnvoller Gedankengang*), inasmuch as it embodies "the entrance into death and into the land beyond as a self-sacrifice of the hero, for the attainment of immortality".[89] Hence in Hölderlin's lines –

> ... and from now on
> A joy it was
> To dwell in loving Night, and in fixed,
> Ingenuous eyes to preserve
> Abysses of wisdom.[90]
>
> *... Freude war es*
> *Von nun an,*
> *Zu wohnen in liebender Nacht, und bewahren*
> *In einfältigen Augen, unverwandt*
> *Abgründe der Weisheit.*[91]

– Jung discerns the message that what "dwells in the depths" is not just "wisdom" in a general sense, but specifically "the wisdom of the mother", a wisdom to be united with, which means that one is granted "an intuition of the deeper things, of all the deposits of primeval times, the strata of which have been preserved in the mind" (*Ahnung ... von den tieferen Dingen, von all den Niederschlägen uralter Zeit, deren Schichten sich der Geist bewahrt hat*).[92]

Although Hölderlin's insights are compatible with those enunciated in Goethe's *Faust*, there is a significant difference: like Faust, Hölderlin "feels something of the greatness of what he has seen", but unlike Faust, he does not bring "what he has found in the depths" into "the light of day".[93] Instead, Hölderlin allows only one hope to glimmer through, formed "in scanty words" – that "Christ lives yet" (*noch lebt Christus*).[94] Yet Jung concludes (in a somewhat forced comparison), just as Gilgamesh, the hero of the ancient Mesopotamian epic, bringing back the magic herb from the West, is robbed of his treasure by the demon serpent,[95] so Hölderlin's poem dies away "in a painful lament", revealing that, in his case, no "victorious resurrection" will follow his "descent to the shadows".[96] This recognition – that

> ... shamefully
> A power is wresting our hearts from us.
> For every one of the Heavenly wants sacrifices[97]

> *... schmählich*
> *Entreißt das Herz uns eine Gewalt.*
> *Denn Opfer will der Himmlischen jedes*[98]

and that "one must sacrifice the retrogressive longing (the incestuous libido) before the 'heavenly ones' wrest from us the sacrifice" (or from the sacrifice, in other words, of one's "entire libido")[99] – came too late to Hölderlin, or so Jung maintains. Hence, this insight was prefigured in his unconscious: that is, *the literary text reveals (and, in a sense, constitutes) the unconscious of the poet.*

Several of the texts by Hölderlin that Jung discusses explicitly foreground the theme of nature and our relation to it. His analysis of them must be understood in terms of the eighteenth-century debate over nature (and, specifically, over the notions of "second" nature and "inner" nature), which informs Jung's formulations – and his thinking – in a number of ways. In his major 1796 essay, *On the Naïve and the Sentimental in Poetry*,[100] Friedrich Schiller outlined his aesthetics, as part of which he develops the idea of art as a "second nature". In this treatise, Schiller diagnoses in modern humans "a double and very unequal longing for nature": on the one hand, for her "happiness", and, on the other, for her "perfection".[101] This dual yearning is related to the alienated condition of modern humankind, which Schiller contrasts with the attitude to nature of antiquity and summarizes thus: "They felt in a natural way, we feel the natural" (*Sie empfanden natürlich; wir empfinden das Natürliche*).[102] On the basis of this distinction, Schiller sets up the contrast (mentioned in the title of his work) between "sentimental" poetry (which feels the natural) and "naïve" poetry (which feels in a natural way).

In an important footnote that discusses the relationship of these two kinds of literature to each other and to the poetic ideal, Schiller remarks that "both modes of feeling ... are related to each other as the first and third categories [in Kant's table of categories] because the latter always comes into being by the first being combined with its exact opposite".[103] Consequently, he continues,

> if one goes through the three concepts according to the categories, then one will always find nature, and the naïve mood which corresponds to it, in the first, art as the suspension of nature through the

> reason working freely in the second, and finally the ideal in which a perfected art returns to nature in the third category.[104]

Hence, in Schiller's synthesizing view, "nature makes [the human being] one with himself, art separates and divides him, through the ideal he returns to that unity".[105]

Precisely such a dialectic of art and nature can be found, less than a century (in chronological terms) but an entire epoch (in intellectual terms) later, in the thought of Friedrich Nietzsche. In a letter written in December 1882 from Rapallo, a small town on the Italian Riviera, to the composer and conductor Hans von Bülow, Nietzsche invoked the idea of the "second nature" he was developing:

> The changed way of thinking and feeling, which I have been expressing in written form for six years, has *preserved* me in my existence and almost *made* me healthy. What does it concern me, if my friends claim that my present "free-spiritedness" is an eccentric *decision*, held in my teeth and wrung and forced from my own inclination? Well, it may be a "second nature": but I still want to prove that it is only with this second nature that I have actually taken *possession* of my first nature.[106]

In Schiller's treatise, the literary-typological problem of the naïve and the sentimental is related to "a very remarkable psychological antagonism among people in a century which is in the process of civilisation" (i.e. the eighteenth), and one which is "without doubt as old as the beginning of culture": the conflict between realism and idealism.[107]

Is this second nature something external or internal to the individual, and how does it relate to the problem of realism and idealism? In *Psychological Types*, Jung hastily passes over Schiller's discussion of the realist and idealist attitudes[108] – rather too hastily, in fact. But the dichotomy of realism and idealism in relation to the conception of nature re-emerges in a figure roughly contemporaneous with the late Nietzsche and the early Jung, the aesthetician and novelist, Friedrich Theodor Vischer (1807–87). Toward the end of the nineteenth century, Vischer achieved considerable fame, thanks to his novel *Auch Einer* (1879), a work that Jung explicitly singled out for praise in *Black Book 3* as "the first attempt to elevate this truth" – that "our most precious life is grotesque and tragic [*grotesk-tragisch*]" – "to a system", arguing that Vischer deserved "a place among the immortals".[109] (Later, in *Psychological Types*, Jung praised Vischer's novel for its "excellent picture" of "animated objects", as well as for its "deep insight" into "the introverted state of the soul" and "the underlying symbolism of the collective unconscious".[110]) Vischer's novel, whose characteristics include a complex structure and multiplicity of styles and narrative voices; a lengthy (and, for most readers, interminable) interpolated story, the so-called *Pfahldorfgeschichte*, about a tribe of prehistoric lake-dwellers, along with laborious references to their mythology; as well as the striking and occasionally moving formulations of its aphoristic reflections, constitutes in part a discussion of the problem of idealism. Early on in the novel, the narrator cites the central fictional character, known by his initials, A. E., as telling him:

> The deeds and activities of the many have carved out something that stands above them, an upper floor, permanent structures, eternal laws, to serve which is to breathe the purest air, because this service lifts the one who serves into timelessness.[111]

Later, in the lengthy concluding section of entries from A. E.'s diary, we read:

> A second world in the world, a second nature above nature, the ethical world [*Eine zweite Welt in der Welt, eine zweite Natur über der Natur, die sittliche Welt*] ... rises above time and beyond time, is something unconditioned, truth in itself, one can ignore, for it is irrelevant, that it arose within time, – eternal substances, that "hang up there inalienable and unbreakable, like the stars themselves" [*ewige Substanzen, die "droben hängen unveräußerlich und unzerbrechlich, wie die Sterne selbst"*].[112]

This notion, found in Schiller, Nietzsche, and Vischer, is closely related to an idea found in Jung's thinking, the idea of an "inner nature". Such an idea can also be found in Freud, who speaks in *Civilization and Its Discontents* (1930) about "a piece of unconquerable nature" forming part of our psychic constitution.[113] This idea crops up time and again in the thinking of the first and second generations of the Frankfurt School, where it is always attributed to Freud. In *Dialectic of Enlightenment* (1944), for example, T. W. Adorno (1903–69) and Max Horkheimer (1895–1973) speak of the "remembrance of nature in the subject" (*Eingedenken der Natur im Subjekt*) as the central point at which the Enlightenment is opposed to tyranny.[114] And in his *Theory of Communicative Action* (1981), Jürgen Habermas (b. 1929) also focuses on this key phrase, albeit as part of *his* critique of Adorno's and Horkheimer's critique of instrumental reason.[115] Yet the concept of the unconscious as our "inner nature" – indeed, the very phrase – is originally found in Jung, who wrote in his paper "Psychological Types" (1923) that "the unconscious is the residue of unconquered nature in us, just as it is also the matrix of our unborn future" (*das Unbewußte ist der Rest unbezwungener Urnatur in uns, so wie es auch der Mutterboden ungeschaffener Zukunft in uns ist*).[116]

And the realization (in both senses) of one's inner nature goes right back to the origins of Jung's thinking in *The Red Book*,[117] where he observes, for example, in the chapter entitled "Soul and God", that "the knowledge of the heart" is "in no book and is not to be found in the mouth of any teacher, but grows out of you like the green seed from the dark earth".[118] In "The Desert", he promises that "if your creative force now turns to the place of the soul, you will see how your soul becomes green and how its field bears wonderful fruit".[119] After a sequence of anticipatory moments – "And behold – Oh miracle – my green garments everywhere burst into leaf", "I turn green like a tree in spring";[120] "I ate the earth and I drank the sun, and I became a greening tree that stands alone and grows";[121] and "I am fully covered in green leaves, which spring from my body"[122] – in one of the most astonishing episodes in this astonishing book, Jung himself becomes a Green Man:

> But I was no longer the man I had been, for a strange being grew through me. This was a laughing being of the forest, a leaf green daimon, a forest goblin and prankster, who lived alone in the forest and was itself a greening tree being … neither beautiful nor ugly, neither good nor bad, merely living, primordially old and yet completely young, naked and yet naturally clothed, not man but nature … utterly inconstant and superficial, and yet reaching deep down, down to the kernel of the world.[123]

Here Jung obeys the injunction issued by Schopenhauer in the famous chapter, entitled "On Death and Its Relation to the Indestructibility of Our Inner Nature", in the second volume of *The World as Will and Representation* (1818;[2] 1844). Here, Schopenhauer tells us: "Know your inner being, precisely that which is so filled with the thirst for existence; recognize it once more in the inner, mysterious, sprouting force of the tree."[124]

In the visionary mode of writing in *The Red Book*, in his theoretical formulations in his scientific papers and essays, and in his analysis of major literary texts belonging to German classicism and Romanticism, Jung situates himself within the *philosophia perennis* that is an *aesthetica perennis*: he participates in the ongoing debate about the relation of art to nature, and he articulates afresh an enduring insight into the relation of Self to World. Thus, analytical psychology (or so I read it) offers a valuable antidote to our current obsession with the (de-historicized) contemporary, reminding us that we cannot understand the present without understanding the past and alerting us to the archaic dimension of our (post)modern world.

Notes

1 K. Kailo, "C. G. Jung's transcendent function and temenos: valid concepts for EcoFeminist literary criticism?" in G. Schmitt (ed.), *Die Welt im Symbol: C. G. Jung Symposium 7–8.9.2000*, pp. 102–26, Oulu, University of Oulu. Quotes from p. 102.

2 *Faust* II, l. 6990, in J. W. von Goethe, *Faust: Part 2*, trans. D. Luke, Oxford and New York, Oxford University Press, 1994, p. 77; and *Faust*, ed. E. Trunz, Munich, Beck.
3 W. McGuire, *Bollingen: An Adventure in Collecting the Past*, Princeton, NJ, Princeton University Press, 1982, pp. 124–7.
4 S. Shamdasani, *Jung Stripped Bare by His Biographers, Even*, London and New York, Karnac, 2005, pp. 47–58.
5 M. Kyburz, J. Peck, and S. Shamdasani, "Translator's note", in Jung, *The Red Book: Liber Novus*, pp. 222–4, New York and London, Norton, 2009. Quote from p. 222.
6 A. Storr, *Jung*, London, Fontana, 1973, pp. 37–8.
7 P. Rieff, *The Triumph of the Therapeutic: Uses of Faith after Freud* [1966], Harmondsworth, Penguin, 1973, p. 110.
8 Ibid.
9 J. Hillman, *Re-Visioning Psychology*, New York, Harper & Row, 1976, p. 215.
10 S. Rowland, *Jung as a Writer*, London and New York, Routledge, 2005.
11 Ibid., p. 1.
12 S. Rowland, "Jung 'performing' the archaic: response to Robert Segal's 'Jung and Lévy-Bruhl'" [2007], in P. Bishop (ed.), *The Archaic: The Past in the Present*, pp. 219–25, New York and London, Routledge, 2011. Quotes from pp. 220–1.
13 E. Jones, *Free Associations: Memoirs of a Psycho-Analyst*, London, The Hogarth Press, 1959, p. 35; cf. R. H. Armstrong, *A Compulsion for Antiquity: Freud and the Ancient World*, Ithaca, NY, and London, Cornell University Press, 2005.
14 C. G. Jung, "The psychopathological significance of the association experiment", in *Experimental Researches*, *The Collected Works of C. G. Jung* (hereafter *CW*), vol. 2, pp. 408–25, London, Routledge & Kegan Paul, 1906/1973.
15 C. G. Jung, "On psychological understanding", in *The Psychogenesis of Mental Disease*, *CW* 3, pp. 388–424, London, Routledge & Kegan Paul, 1915/1960.
16 C. G. Jung, "On the importance of the unconscious in psychopathology", in *The Psychogenesis of Mental Disease*, *CW* 3, pp. 438–465, London, Routledge & Kegan Paul, 1914/1960.
17 C. G. Jung, "On the problem of psychogenesis in mental disease", in *The Psychogenesis of Mental Disease*, *CW* 3, pp. 466–95, London, Routledge & Kegan Paul, 1919/1960; and "On the psychogenesis of schizophrenia", in *CW* 3, pp. 504–41, London, Routledge & Kegan Paul, 1939/1960.
18 C. G. Jung, *Psychology of the Unconscious: A Study of the Transformations and Symbolisms of the Libido*, trans. Beatrice M. Hinkle, London, Routledge, 1911–12/1991, p. 566; cf. *Symbols of Transformation*, *CW* 5, London, Routledge & Kegan Paul, 1952/1967, p. 553.
19 C. G. Jung, "The stages of life", in *The Structure and Dynamics of the Psyche*, *CW* 8, pp. 749–95, London, Routledge & Kegan Paul, 1930–31/1969, p. 778.
20 C. G. Jung, *The Red Book: Liber Novus*, ed. S. Shamdasani, trans. M. Kyburz, J. Peck, and S. Shamdasani, New York and London, Norton, 2009, p. 232.
21 Ibid., p. 233.
22 Ibid., pp. 233–4.
23 J. W. von Goethe, *Selected Poems*, trans. J. Whaley, London, Dent, 1998, p. 123.
24 J. Suglia, "On the nationalist reconstruction of Hölderlin in the George circle", *German Life and Letters*, 2002, vol. 55, pp. 387–97.
25 See my brief discussion of how, in *Transformations and Symbols of Libido* (and in its revised version, *Symbols of Transformation*), Jung juxtaposes a case study, involving a young male labourer suffering from schizophrenia, with a discussion of Hölderlin. P. Bishop, "Jung looking at the stars: chaos, cosmos and archetype", *International Journal of Jungian Studies*, 2009, vol. 1, pp. 12–24; Jung, "Psychology of the unconscious", p. 645, n. 3; cf. Jung, *Symbols of Transformation*, *CW* 5, p. 624, n. 15.
26 F. Hölderlin, *Poems and Fragments*, trans. M. Hamburger, London, Anvil, 1994, pp. 46–7.

27 Jung, *Psychology of the Unconscious*, p. 268. Translation modified.

28 Ibid., p. 236. Steinthal, a German philologist and philosopher, was a pupil of Wilhelm von Humboldt, whose writings on linguistics he edited. Himself a Jew, and one of the directors of the Deutsch-Israelitische Gemeindebund, in 1860 he founded, together with the German philosopher and psychologist (and his brother-in-law), Moritz Lazarus (1824–1903), the *Zeitschrift für Völkerpsychologie und Sprachwissenschaft*, a journal dedicated to the "science" of racial psychology. In *Transformations and Symbols of the Libido*, Jung cites two papers by him: H. Steinthal, "Die ursprüngliche Form der Sage von Prometheus", *Zeitschrift für Völkerpsychologie und Sprachwissenschaft*, 1862a, vol. 2, pp. 1–29; and "Die Sage von Simson", *Zeitschrift für Völkerpsychologie und Sprachwissenschaft*, 1862b, vol. 2, pp. 129–78.

29 P. Watson, *The German Genius: Europe's Third Renaissance, the Second Scientific Revolution, and the Twentieth Century*, London and New York, Simon and Schuster, 2010; cf. N. Boyle, *Goethe: The Poet and the Age*, vol. 1, *The Poetry of Desire*, Oxford and New York, Oxford University Press, 1991, p. 605.

30 H. A. Korff, *Geist der Goethezeit: Versuch einer ideellen Entwicklung der klassisch-romantischen Literaturgeschichte*, vol. 2, *Klassik*, Leipzig, Weber, 1930, p. 149. Even in 1975, the British Germanist W. H. Bruford (1894–1988) was still able to dismiss this "ethical view" as "disappointingly vague and question-begging". (See *The German Tradition of Self-Cultivation: "Bildung" from Humboldt to Thomas Mann*, Cambridge, Cambridge University Press, 1975, p. 47.) Perhaps the gap between British expectations and German ambition is best revealed by the response of Henry Sidgwick, the late nineteenth-century utilitarian philosopher and economist at Cambridge, to a German visitor who had observed there was no equivalent in English to the word *gelehrt*: "Oh yes there is, we call it a prig" (Watson, *German Genius*, p. 120).

31 Jung, *Psychology of the Unconscious*, p. 636. Translation modified.

32 F. Hölderlin, *Sämtliche Gedichte*, ed. J. Schmidt, Frankfurt am Main, Deutscher Klassiker Verlag, 2005, p. 147.

33 Trans. Hinkle in Jung, *Psychology of the Unconscious*, p. 637.

34 Circa 1771, p. 1789; cf. J. W. von Goethe, *Selected Verse*, trans. D. Luke, Harmondsworth, Penguin, 1964, pp. 10–11.

35 See Homer, *The Iliad*, book 14, lines 292–351, trans. R. Lattimore, Chicago and London, University of Chicago Press, 1951, pp. 302–3. Compare with Jung's remarks in *Transformations and Symbols of the Libido* (Jung, *Psychology of the Unconscious*, pp. 368–9, esp. n. 66). The presence of various details, Jung suggests, categorizes the text as an example of the *hieros gamos* (literally, "sacred marriage"), a motif of rejuvenation and rebirth. Cf. "the end (346–51) – particularly beautiful in its description of nature in springtime sending forth its new flowers and grass, in symbolic sympathy with the amorous god – has given some scholars the idea that behind this light-hearted tale lies a spring ritual connected with the reawakening of fertility and the rebirth of nature" (M. M. Willcock, *A Companion to the Iliad*, Chicago and London, University of Chicago Press, 1976, p. 159). And compare with the vision subsequent to Jung's near-death or out-of-the-body experience in 1944, recounted in *Memories, Dreams, Reflections* (C. G. Jung and A. Jaffé, *Memories, Dreams, Reflections of C. G. Jung*, trans. R. and C. Winston, London, Collins and Routledge & Kegan Paul, 1963, p. 325).

36 See Plutarch, "On Isis and Osiris", in F. C. Babbitt (trans.), *Moralia*, vol. 5, 351c–384c, pp. 6–191, London, Heinemann, and Cambridge, MA, Harvard University Press. Compare with Jung's remarks in *Symbols and Transformations of the Libido* (Jung, *Psychology of the Unconscious*, p. 358).

37 Hölderlin, *Sämtliche Gedichte*, p. 207.

38 Hölderlin, *Poems and Fragments*, p. 65.

39 Jung, *Psychology of the Unconscious*, p. 639.

40 Ibid.
41 Ibid.; cf. L. Frobenius, *Das Zeitalter des Sonnengottes*, Berlin, Reimer, 1904, p. 68.
42 Jung, *Psychology of the Unconscious*, p. 641. Is Jung thinking of the following passage in Plutarch, where he explains that, although the Egyptians do not "believe that the sun rises as a new-born babe from the lotus", they "portray the rising of the sun in this manner to indicate allegorically the enkindling of the sun from the waters" ("On Isis and Osiris", 355c, in Plutarch, *Moralia*, p. 29; cf. "The Oracles at Delphi", 400a: "The Egyptians, to show the beginning of sunrise, paint a very young baby sitting on a lotus flower" [p. 291])?
43 Alluding to Nietzsche's poem "Sils Maria", Jung writes that, "when a summit of life is reached, when the bud unfolds and from the lesser the greater emerges, then, as Nietzsche says, 'One becomes Two,' and the greater figure ... appears to the less personality with the force of a revelation". C. G. Jung, "Concerning rebirth", in *The Archetypes and the Collective Unconscious*, *CW* 9/i, pp. 199–258, London, Routledge & Kegan Paul, 1940–50/1959, p. 217.
44 Jung, *Psychology of the Unconscious*, p. 642.
45 Hölderlin, *Poems and Fragments*, p. 61; *Sämtliche Gedichte*, p. 204.
46 See Genesis 49:11: "Tying his foal to the vineyard, and his ass, O my son, to the vine" (DRV).
47 See J. M. Robertson, *Die Evangelien-Mythen* [trans. of *Christianity and Mythology*, vol. 3], Jena, Diederichs, 1910, p. 92; cf. "A Gnostic gem representing an ass suckling its foal, with the figure of the crab (Cancer) above, and the inscription D. N. IHV. XPS.: *Dominus Noster Jesus Christus*, with the addition, DEI FILIUS" (J. M. Robertson, *Christianity and Mythology*, 2nd edn, London, Watts, 1910, pp. 340–1). For Robertson, Christianity was essentially "neo-Paganism grafted on Judaism" (p. 338).
48 Jung, *Psychology of the Unconscious*, p. 642.
49 Hölderlin, *Sämtliche Gedichte*, pp. 163–5.
50 Hölderlin, *Poems and Fragments*, pp. 88–9.
51 Jung, *Psychology of the Unconscious*, p. 646.
52 Trans. Hinkle in ibid., p. 645; cf. Hölderlin, *Sämtliche Gedichte*, p. 165.
53 Jung, *Psychology of the Unconscious*, p. 645, fn. 6. Translation modified.
54 Ibid., p. 646.
55 Hölderlin, *Poems and Fragments*, pp. 12–13.
56 Jung, *Psychology of the Unconscious*, p. 647.
57 Ibid., p. 284; and C. G. Jung, *Wandlungen und Symbole der Libido* [1911–1912], Munich, Deutscher Taschenbuch Verlag, 1991, p. 176.
58 Jung, *Psychology of the Unconscious*, p. 648. Elsewhere in *Transformations and Symbols of the Libido*, Jung detected this dynamic in Goethe and in Nietzsche.
59 See Hölderlin, *Poems and Fragments*, pp. 98–9, where the poem is published under its opening line as its title, "Though Every Day I Follow" (*Wohl geh' ich täglich*).
60 Jung, *Psychology of the Unconscious*, p. 648; translation modified. Jung, *Wandlungen*, p. 379.
61 Jung, *Psychology of the Unconscious*, p. 648.
62 Hölderlin, *Sämtliche Gedichte*, p. 213.
63 Jung, *Psychology of the Unconscious*, p. 649; translation modified.
64 Ibid., p. 650.
65 Ibid.
66 Ibid., translation modified.
67 Hölderlin, *Poems and Fragments*, p. 483.
68 Hölderlin, *Sämtliche Gedichte*, p. 350.
69 M. Heidegger, *Elucidations of Hölderlin's Poetry*, trans. K. Hoeller, Amherst, NY, Humanity Books, 2000, p. 40; cf. pp. 185, 204, 213.
70 Jung, *Psychology of the Unconscious*, p. 652. In *Mysterium Coniunctionis*, Jung returns to and cites these lines in his discussion of imagery of ascent and descent in the *Tabula smaragdina*,

claiming that "in moments of crisis ... the symbol of unity, for instance the mandala, occurs in a dream": C. G. Jung, *Mysterium Coniunctionis*, *CW* 14, London, Routledge & Kegan Paul, 1955–6/1963, p. 294.

71 Goethe, *Faust* II, line 6291; J. W. von Goethe, *Faust*, ed. C. Hamlin, trans. W. Arndt, 2nd edn, New York and London, Norton, 2001, p. 178.

72 In *Psychological Types*, Jung cites these same lines in the context of an explanation of the symbol as a redeeming factor (C. G. Jung, *Psychological Types*, London, Routledge & Kegan Paul, 1971, p. 446): "The redeeming symbol is a highway, a way upon which life can move forward without torment and compulsion" (p. 445).

73 Hölderlin, *Poems and Fragments*, p. 483.

74 Hölderlin, *Sämtliche Gedichte*, p. 350.

75 Jung, *Psychology of the Unconscious*, p. 652.

76 See the chapters in *The Red Book* entitled "Death", "The Remains of Earlier Temples", and "The Opening of the Egg" (Jung, *Red Book*, pp. 274, 277, 287).

77 Hölderlin, *Poems and Fragments*, p. 483.

78 Hölderlin, *Sämtliche Gedichte*, p. 350.

79 Hölderlin, *Poems and Fragments*, pp. 64–5.

80 For an attempt to rehabilitate, not so much Jung himself as a literary critic, as his ideas as a set of tools for literary commentary, see G. Schmitt, *Text als Psyche: Eine Einführung in die analytische Psychologie C. G. Jungs für Literaturwissenschaftler*, Achen, Shaker, 1999.

81 *The Odyssey*, book 11, lines 204 ff; see Homer, *The Odyssey*, trans. W. Shewring, Oxford, Oxford University Press, 1980, p. 132.

82 Jung, *Psychology of the Unconscious*, p. 654.

83 Ibid.

84 See "The Opening of the Egg" in *The Red Book*: "I wandered toward the East where the sun rises. ... My God ... had taken my wings from me ... cruelly and unthinkingly the sunbird spread its wings and flew up into infinite space" (Jung, *Red Book*, p. 287).

85 Jung, *Psychology of the Unconscious*, p. 655; translation modified.

86 Hölderlin, *Sämtliche Gedichte*, p. 352; and *Poems and Fragments*, p. 487.

87 Jung, *Psychology of the Unconscious*, p. 658.

88 Ibid.; translation modified.

89 Ibid., p. 660; translation modified.

90 Hölderlin, *Poems and Fragments*, p. 489.

91 Hölderlin, *Sämtliche Gedichte*, p. 353.

92 Jung, *Psychology of the Unconscious*, p. 661; Jung, *Wandlungen*, p. 385.

93 Ibid.; translation modified.

94 Ibid., p. 662; cf. Hölderlin, *Poems and Fragments*, p. 495, and *Sämtliche Gedichte*, p. 356.

95 See the standard version of Babylonian Gilgamesh Epic, Tablet XI, "Immortality Denied". Having discovered "Ur-shanabi, the 'Plant of Heartneat,'" Gilgamesh "found a pool whose water was cool, / down he went into it, to bathe in the water. / Of the plant's fragrance a snake caught the scent, / came up [in silence], and bore the plant off": *The Epic of Gilgamesh: The Babylonian Epic Poem and Other Texts in Akkadian and Sumerian*, trans. A. George, Harmondsworth, Penguin, 1999, p. 99.

96 Jung, *Psychology of the Unconscious*, p. 663.

97 Hölderlin, *Poems and Fragments*, p. 495.

98 Hölderlin, *Sämtliche Gedichte*, p. 356. These lines are also cited in Jung and Jaffé, *Memories, Dreams, Reflections*, p. 390.

99 Jung, *Psychology of the Unconscious*, p. 664; translation modified.

100 In *Psychological Types* (1921), Jung considered this work from a typological perspective (pp. 213–22).

101 F. Schiller, *On the Naïve and Sentimental in Literature*, trans. H. Watanabe-O'Kelly, Manchester, Carcarnet New Press, 1981, p. 31.

102 Ibid., p. 34; F. Schiller, *Über naive und sentimentalische Dichtung*, ed. W. F. Mainland, Oxford, Blackwell, 1957, p. 17.

103 Schiller, *On the Naïve and Sentimental*, p. 104. See the table of categories in Kant's first critique, A 80/B 106 (I. Kant, *Critique of Pure Reason*, ed. and trans. P. Guyer and A. W. Wood, Cambridge, Cambridge University Press, 1997, p. 212).

104 Schiller, *On the Naïve and Sentimental*, p. 104.

105 Ibid., p. 40.

106 F. Nietzsche, *Sämtliche Briefe: Kritische Studienausgabe*, ed. G. Colli and M. Montinari, vol. 6, Berlin and New York, de Gruyter, Deutscher Taschenbuch Verlag, 1986, p. 290. Compare with Nietzsche's letter to Erwin Rohde of December 1882: "I have a 'second nature,' but not to destroy the first, rather to make it *bearable*. My 'first nature' would have destroyed me long ago – it did almost destroy me" (p. 291).

107 Schiller, *On the Naïve and Sentimental*, p. 81.

108 Jung, *Psychological Types*, p. 222.

109 Jung, *Red Book*, p. 286, n. 135.

110 Jung, *Psychological Types*, pp. 501, 627.

111 F. T. Vischer, *Auch Einer: Eine Reisebekanntschaft* [1879], Stuttgart and Leipzig, Deutsche Verlags-Anstalt, 1904, p. 33.

112 Ibid., p. 337, cf. pp. 340 and 443–4. Vischer is alluding here to the famous lines spoken by Stauffacher in Schiller's *Wilhelm Tell*, Act 2, Scene 2.

113 S. Freud, *Civilization and Its Discontents*, *Standard Edition of the Complete Psychological Works*, vol. 21, ed. James Strachey and Anna Freud, pp. 57–147, London, Hogarth Press, 1930/1964. Quote from p. 86.

114 M. Horkheimer and T. W. Adorno, *Dialectic of Enlightenment: Philosophical Fragments*, trans. J. Cumming, New York, Continuum, 1996, p. 40.

115 J. Habermas, *The Theory of Communicative Action* [1981], vol. 1, *Reason and the Rationalization of Society*, trans. T. McCarthy, London, Heinemann, 1984, pp. 382 and 385. Habermas notes that "Adorno is in the end very similar to Heidegger as regards his position on the theoretical claims of objectivating thought and of reflection: the mindfulness [*Eingedenken*] of nature comes shockingly close to the recollection [*Andenken*] of being". Of course, the shared legacy with Heidegger could alternatively be seen as a strength, not a weakness, and as evidence of the global appeal and universal truth of this topos.

116 C. G. Jung, "Psychological types", in *Psychological Types*, *CW* 6, pp. 883–914, London, Routedge & Kegan Paul, 1923/1971, p. 907.

117 The rhetorical gesturing of Jung's *The Red Book* is, strangely enough, echoed in Wilhelm Reich's *Listen, Little Man!*: "Build your house on granite. By granite I mean your nature that you're torturing to death … And first and foremost, *think straight*, trust the quiet inner voice that tells you what to do." W. Reich, *Listen, Little Man!* [1945], trans. R. Manheim, New York, Farrar, Straus and Giroux, 1974, pp. 68 and 70. For further discussion, see J. P. Conger, *Jung and Reich: The Body as Shadow*, Berkeley, CA, North Atlantic Books, 2005.

118 Jung, *Red Book*, p. 233.

119 Ibid., p. 236.

120 Ibid., pp. 260, 261.

121 Ibid., p. 273. See the continuation in the *Draft* and *Corrected Draft*, p. 273, n. 67.

122 Ibid., p. 275.

123 Ibid., p. 276. Cf. these other passages: "Within myself I had become one as a natural being, but I was a hobgoblin who frightened the solitary wanderer, and who avoided the places of men. But I greened and bloomed from within myself" (p. 277); "I was a child and grew like a greening tree and let the wind and distant cries and commotion of opposites / blow calmly through my branches" (p. 280).

124 A. Schopenhauer, *The World as Will and Representation*, trans. E. F. J. Payne, vol. 2, New York, Dover, 1966, p. 478.

5

READING JUNG FOR MAGIC

"Active Imagination" for/as "Close Reading"

Susan Rowland

Jung's imaginative and symbolic writing is neither a literary device nor an embellishment, but is his psychology's most complete expression, according to Susan Rowland. Closely examining what Jung wrote about his foremost therapeutic method, which he called "active imagination", she intuitively grasps its family resemblance to a method of literary criticism called "close reading". In this essay, Rowland carefully traces the nature of each method, approximating their analogous contours, and bridging the gap between them where fruitful exchanges might begin to occur for their mutual enrichment. By holding the two methods face to face, Rowland creates magic. She inspires the literary scholar to gain familiarity with Jung's writing and thus enhance his or her skill as a critic and the Jungian analyst to contemplate the dual nature of his or her work and narrative competence. She does so with her own imaginative and symbolic writing.

J. K.

A note: why I read Jung

One advantage of being trained as a literary scholar is the habit of reading in the mode of a quest: reading as asking what writing *is* or could be. Of course, any form of academic training involves exploring different models of writing and the history of literary representation. We all read with presuppositions of what a particular kind of writing should contain or offer. On the other hand, an education in literary studies encourages a questioning, an opening up to scrutiny of habits and conventions in the way we write. For example, fiction is not wholly separable from factual prose if both use many of the same techniques. Imaginative writing and scientific accounts are not as distinctly different as parts of our culture assume.

When reading Jung for the first time, I found myself experiencing some of the pleasures frequently associated with creative writing, such as evocative symbols, mythical tropes, speculation, and humour. In particular such "literary" devices appeared not to be ornamental nor did they detract from the "psychology". Rather imaginative, dramatic, and symbolic writing proved fundamental to the psychology's expression. Jung, I concluded, was intrinsically literary. I began to recognize that not only was his writing especially suitable to literary analysis, but also it *belonged* to literary categories. Above all, I saw that Jung's writing was responsive to reading as quest because it was writing *as* quest. Jung's work belonged to post-Romantic literature, when writing stopped being valued for its strict adherence to past models. Romantic works do not obey rules. Rather, Romantic writing is in search of the rules and theories by which it might be comprehended.

Here is writing that fulfils Romanticism's radical agenda. It proffers a psychic revolution that undoes the dominant conventions that have calcified psyche and society. Jung's writing frees the reader's psyche from too narrow notions of rational truth. It does so by seeking knowledge as a quest for its rules rather than an enactment of them.

To me, Jung's writing is also a quest for meaning – a quest that embraces fictional, poetic, mythic, rhetorical, logical, and empirical strategies. Part of its quest nature is to address and unravel distinctions between science and art. Reading Jung is to engage the *whole* psyche since much of the so-called literary qualities invoke the "other", those parts of ourselves that modernity has sited/cited beyond the ego along our developmental path. For Jung's writing is historically acute. Not only does it map the hardened ego of post-Enlightenment definitions of reason, but also it seeks to overcome that very ego's too rigid boundaries. Jung's writing is literature that incorporates the reader's psyche, remaking the structures of the soul within modernity. It is for these reasons that my reading of Jung has never been concerned with issues of translation. While the study of "original" manuscripts is a fine and legitimate act of scholarship, it is nevertheless built on an ideal of knowledge as something that is ultimately fixed, pure, and knowable. If the essays that make up *The Collected Works*, Volume 12, were originally written in German, then some consider that a study of the translation and the related search for Jung's original manuscript will produce a *truer* text than the English version. Although such scholarly research is undeniably valuable as a contribution to a larger picture consisting of different kinds of knowing, its epistemological basis in translation is partial. Such a pursuit of a creation myth of truth from the first manuscript presupposes that writing is meaningful only insofar as it can be related to the embodied presence of an author. "Original" writing is supposedly sealed hermetically and possessed of full and rational meaning, *and that is all that can be construed as knowledge.*

I suggest that if we read Jung as a challenge to the divisions between literature and science, the search for an original version or Jung's pure and knowable intentions (as author) is unnecessary. It misreads the radical possibilities of his writing. I do not want to read Jung for what the rationalized ego of the once living man might have meant, for this goal in all its fantasy of completeness is not realizable given the complexity of authorship and revisions, let alone the mixture of conscious and unconscious functions within the writer. My proposal is to read Jung for what the non-ego qualities of the writing might offer us *now*. What multiple possibilities might be discovered by the living psyche of the twenty-first-century reader in the enigmatic qualities of Jung's texts?

In short, I want to read Jung as a quest to fertilize and sow the contemporary imagination. His words are seeds that blossom in readers today and in the unimaginable future. In such a spirit the following essay is my attempt to explore and develop the fecundity of Jung as a writer.

Introduction

In this essay, I want to pivot the topic of C. G. Jung and "reading" into a bold argument about the evolution of academic disciplines (and later about evolution itself). Relatively recent forms of academic study, such as psychology, were constructed by dividing a heritage along lines of "respectable" proto-scientific ideas versus esoteric practices better forgotten and darkened. After all, how we read Jung and why concerns not just reading *The Collected Works of C. G. Jung*, but also how such work might affect reading texts of all kinds. The act of reading might be defined as interpreting words and other signifying material such as dream images. This definition opens up large spheres of knowledge: hermeneutics; the study of imaginative literature; and, in pre-Enlightenment eras, reading arts such as alchemy and magic.

My core proposition is that Jung proposed a method of working with unconscious images – "active imagination", he called it – that was simultaneously an act of liberation and repression. Comparing active imagination with its historical parallel from the discipline of vernacular literary studies, "close reading" makes visible its structure of reduction and expansion. As offered by Jung, active imagination represses its nature as an art, while proposing an expansion of reading sorely needed by literary studies. In turn, an examination of close reading and its antecedents reveals a structurally similar *and opposite* repression, that of the creative psyche, while expanding the role of reading as an art of *making*. In this way, Jung's psychology and literary studies may re-form each other to show both active imagination and close reading as acts of magic for the twenty-first century.

We begin by recognizing that positing an unconscious subverts conventional assumptions about reading. Words and images are not unproblematically paired with "meaning" if a part of the psyche resists conscious control. Therefore, Jung devised active imagination to "read" images generated primarily by the unconscious as symbols. Suggestively, active imagination arises contemporaneously with another development of reading from another recently founded academic discipline. Because literature was traditionally a staple of universities, albeit in Latin and Greek, the newness of literary studies or "English" as a degree in higher education has often been overlooked. However, literary studies, a degree subject invented in the late

1890s, differs radically from the classics in constructing *vernacular* literature as a basis for knowledge. My essay argues that Jung's method of subjecting unconsciously generated symbols to the process of active imagination has a deep historical relationship with literary studies and its originating research method, known today as *close reading.*

By examining the roots of close reading and active imagination in hermeneutics, Renaissance philosophy, and magic, I explore how Jung re-oriented the reading of symbols in the service of cultural transformation. Furthermore, I show that this cross-disciplinary comparison allows active imagination to be reimagined as a *skill to be practised.* In effect, I am suggesting that active imagination be regarded as magic, for it becomes an imaginative reweaving into the body of the earth.

Wild and (un)disciplined

For centuries, literary scholarship meant the examination of classical texts and their languages. By the close of the nineteenth century, emancipatory pressures generated the need to open the universities to new categories of students, such as women and lower-class men. They were admitted with accompanying anxiety about their fitness for such robust study as the classics. Therefore, as a compromise, a new degree of literary studies was invented using the students' own language and literary history.[1]

Both the psychology of the unconscious, known here as *depth psychology*, and literary studies began in a previously neglected wilderness, which they set about "disciplining" as quickly as possible. Depth psychology began to listen to feminine voices in hysteria; literary studies to consider the "feminine" domesticities of native fiction. "Wild writing" is a term taken from the poet Gary Snyder, who argues that language is rooted in the human body and, therefore, "wild" in essence.[2] It becomes "cultivated" by practice, education, and artfulness, and thereby transitions into culture. Human language is here a medial realm by which boundaries of nature and culture are negotiated. Art, in particular the intensities of poetry, may open up its roots in the nature of our biological being shared with other creatures, who themselves have languages we can only dimly appreciate.

Jung becomes important here in the context of his drive for *cultural* as well as *individual* healing. His concern for the psyche in an age of accelerating technological change can be traced back to the literary and philosophical anxieties of late eighteenth-century Romanticism. Here, it is useful to look at Ross Woodman's magnificent study of Romanticism and Jungian psychology, *Sanity, Madness, Transformation: The Psyche in Romanticism.*[3] This work compares literature a century prior to its vernacular "disciplining" to Jung's very similar treatment of the "wild" in writing. Woodman starts revealingly with Jung and Northrop Frye, a literary scholar rooted in the process of making the new discipline.

Influenced by Jung, Frye was equally fearful of breakdown in the collective psyche. Both Frye and Jung, therefore, adopted the term "archetype" to offer a new understanding of symbols as healing containers of psychic energy. However, there is a crucial difference between Jung and Frye. Although both agreed that the decline of Western Christendom had dangerously weakened social health, the literary critic found alternative sources of the sacred in Romantic poetry, notably that of William Blake. Frye, also like Jung, identified the mythopoetic imagination with the experience of the numinous. Unlike Jung, Frye believed that existing symbols are still communicable to the world. Frye's archetypes are entities, within great literature, that contain "presence", an intensity of meaning that endows the receiver of the symbol with authentic being. Frye identified the presence of the mythopoetic in Romantic literature with the Logos of Christ. He found his new gospel in existing literature.

I want to consider further Woodman's distinction between Jung and Frye on the symbol and its social function. What is more symptomatic of a fractured psyche than the failure of the great codes in religion and the arts? If they are no longer read in a way that knits the collective together, then society is indeed fragmented.

> From Jung's point of view, Frye's notion of the archetype as "the communicable symbol" ignores the historical fact that the symbol is no longer communicable. The unified and integrated symbolic life embodied in the Catholic Church, he argues, has been squandered by, among other things, the Protestantism that replaced it . . . "Only an unparalleled impoverishment of symbolism", he then goes on to explain in *The Archetypes of the Collective Unconscious*, "could enable us to rediscover the gods as psychic factors, that is, as archetypes of the unconscious."[4]

Woodman makes a vital point that Jung's notion of archetype inheres in humanity through the body's connection to the psyche, whereas, for Frye, it can still be found in the reading of great vernacular literature. "Herein lies the difference between Frye's notion of the archetype and Jung's: whereas Frye locates the archetype in 'the metaphysics of presence', Jung locates it in the unconscious operations of the human body."[5]

In this analysis, Frye invokes literature as a source of the mythopoetic numinous to counter the abyss of unsignifying that is the unconscious. Woodman regards Jung as more realistically offering the human body as repository of archetypal energies of patterning against the abyss. Although I find Woodman's reading of Frye and Jung entirely persuasive, I want to offer two counterarguments as more optimistic responses to Jung's appreciation of the unconscious void.

Woodman's acute sense of both Jung's psychology and Romantic literature as being built upon the absolute void (the absence of signifying in the unconscious) is powerfully explored through the cultural theory of deconstruction and the work of Jacques Derrida in particular:

> Not until my immersion in deconstruction during my final teaching years did I fully confront the depth of the "secret unrest" that ... gnaws at the roots of Romantic being, or recognize in Jung's psychological views of the archetype the way in which Frye's essentially Christian view aesthetically insulated him from the global psychosis that threatened to invade it.[6]

This entirely persuasive portrait of the radically deconstructive nature of Jung's unconscious provides a starting point, I argue, for two countering notions of how this terrifying void has an-other kind of being altogether: first, the role of the unconscious in magic, and second, the imbrication of the human body with nonhuman nature through evolutionary complexity science. Both of these arguments provide major recuperative frameworks for reading symbols *with* the body and nature. Symbols can be viewed as a communicating link between the human body and nature.

Active imagination and amplification vs. New Criticism and close reading

Both active imagination and what I have been calling "close reading" are responses, in different disciplinary locations, to the perceived loss of the communicable symbol in culture. It is time to look at just what these different epistemologies, as ways of making and justifying knowledge, entail.

Of course, Jung does not present active imagination as a theory of reading, but as a way of encouraging the spontaneous growth of images from the unconscious and of using them as a mode of healing. Here, he envisages a number of modes of active imagining in ways that envelop the body as home of the ensouled psyche:

> I therefore took up a dream-image or an association of the patient's, and, with this as a point of departure, set him the task of elaborating or developing the theme by giving free rein to his fantasy. This, according to individual taste and talent, could be done in any number of ways, dramatic, dialectic, visual, acoustic, or in the form of dancing, painting, drawing, or modeling.[7]

When a patient is depressed or overwhelmed by a feeling of dread, he or she is prompted to allow the sheer power trapped in the unconscious to produce an image or to meditate upon a potent dream symbol. By relaxing conscious control, the overwhelming "other" develops the images of its own accord. Either with the analyst or alone, patients can then work on finding a rapprochement with this "active", previously alien, part of themselves. Ultimately, the "active" in active imagination encompasses ego as well as the unconscious. In this sense, active imagination is a way to improve and enhance individuation, that healing development of an ever-deeper connection between ego and unconscious archetypal energies. "But active imagination, as the term denotes, means that the images have a life of their own and that the symbolic events develop according to their own logic – that is, of course, if your conscious reason does not interfere."[8]

None of this looks like reading in its everyday sense, except for the insistence on beginning by treating the other as *other*. Active imagination is a kind of reading when it insists upon symbolic images being treated as *the text of another*. During the process of integrating these symbols into ego consciousness (individuation), it may cease to be seen as a kind of reading. In fact, though, active imagination remains allied to reading if its resemblance to depth psychology's nonidentical twin, literary studies, is pursued.

Contemporary to Jung in the early twentieth century and out of the developing field of literary studies there arose another response to the loss of the communicable symbol, a literary theory known as New Criticism (*c.*1900–60). The New Critics pioneered the method known as *close reading* (sometimes called *practical criticism*), a practice still indigenous to literary studies today and, therefore, greatly influencing the teaching of literature in schools and colleges throughout the anglophone world. I suggest that recognizing the resemblance of close reading to active imagination will augment both depth psychology and literary studies.

"New Criticism" is a theoretical label applied to American and British scholars with a range of attitudes to vernacular literary study including, in Britain, I. A. Richards, F. R. Leavis, and the poet, T. S. Eliot; and, in the United States, J. C. Ransom, Cleanth Brooks, and W. K. Wimsatt.[9] What linked those theorists was the belief that a work of literature forms an organic and semantic whole that transcends its origins either in an author or a historical context. To the New Critics, a literary text needs nothing outside of itself. It is autonomous as to its meaning. New Critics are, by default, liberal humanists because they argue that a literary work can speak to an attentive reader in any historical setting by reason of its *communicative* ability to a common human essence. What holds potential conflicts of meaning in a work together is the power of symbols operating as verbal icons.

While faith in the symbol to *transcend* conflicts of meaning in the text is seductively close to Jung's notion of a psychic symbol possessing a transcendent function, the New Critics unhelpfully disowned psychology altogether. They dismissed the psyche of the author *and reader* in interpreting a work of literary merit. It is not their approach to the reader that brings them to depth psychology, but to the *act of reading* that so resembles active imagination. In effect, the New Critics endorsed active imagination technically, yet not ontologically (philosophically). For in order to restrain a literary work from spilling its meaning or its historical and cultural considerations into the reader's conscious mind (all anathema to New Critics), "close reading" was developed as a way of *othering* the text. Close reading is a *perverse* counterintuitive practice. It involves focusing on words and phrases, their sounds and shapes on the page, to thus invoke their almost infinite possibilities to spark interpretations. For close reading, everyone's interpretation of a particular text is unique.

Here, I want to offer a perverse argument. For despite these literary theorists' disavowal of psychology and, in particular, the psychology of the unconscious, I suggest that, nevertheless, a secret kinship exists between New Criticism and Jungian depth psychology. The incestuous closeness between close reading and active imagination inheres in their disciplinary "cousinship" and, as I will show later, in common ancestry. For now I want to focus on a possible link between close reading and active imagination, beyond and despite the New Critics' insistence on ignoring the reading psyche. In particular, I argue for a link between close reading as a literary technique (once New Criticism's theoretical orthodoxies have been left behind) and active imagination plus amplification as a psychological method. The New Critics invented close reading, but the practice survived their dominance of the academy.

Even as new theories emerged to leave their mark upon the junior discipline of literary studies, the perverse "closeness" of the New Critics' reading has survived, although severed from New Critical doctrine and modified by all subsequent literary theories such as Freudian psychoanalysis, feminism, Marxism, structuralism, cultural materialism, Queer Theory, poststructuralism, postmodernism, postcolonialism, ecocriticism, and so on. Because close reading gives *the words on the page themselves* the authorizing power for interpretation, it remains a valued research method, supporting various epistemological diversities. Close reading frames words (and their grammatical constructs) into images that must be regarded as autonomous in constructing meaning. Considerations of the author's "intention" or the reader's "preference" are illegitimate. Like active imagination, close reading construes the words (of literature and whole literary works) as images with their own signifying strategies, independent of their "location" in culture and history or in any one psyche. As a result, close reading endows the words of literature with the highest creative potency, so expanding almost infinitely their potentials for interpretation. After New Criticism, later theories retained this original source of creative energy in literary interpretation, only changing the parameters of close reading to give permission to follow the signifying of the text beyond its boundaries. For the later theories, the literature-as-potent-image-through-close reading was enabled to *add* meaning to cultural topics of power, identity, politics, history, sexuality, and so on.

In effect, close reading as practised today unwittingly has added Jung's method of cultural *amplification* of the symbol to its active imagination-like generation of its *own*, or *othering* significance. I suggest that close reading has survived, at least in part, because of its underground kinship to active imagination: their *secret history in the psyche*. In turn, depth psychology may benefit from knowledge of the way literary scholars explore the hidden dark impulses that determine patterns of thought and action.

For while the methodology of close reading represses a *conscious* role for the reading psyche, it actually draws upon the structural precepts of active imagination and the symbol as understood by Jung. In close reading, the literary work must be allowed to manifest *its own* imaginative powers. In contemporary literary studies, the term "symbol" has fallen out of favour, but the notion that literature is language that possesses multiple, hidden, or repressed directions for making meaning is inescapable. Like active imagination, students of literature are directed to put aside their conscious concerns and allow the text to speak through them, not just to them.

Close reading (called *literary studies*) discourages personal associations to the text, while cultural and historical connotations are encouraged. What follows with close reading is the student's own written interpretation. This is a new synthesis, different for each person, and should be guided by the symbolic power of the text, not the ego of the reader. When active imagination (called *psychology*) adds "amplification" to the initial active imagination, allowing the words on the page, the *symbols*, to manifest their own power and energy, what follows is a new synthesis of psyche through the activity of images imbued with unconscious energy. As Jung ultimately emphasized, the ego is renewed by accepting the actions of images and interacting with them. *Amplification* is a form of interrelating with images that draws on historical and cultural paradigms to *ground* the ego as it becomes newly embodied in the collective by the grace of images.

I have been describing the basic technique of close reading as it evolved from the New Critics. Early on, other literary critics recognized that New Criticism itself derived from Romanticism, but it deliberately cast off those Romantic theories of mind, theories that, in turn, re-emerged in depth psychology. In 1952, the literary scholar R. S. Crane critically examined New Criticism, in general, and the work of Cleanth Brooks, in particular.[10] His essay focused on Brooks's debt to and divergence from the Romantic poet S. T. Coleridge. The latter was the author of *Biographia Literaria*,[11] a work of Romantic aesthetic theory that anticipated depth psychology.

Crane found New Criticism wanting for its unwarranted diminishing of the category of imaginative writing into fictional literature only. To the Romantics, as to Coleridge, poetry implied a larger activity than simply the making of poems. Poetry is a *quality* of writing that emerges from the creative imagination, whether directed to scientific, philosophical, or literary ends. In fact, to me, Coleridge's view of the imagination is very close to that of Jung's, in seeing it as a creative power adding to the conscious will and ego's directed thinking.[12] Coleridge argues: "The reason is that 'poetry' comes into being, no matter what the medium, whenever the images, thoughts, and emotions of the mind are brought into unity by the sympathetic power of the secondary imagination."[13]

For Coleridge, primary imagination is the creative energy of God: it makes the world; the "secondary imagination" corresponds to what Jung later calls the unconscious, for it is the creative force in humans that is not always accessible to the rational faculties. Crane points out that, for Coleridge, and by extension the Romantics, three kinds of knowing are needed for literary study: logic, grammar, and psychology.[14] These three are equal potentates in examining a literary work. Grammar thus invades psychology by way of rhetoric.[15] By contrast, for Cleanth Brooks, and by extension the New Critics, only grammar is needed for literary criticism. Unable to locate an originating cause in the human psyche, they are reduced to positing the origins of imaginative literature in the properties of language.[16]

Here, New Criticism and Jungian psychology divide the heritage of literary and philosophical Romanticism. New Criticism founded close reading, but denied it an epistemology in the psyche conceived of as intrinsically imaginative. It did so because of its urge to separate "literature" from other kinds of writing. Arguably, this collective insistence can be traced to the founding anxiety of the "new" discipline of vernacular literary study. For how could scrutinizing imaginative works in their own language be justified as *knowledge*, epistemologically, if literature were not in some way a special category? Literature *has* to be elevated from the trivial, the journalistic, the contingent immanence of the everyday, into something sublime and transcendent of dependence upon time, place, or person.

What was achieved, I suggest, by this thankfully short-lived denial of psyche in literary studies, was a concentration upon technique. Indeed, it was the *perversity* of the exclusion of the reading psyche from reading that led to the corresponding energy being applied to the words on the page. As a result, it bequeathed to subsequent theories of literary study the notion of developing a counterintuitive skill. Close reading is a skill, an art that has to be learned over time by consciously repressing parts of the ego and repressing conventional ideas about what pleasurable reading is *for*.

Close reading does its (founding) disciplinary job of converting reading literature from an act primarily given to pleasure to a mode of exegesis. It is this achievement of expertise, skilfulness, and art that keeps the practice vibrant in literary studies today. I want to suggest that the development of this disciplined skilfulness has something to offer the idea of active imagination. In order to make my argument for a reciprocal exchange between literary studies and depth psychology, I need to go further back into their mutual lineage in the mythical and esoteric realms of hermeneutics and magic.

Hermeneutical problems, magical texts

R. S. Crane notes that Coleridge's Romantic theory of mind was indebted to Plato in the notion of imitation. Just as Plato erected a dualist sense of the world through an ultimate reality of transcendent forms to be imperfectly imitated by humans, so Coleridge gave us a secondary imagination by which we might learn to imitate the primary creative imagination of God.[17]

Hermeneutics, the art of creating meaning from texts, also contains a Platonic notion in its various citations of recollection. Plato described a process of "anamnesis", or learning about the unknown by recognizing it as or through the already known. This idea becomes a principle in hermeneutics, where meaning is constructed by placing the unknown within an already known context.[18] Another key element in the development of hermeneutics is the notion of the "hermeneutical circle", which, although having roots in Plato, was actually formulated by Friedrich Schleiermacher in the nineteenth century.[19] Here textual apprehension moves from focus upon parts to realizing its context in the whole work, and vice versa. By erecting a circle of epistemological acts, such hermeneutical analysis enhances Plato's concept of recollection, placing the unknown in the text in the context of the known.

In his book, *Freud and Philosophy*, Paul Ricoeur significantly redefines hermeneutics by refocusing the practice on the interpretation of texts and by incorporating some depth psychology. It was Ricoeur who famously announced a "hermeneutics of suspicion" congruent with Freud's assertion that a dream *conceals* a wish. By contrast, he also announced a "hermeneutics of trust", closer to Jung's belief in treating an image as meaningful in itself, thus building meaning by amplifying it.[20]

Already in Ricoeur, we see hermeneutics learning from depth psychology. Less recognized is New Criticism's debt to the hermeneutic circle, in close reading's tradition of placing the unknown in the context of the already known or recollected. Close reading in New Criticism depended on the literary text being regarded as an autonomous entity whose meaning could be gleaned by scrutinizing its parts minutely in the context of the entire work. Just as in the elaboration of the hermeneutic circle, close reading moved from parts to whole and from whole to parts, New Criticism's close reading had to stay within that circle for the boundary of the text was, indeed, "sacred" to it. Post-New Criticism's close reading freely expands the hermeneutic circle of interpretation beyond the text, and even into the psyche.

Now I will look at what we might call "the psyche" before psychology and Romanticism – in Renaissance magical lore.

Renaissance magic and alchemy: twentieth-century transformation and individuation

In *Eros and Magic in the Renaissance*, Ioan P. Couliano draws on Freudian depth psychology to a greater degree than upon that of Jung in his study of those master magicians of the Renaissance, whose arts of darkness he likens to the hucksters who now bewitch the public with advertising and mass media manipulation.[21] He, therefore, applies Ricoeur's "hermeneutics of suspicion". While appreciating Couliano's moral distaste for those who manipulate people by exerting control over psychically potent symbols, I see other possibilities for his research on magic by applying a "hermeneutics of trust". The Renaissance treatment of psyche may reveal a magic potent enough to revise close reading with/and active imagination.

Like hermeneutics, Couliano traces a lineage back to Plato's separation of true reality of ideal forms, dwelling in an imperceptible realm, from their imperfect shadows in the everyday. By the Renaissance, this dualist heritage had become what today we might recognize as a form of sophisticated psychology that viewed humans as possessed of a soul that was in essence *phantasmic*, neither of bodily substance nor destroyed by death. This phantasmic soul shared something of the inaccessibility of Plato's ultimate forms. The soul did not understand the body's language, which was dependent on the physical senses. The soul only comprehended a language made of phantasms – one that the body did not know. Only what was called the "intellect" had the capacity to perceive phantasmic language as well as the sensual. Again, we return to the problems of communicating the symbols because that is what the esoteric phantasmic language consists of.

As Couliano puts it:

> Fundamentally all is reduced to a question of communication: body and soul speak two languages, which are not only different, even inconsistent, but also *inaudible* to each other. The inner sense alone is able to hear and comprehend them both, also having the role of translating one into the other. But considering the words of the soul's language are phantasms, everything that reaches it from the body – including distinct utterances – will have to be transposed into a phantasmic sequence. Besides – must it be emphasized? – the soul has absolute primacy over the body. It follows that the *phantasm has absolute primacy over the word*, that it precedes both utterance and understanding of the linguistic message. Whence two separate and distinct grammars, the first no less important than the second: a grammar of the spoken language and a grammar of phantasmic language. Stemming from the soul, itself phantasmic in essence, intellect alone enjoys the privilege of understanding the phantasmic grammar.[22]

Here, we can see why Jung was so attracted to Renaissance symbolic practices such as alchemy. For, in its intellect that stemmed from the soul and was phantasmic in essence is an ego deeply rooted in what Jung much later termed the Self. In seeking out the symbolic texts of alchemy, which predated the historical elevation of logical rationality, Jung sought to heal the modern psychic split by evoking a past with an "other" architecture of psychic being. Notably, in placing so much importance on alchemical texts, Jung implicitly structures active imagination as a kind of reading with the aim of transforming the psyche.

Significantly, here "intellect" is not the rational ego of post-Enlightenment reason. In Jung's view, this rational ego is fallible because it has been constructed through cultural discourses of reason that repress too much that is "other". Jung calls for this ego to remake its relation with the unconscious by converting a strategy of repression into one of relationship, thus transforming the libido (or affective life force) through an active and imaginative engagement with its symbols. This is "individuation", and a nice illustration of Jung preferring a hermeneutics of trust to that of suspicion (that "distances" the other).

Couliano's explication of phantasms offers an understanding of the Renaissance alchemist's sense of working simultaneously in body, psyche, and material substance. In this era, the phantasm is a language that is also a material realm of being in which the soul can be manipulated by the intellect of a skilled practitioner. This "art" as it was called, encompassed what we now call science; for it also operated on, and from, the material world. For the Renaissance practitioner of the art of phantasmic manipulation, it was possible to mutate material substances and even to affect the world at a distance. In one sphere, this was "alchemy" (from the Egyptian *Khemia*, "land of black earth"), but in another, "magic".

Central to the notion of phantasms and magic is the belief that there is no essential separation between an individual human, the material world, and the spiritual heavens. Phantasms offer the individual a soul that engenders an intellect, which is, after much study, capable of apprehending the soul and the spiritual realm. In this system, soul and intellect (ego-with-self, in Jung's vocabulary) also belong to a cosmic unity that is structured through and with the stars. Hence, the individual soul is caught up in a dynamic universe of subtle, part material, part spiritual potential entities. As Couliano explains:

> [M]agic makes use of the continuity between the individual pneuma and the cosmic one ...
>
> Reciprocity or the principle of inversion of action, is the guarantee that a process that takes place in the phantasmic mind and spirit of the individual will result in obtaining certain gifts the stars grant us by virtue of the consubstantiality and intimate relationships existing between us and them.[23]

That Jung had a very real sense of this aspect of Renaissance alchemy is shown by his depiction of the "subtle body", which is, in fact, the dimension of psychic and material phantasms.

> The singular expression "astrum" (star) is a Paracelsan term, which in this context means something like "quintessence". Imagination is therefore a concentrated extract of the life forces, both physical and psychic.... But, just because of this intermingling of the physical and the psychic, it always remains an obscure point whether the ultimate transformations in the alchemical process are to be sought more in the material or more in the spiritual realm. Actually, however, the question is wrongly put: there was no "either–or" for that age, but there did exist an intermediate realm between mind and matter, i.e. a psychic realm of subtle bodies whose characteristic it is to manifest themselves in a mental as well as material form.[24]

Fascinatingly, here Jung calls "imagination" what Couliano terms "Renaissance intellect". Today, depth psychology would recognize Jung's "imagination" here and Couliano's "intellect" as that desired result from the ego's individuation into the numinous unconscious, that is, an individuated ego/self. Not only is this an era in which there is no secure division between the sciences and imaginative arts, but also there is little sense of psychic differentiation between these activities.

Taking his *Collected Works* as a whole, Jung remains ever wary of the shocking departure of endorsing magic. Much of his depiction of alchemy relies upon the post-Cartesian division of self as intrinsically separate from the world. In particular, Jung bases his conceptual scheme on his historically inherited dualism of conscious versus unconscious, with terms like ego, archetype, anima, animus, and shadow belonging on either side of the divide. Yet, at the heart of his project are processes that signify a momentous *undoing* of dualism within the psyche and between the psyche and material world, such as individuation. *Projection*, at least here, is Jung's retention of epistemological respectability, in suggesting that, for the Renaissance alchemists, the psyche was projected into matter.

It is in Jung's later work on synchronicity that we find his more authentic alchemical and, I suggest, magical sensibility. In synchronicity, mind and matter reveal themselves as intimately related. Jung describes as synchronous, phenomena in which a psychic event and a material one reveal a meaningful, not causal, connection.[25] For example, I dream of a long-lost relative, whose e-mail then arrives, and I note with surprise that it was typed *while I was dreaming of her*. To Jung, synchronicity is a phenomenon that reveals the possibility of a universe similar to the one invoked by the Renaissance alchemists and magicians, as well as by modern quantum physicists.

Perhaps it was Jung's very proper moral reservations that preserved the difference between his work on synchronicity and Renaissance magic. Synchronicity is a revelation of a property of reality, whereas both alchemy and magic were *arts*, thus deliberate attempts to manipulate actual conditions. Jung aligns his psychology with Renaissance alchemy by the linking hypothesis that its unconscious goal was the personal development of the alchemist, projected onto matter, hence constituting a pre-psychological form of individuation. Provided alchemy shows the possible individuation of an individual psyche, it is safe from the moral dubiousness of magical attempts to intervene in the physical world. Couliano, operating from a hermeneutics of suspicion, is explicit about what he calls Eros and magic as manipulative practices against unknowing populations. Today we possess and are possessed by "magicians" who manipulate, even sculpt, our embodied psyches in the magical symbolic images of the media.

Preferring a hermeneutics of trust, Jung does not explicitly consider the proximity of individuation to magic. However, I argue that active imagination, another process by which a dualistic psyche surmounts its dichotomy, is potentially friendly to a magic that comes by way of literary study's close reading. Indeed, Jung's sense of individuation as "transformation" begins to look like what the Renaissance called magic.

Close reading and magic: making active imagination an art

Nothing could be further from the intentions of the devisers of "close reading" than the rediscovery of Renaissance magic. Denying psyche's creativity in the reading process, New Critics repressed all the esoteric possibilities of the hermeneutical circle to that of language regarded as a disembodied system. And yet the stripping of psyche from language created the essential psychic perversity embedded in close reading. Subjecting the reader to an impersonal system dissolves psychic identity. Close reading is a defeat of the ego or it is *not close enough*.

At this point, it is time to rethink one of Jung's dualisms: his binary division of literature, and by extension art, into two categories. In "Psychology and Literature",[26] he divides literary works into two psychological categories. One is confusingly called "psychological" and refers to literature in which the unconscious psyche has been fully processed into the work. Psychological literature knows its own world and builds it out of signs: images that denote a stable conscious meaning. Standing opposite is "visionary literature", saturated by the raw symbols of the collective unconscious. Less noticed than this stark division is Jung's acknowledgement that literature may change categories over time. A work of art may be *read* as visionary in one era, psychological in another, and vice versa. This leaking of categorization into *the circumstances of reading* has inspired me to propose a revision of Jung's psychological and visionary reading into *modes of reading* that could be applied to any work of art, not just literature, of any time.[27]

Psychological reading, then, reads art for its conscious intervention into psyche and world. It reads for known signs of the collective consciousness. *Visionary reading* reads for symbols that point to the unknown, not yet known, or unknowable. To read in a visionary manner is to read in the service of the collective unconscious, or soul. Of course, these two types of reading are epistemological strategies that both preserve and defeat a dualistic notion of psyche and world. Psychological reading adheres to faith in consciousness as separable from unconsciousness, if not wholly distinct from it. Visionary reading is a process by which an ego that considers itself as separate from the unconscious is, through reading its symbols, integrated into it.

Furthermore, visionary reading cannot retain a psyche distinct from body or nonhuman nature. For visionary reading describes a practice of working with symbols in art that are simultaneously *known* in the body – and through the body to the nonhuman – and that signify cosmos. Here, I must insist that visionary reading requires the practice of close reading in order to be *visionary*. It is close reading in the visionary mode that deconstructs the ego as a disembodied island of rationality. Uncanny is the similar argument: that active imagination also deconstructs ego as a disembodied island of rationality. Vital to my argument is close reading as an *acquired skill*. As taught in literary studies, close reading requires little in the way of natural aptitude. Anyone with a normal attention span can learn to do close reading, to let the words of the text become alive and guide the reading psyche, rather than vice versa, yet it is a skill that usually takes years of study and practice.

Overarching the notion of learning skills is the great theme of evolution in both natural and cultural terms. In particular, evolution has generated a new ecological complexity science, arguing that creativity and skilfulness are not limited to human beings. What might reading for magic mean if signifying and creative enmeshment mean embracing the whole planet?

Magic through complexity science: symbols as nature speaking

To further consider the connections among psyche, nature, evolution, and magic, I will draw upon two emerging fields of study: *complex adaptive systems* (as they are changing the study of ecology) and *biosemiotics*. The latter term refers to new research in biology that counters centuries of assumptions about "dumb" nature, by proposing that the biosphere communicates on a basic cellular level both within and across species. Nature has systems of signification that are "read" intelligently by plant and animal organisms. This remarkable field of study enhances what used to be called *chaos theory* and is now called *complexity evolution* – the notion that evolution proceeds not by competition among individual species but by the interaction of incredibly complex environments. So-called complex adaptive systems behave "intelligently" in generating their own complex responses to environments, and their version of creativity even extends to mapping processes between groups in human societies. Biosemiotics may reveal *how* complex adaptive systems in nonhuman locations creatively coevolve, and both offer models for exploring what Jung calls *synchronicity.*

For Jung's notion of synchronicity implies an ordering in nature that is accessible to the human psyche. A parallel perspective is to be found in literary scholar Wendy Wheeler's *The Whole Creature.*[28] Looking for a continuity between nature's fecundity and what is defined as creativity in humans, Wheeler draws on notions of tacit bodily knowledge, such as craft skills, to resituate the body in nature as an organ of knowing indivisible from the psyche. Wheeler argues that art and culture advance through intuited embodied knowledge. It is through the incarnated creative unconscious that the "new" happens. Tacit bodily knowledge implies a complexity greater than can be comprehended at the time. This complexity is not confined to cultural change; complexity is now regarded as key to evolution in nature.

Here is an important development in the theory of evolution after Darwin. Evolved nature is not so much a result of competition among species. Rather, nature changes through ever more complexly interpenetrating environments.

> Complex systems evolve via the emergence of strata of increasing complexity. Biological evolution proceeds in this fashion, as, we have now seen, does human culture and human knowledge. Human discovery and invention – human creativity – proceeds via tacit knowledge and our sense that we are in contact with a complex reality of which there is more to be known.[29]

What Wheeler does not say is how far Jung, particularly with reference to synchronicity, anticipates her fruitful gatherings from the field of "biosemiotics".

Jung's unconscious psyche, like Wheeler's, is also embodied. His "synchronous events" are apprehended through/as tacit knowledge in the body. Effectively, he too embraces the creativity of nature through tacit *significance* into culture. Biosemiosis offers another model for looking at the natural phenomena Jung describes as examples of synchronicity, another way of viewing the links between language and nature. Effectively, Jung embraces the idea of the creativity of nature. Biosemiosis is a parallel way of describing nonhuman nature as animate, as *communicating* with humans in the reciprocal formation of symbols in culture.

We are back to the issue of the communicability of the symbol, now seeing it as possible on a truly cosmic scale. Symbols, as Jung described them, are archetypal images rooted in the human body, and through its tacit knowledge, in the nonhuman. Nature is a web of co-evolving complex adaptive systems of which the human embodied psyche is one system, creatively interacting with nonhuman nature. Symbols may arise from biosemiosis when human cultures are rooted in a *reciprocal communication* with the nonhuman. Jung called these occurrences *synchronous.* It is a small step to move from *reciprocal communication* to *reciprocal influence*, or magic.

Active imagination and close reading as skilful magic: the mythological frame

I propose that close reading is the practice of magic when it involves symbolic images. When not confined to writing in words, we could term such close reading "active imagination", for encouraging the image to reveal its potential being in the soul spontaneously. Active imagination then overcomes its origin in one of Jung's dualist paradigms of dividing psyche into ego and other. It does so by welcoming the soul matter into the image as a symbol that actively unites the psyche.

My suggestion in this essay is that we allow a reciprocal *influence* or magic between literary studies' close reading and depth psychology's active imagination. The *grounds* for this cross-disciplinary fertilization come from the Complex Adaptive System's theory of the embodied psyche, the mutual inheritance of these disciplines in Plato, hermeneutics, and Renaissance magic. For example, Jungian Helene Shulman, in *Living at the Edge of Chaos*,[30] considers the collective unconscious as a Complex Adaptive System that offers human co-evolution with the natural environment. Because Jung's unconscious is rooted in the body, but not limited to it, the psyche in all its unmappable complexity is the meeting place of human and other that teems with fertility and productivity. Moreover, behind all these epistemologies of psychology, philosophy, and magic, I suggest, is the founding role of the two entwined creation myths that have shaped the modern Western psyche.

Borrowing heavily from Ann Baring and Jules Cashford's *The Myth of the Goddess*,[31] I have inferred that depth psychology, and Jung's project in particular, is one among many attempts to re-orient modernity through its great myths of consciousness.[32] Dominant in the West, via Christianity, has been a sky father myth based on separation and differentiation from the other that reinforced Platonic dualism and structured consciousness as masculine. Repressed for centuries has been a myth deriving from premonotheistic animism, with the earth seen as a divine mother. Earth mother consciousness lies in the *grounding* of consciousness and spirituality through connection, body, the unconscious, sexuality, and an animistic relation to nature.

In this version, myths operate as grand narratives in making paradigms for knowledge. "Magic" in this context is a practice of the repressed myth of earth mother consciousness. Such a perspective uncovers major trends in late modernity to revive "her". Depth psychology brings "her" back as the pre-Oedipal (m)other, with Jung's creative androgynous unconscious as source. Jung also cites/sites her as Eros and synchronicity. Beyond psychology, earth mother consciousness arises in the very theory of evolution (earth generates all life and consciousness) and particularly intensifies with the development of biosemiotics and its theory of nature evolving through creative complexity.

With such epistemological support to a mythic heritage, I propose that both active imagination and close reading might undergo a creative co-evolution, within and between psychology and literary studies, when brought together in the context of a Complex Adaptive System (such as this chapter) and together move toward restructuring our consciousness. Put simply, as the skilful practice of close reading enters the threshold realm of active imagination, it becomes an *art of psychic complexity evolution.* Close reading becomes active imagination through the reciprocity of human and nonhuman nature in embodied symbols. Similarly, active imagination can take on close reading's habits of disciplined skilfulness.

Thus, active imagination becomes an *art to be learned and practised* in the service of soul as connected to cosmos. Both practices are magic because they constitute active interventions into the creativity of nature, human, and non-human. Because both are skills practised until they become arts, close reading and active imagination, now indistinguishable from each other, are activities of what the Renaissance called the intellect – not the ego, but ego-united-with-soul by training and practice in imaginative creativity. To be precise, then, close reading and active imagination are magic because the division between ego and unconscious has been eroded through the art. Practising this magic remakes who we are, as children of a creative earth.

I began this essay with my long attachment to reading Jung as a quest for knowing, not a map of it. In amplifying, actively imagining, and close reading Jung's concept of "active imagination", I have been on a quest for that which is not amenable to disciplinary endeavour through the academic disciplines of psychology and literary studies. Perhaps it is a quest to evoke what Jung indicated when he suggested that analytical psychology was one way of knowing in a long history of symbolic arts, a way also susceptible to change when historical conditions require. In so positioning his work, Jung suggests *how* one might read him – as an invocation to the other – and *why*, that we might continue the pursuit of creativity in (our) nature to find a magic by which to live.

Notes

1 T. Eagleton, *Literary Theory: An Introduction*, Oxford, Blackwell, 1983.
2 G. Snyder, "Language goes two ways", in L. Coupe (ed.), *The Green Studies Reader: From Romanticism to Ecocriticism*, London and New York, Routledge, 2000, pp. 127–31.
3 R. G. Woodman, *Sanity, Madness, Transformation: The Psyche in Romanticism*, Toronto, University of Toronto Press, 2005.
4 Ibid., 11; C. G. Jung, *The Archetypes and the Collective Unconscious*, in *The Collected Works of C. G. Jung* (hereafter *CW*), vol. 9i, Princeton, NJ, Princeton University Press, 1968, p. 150.
5 Woodman, *Sanity, Madness, Transformation*, p. 104.
6 Ibid., p. 15.
7 C. G. Jung, "General aspects of dream psychology", in *The Structure and Dynamics of the Psyche*, *CW* 8, Princeton, NJ, Princeton University Press, 1952, p. 400.
8 C. G. Jung, "The Tavistock Lectures", in *CW* 18, Princeton, NJ, Princeton University Press, 1968, p. 397; quoted in J. Chodorow, *Jung on Active Imagination*, Princeton, NJ, Princeton University Press, 1997, p. 145.
9 Eagleton, *Literary Theory*.
10 R. S. Crane (ed.), *Critics and Criticism: Ancient and Modern*, Chicago, University of Chicago Press, 1952.
11 S. T. Coleridge, *Biographia Literaria, or, Biographical Sketches of My Life and Opinions*, London, William Pickering, 1847.
12 Crane, *Critics and Criticism*, p. 89.
13 Ibid., p. 87; Coleridge quoted in Crane.
14 Ibid., p. 93.
15 Josephine Evetts-Secker superbly explores psychology's coopting by grammar in *At Home in the Language of the Soul: Exploring Jungian Discourse and Psyche's Grammar of Transformation*, New Orleans, Spring Journal and Books, 2012. In my own book, *Jung as a Writer*, I explore Jung's counterattack on grammatical pressures in psychology, his "trickster" writing. S. Rowland, *Jung as a Writer*, New York and London, Routledge, 2005.
16 Crane, *Critics and Criticism*, p. 92.
17 Ibid., p. 85.
18 S. Gallagher, *Hermeneutics and Education*, SUNY Series in Contemporary Continental Philosophy, Albany, State University of New York Press, 1992.
19 R. E. Palmer, *Hermeneutics: Interpretation Theory in Schleiermacher, Dilthey, Heidegger, and Gadamer*, Evanston, IL, Northwestern University Press, 1969.
20 P. Ricoeur, *Freud and Philosophy: An Essay on Interpretation* (The Terry Lectures), New Haven, CT, Yale University Press, 1970.
21 I. P. Couliano, *Eros and Magic in the Renaissance*, Chicago, University of Chicago Press, 1987.
22 Ibid., pp. 5–6.
23 Ibid., pp. 23, 27
24 C. G. Jung, "The philosophical tree", in *Psychology and Alchemy*, *CW* 12, trans. R. F. C. Hull, ed. Sir Herbert Read, Dr Michael Fordham, and Dr Gerhard Adler, London, Routledge, and Princeton, NJ, Princeton University Press, 1968, p. 394.
25 Jung, "General aspects of dream psychology", p. 864.
26 C. G. Jung, "Psychology and literature", in *The Spirit in Man, Art, and Literature*, *CW* 15, trans. R. F. C. Hull, ed. Sir Herbert Read, Dr Michael Fordham, and Dr Gerhard Adler, London, Routledge, and Princeton, NJ, Princeton University Press, 1930/1950; *Modern Man in Search of a Soul*, London and New York, Routledge, 1933/2001.
27 S. Rowland, *C. G Jung in the Humanities*, New Orleans, Spring Journal and Books, 2010.
28 W. Wheeler, *The Whole Creature: Complexity, Biosemiotics and the Evolution of Culture*, London, Lawrence & Wishart, 2006.

29 Ibid., pp. 67–8.
30 H. Shulman, *Living at the Edge of Chaos: Complex Systems in Culture and Psyche*, Zurich, Daimon Verlag, 1997.
31 A. Baring and J. Cashford, *The Myth of the Goddess: Evolution of an Image*, New York and London, Vintage, 1991.
32 Rowland, *C. G. Jung in the Humanities.*

6

READING FRYE READING JUNG

Craig Stephenson

Continuing the theme of Jung's contribution to the humanities, in this essay, the Canadian analyst Craig Stephenson examines why and how his famous countryman, the literary critic Northrop Frye, read and reread Jung over a lifetime of scholarly pursuit. Offering a straightforward account of Frye's initial enthusiastic use of Jung's method, his subsequent criticism, disillusionment, and distancing, and his ultimate acknowledgement of Jung as a major influence on his writing, Stephenson gleans for us the most relevant material from Frye's diaries, notebooks, and published works. What is presented for us, then, are traces of the lifeline of one man who was "bitten" by the creative unconscious and who found in Jung a guide to that underworld, a comrade and a worthy foe, one from whom he learned and with whom he connected, wrestling competitively with Jung's writing for his own strength and growth.

J. K.

How does reading change us? How does our reading change? Do we understand that we have been changed by a certain reading? I first read William Blake's *The Marriage of Heaven and Hell* when I was 16, and it turned my world upside down. In it, Blake acknowledges how one can read Milton's *Paradise Lost* as a conventional Christian allegory of good and evil, but he demonstrates how to read it archetypally. The reader can then see that the angels are actually promoting death, the devils are defending the life principle, and Milton, as poet, is of Satan's party without knowing it (inasmuch as he intends to justify God's ways to man, but privileges poetically all the energy and delight and fire banished to an infernal netherworld). With his archetypal reading, Blake tore the roof off my adolescence. It was one of my first experiences of the numinous evoked by a text, and it was liberating and terrifying at the same time. There was much to learn from reading how a great reader such as Blake reads Milton.

Northrop Frye, an important literary critic and cultural commentator, was one of the penultimate readers of Blake in the twentieth century. With the recent publication of his diaries and notebooks, we now have the opportunity to track his personal reading responses as he read Blake and as he read Carl Gustav Jung. In his notebooks, Frye tested the utility of

Jung's concepts for his own theorizing, and in his diaries he recorded more subjective responses, even interpreting his dreams and feelings during the time he read Jung. Together, these documents establish that in the 1940s and 1950s Frye was carefully familiarizing himself with Jung's work. By 1949, he had read *Psychology of the Unconscious*, *Psychological Types*, and *The Integration of the Personality*, as well as Jung's commentaries on Richard Wilhelm's translation of the Chinese alchemical text, *The Secret of the Golden Flower* and on the Walter Evans–Wentz edition of *The Tibetan Book of the Dead.* And, in 1954, he reviewed *Two Essays on Analytical Psychology* (in its revised form as a Bollingen Foundation publication) and *Psychology and Alchemy* for an important academic journal, the *Hudson Review.* But then he stopped reading Jung. What can we learn by following a great reader like Frye as he makes his way through Jung's works, sometimes enthralled by a text, other times vowing angrily never again to open the volume?

Frye reading Jung

In 1949, as Frye reads Jung's *Psychological Types*, he records in his diary his enthusiastic engagement with Jung's argument about dreams, identifying himself as "progressing" according to Jung's psychological concept of individuation. Almost paraphrasing Jung, Frye distinguishes between Freudian sex-dreams or Adlerian power-dreams, which indicate unconscious regressive tendencies, and other dreams that work differently, centring the personality with images of self:

> Tuesday, January 4, 1949: Everyone admits that the dream comments on the previous day, & everyone knows that the problems of that day are sometimes solved by sleep alone. Does not this imply that the dreaming consciousness rearranges material from waking consciousness in a wish-fulfilment form, & that this material, now dramatized, is assimilated to the archetypes below it, from whence it reemerges to consciousness? This would explain how dreams hook themselves onto the key experiences of childhood, as I'm convinced that impressions taken in the first few years of life recreate for the individual all the primary archetypes. Thus the dream assimilates the haphazard and involuntary experiences of waking life, the becoming world, into the archetypal world of being where everything is a wish-fulfilment comedy. Each dream is a personal episode of a universal comedy of the human collective unconscious, a drama broken off from the one great epic. If the individual is not progressing, then his dreams will be Freudian sex-dreams or Adlerian power-dreams, concerned only with an antithesis between reality and desire. These fall into the childhood archetypes & reemerge

> autonomously in life: the whole process is involuntary, sterile, & regressive – or rather, it follows the organic curve of life, & becomes regressive from 35 on, in the dismal poverty of ideas one sees in age. If he is progressing, his individuality, Jung's self, takes form at the centre of the wheel, instead of being one of the foci of an ellipse, the other being a point in the dark.[1]

It sounds here as if Frye were aligning Jung's concept of a collective unconscious with Percy Bysshe Shelley's notion of "that great poem, which all poets, like the co-operating thoughts of one great mind, have built up since the beginning of the world".[2] But it is important to note that Frye's notion of mythology as shared imaginative vision stems neither from Shelley nor from Jung but from his reading of William Blake.

Frye had recently published *Fearful Symmetry* (1947),[3] in which he rendered accessible and intelligible to the common reader the visionary writings of Blake. It was his first book, the product of over a decade of working his way in and out of the labyrinths of Blake's texts, and his argument countered the still widespread critical dismissal of Blake's writings as a private mythology, subjectively idiosyncratic, and incomprehensible:

> Friday, January 21, 1949: It occurs to me that what I did in writing *Fearful Symmetry* was perform the act described in much the same way by Freud and Jung. This is the act of swallowing the father, integrating oneself with the old wise man. Presumably I shall never find another father, not even in Shakespeare, and should realize I am essentially on my own. I've really reached an individuated stage of thinking, if not of personal life. There's more to it than that – Blake is right in a way no one else is – but that's the psychological aspect of the book.... Perhaps too, if every poem is necessarily a perfect unity, every thinker is necessarily perfectly right. That is doubtless just another way of saying that one seeks understanding rather than a judgement of value.[4]

Here Frye acknowledges that, if Freud and Jung were right (psychologically) about fathers and sons, then writing *Fearful Symmetry* was Frye's act of consciously ingesting the father imago, ruminating on his memories of a conventionally pietistic Methodist upbringing, particularly at the hands of his oppressive reactionary preacher-grandfather, the Reverend Eratus Seth Howard, and taking up an adult stance that he associates with the archetypal images of Blake's nonconformist revolutionary wisdom. In this passage, Frye also redefines his professional task as cultural critic: not so much to assign value to a particular work or identify which works have merit, but more to understand where and how any work fits within the collective cultural imagination. In this regard, Frye would defend Jung's interest in the archetypal structures laid bare by crude "hack" writers such as Rider Haggard, arguing that "value-judgements are worn as blinders by conventional critics to prevent themselves from seeing the real facts of literature".[5]

Around the same time that Frye records in his diaries his psychological responses to Jung, in his notebooks, he positions Jung in the planning for his second major book, *Anatomy of Criticism* (1957).[6] For instance:

> #131: The work of art is literally a product of its author, & should be examined in terms of the mental archetypes of that author as provided by Freud & Jung. Note carefully that the author is not man but poet, & the archetypes are not psychoanalytic & therapeutic but objectively to be seen in the work of art as a microcosm of human or individual experience. As an *allegory*, the work of art is a symbol of its age, & should be examined in the historical archetypes provided by Spengler ... As *moral*, the work of art is a myth, the articulation of a ritual.... As *anagogy*, the work of art is an entity or microcosm of the Word of God, a cyclic panorama of universal existence.... They are the four real forms of criticism: the author's mind, the age, the genre & the unity of the work of art itself as a mirror of universal reality.[7]

> #245: Now let's see what, in summary, stands out. Chapter 1 makes four major points. One, criticism is autonomous; two, it relates to other descriptive verbal disciplines, but controls its own relations; three, it's a comprehensive systematic progressive scientific study; four, it's based on the conception of an order of words. These four points are expanded in Chapter 2 to a conception of four levels of criticism. First, rhetorical, divided into biographical & topical, depending on whether the work of art is in time or not (is taken that way, I mean). Second, dialectic, divided into historical & ethical, Spenglerian & Marxist, wheel of history & classless society, image of the wheel & spiral that comes later. Third, structural & archetypal, Frazer & Jung, the poetic level proper. Fourth.... A level of pure association where there is no coincidental analogy.[8]

In the notebooks, Frye drew up schematic plans, not only for *Anatomy of Criticism* but also for writing his *magnum opus*, his "ogdoad project", eight great books. But perhaps because he wrote as a scholar in academic prose rather than in the mythopoeic language he so privileged in his arguments about the imagination, he never felt that he could cross one of the great eight books off his list as completed. As a result, in his diaries, Frye fantasized continually about writing fiction:

> Saturday, July 8, 1950: I'm just at the "change of life" period in Jung's psychology, I suppose. They now take the form of wishing

> I'd spent my youth practising writing fiction; it's silly, of course, but it's part of a general recognition of the damage I did my future life in my earlier years. A certain amount of daydreaming is normal, I suppose, but I daydreamed to excess, and hesitated to start any real work on fulfilling my ambitions because I was so afraid my first efforts wouldn't show true genius. I worried a lot about genius. I think too that my present excess of embarrassment over various failures to achieve perfect life rhythm in social behaviour is largely due to an exaggerated picture of myself built up in reverie during adolescence. I suppose that repentance ... consists first of all in determining the conditions under which your life must henceforth operate.[9]

In this entry, Frye describes how, with regard to writing fiction, worrying so much about genius prevented him from ever getting down to work in the here and now. On the one hand, the current publication of his *Collected Works* in 29 volumes counters the remorse expressed by the 37-year-old Frye. On the other hand, the unpublished fiction now gathered in Volume 25 of his *Collected Works* is notably lifeless and awkward.[10]

Frye's recorded dreams suggest he may have had a better chance to free himself up (in a compensatory way from the creative academic thinking in his essays and notebooks) through his piano playing. He had sometimes fantasized about music as an alternative career.[11] As an adult, however, he experienced that part of himself as negative and inferior and somehow shallow, not informed enough to allow itself to be seen, but embarrassingly, impulsively performative (as Frye scholar Robert Denham points out in his introduction to the diaries). For instance, Frye notes in a dream recorded on 3 January 1949:

> I was playing the Schumann *Papillons*, which I seemed to remember fairly well, except that I substituted one of the Novelettes for the last long one. At first I seemed to be playing opposite Marie Bond on another piano (the name may be significant as well as a recent meeting with her) on my right, then Connie Blewett got mixed up with it, & finally was lying on her back on top of the piano with a mysterious dark girl standing behind me. All these things are I think dramatizations of Jungian ideas I've recently been reading about. It's curious how dreams seem to point silently to certain things, like the ghost of Christmas Future.[12]

The dream begins with *Papillons* (butterflies), a classic image of hope for psychic transformation, but the dream protagonist has slipped in a Novelette instead of meeting the challenge of that last long *Papillon.* Frye finds himself playing a four-handed, two-piano duet with a woman to his right named

Marie Bond (her presence provides a nice wordplay on Eros as connection). There is some mixing and heating of elements, with a personal feminine colleague eventually on top of the piano like a vamp. A third darker feminine figure emerges from behind – perhaps mysterious, unknown, certainly not someone from his personal circle of friends. In his commentary, Frye takes Jung's prospective interpretation of dream-narratives seriously, noting that this dream of two pianos points to where things could go, like Dickens's Ghost of Christmas Future pointing to Scrooge's tombstone. Three months later, the symbolic doubling of the piano is repeated even more emphatically:

> Friday, April 22, 1949: Last night I dreamed I said to a Dr Gopal of India (there was such a person, but I never met him) that I wanted a piano, & he took me too literally and sent one up to 205 Fulton Ave, where I found my mother-in-law, metamorphosed to Kay Morris, warding off its delivery. There was quite a fuss: Ken McLean was most prominent among my sympathizers, but I was aware simultaneously that our piano was there & I couldn't have another one in, & that our piano wasn't there but had been moved to our own place. The prototype, & part of the name Gopal, was Goggio who so kindly *lent* me an Ariosto instead of telling me where I could get one for myself. I'd have to buy this piano, though, evidently, & thought I was lucky to get off with cartage charges of $16.64, plus a $3 tip given to one of the movers ... I record this dream because it puzzles me, & because I remember so very few dreams these days. Well, I went to the Reference Library, & in spite of it (the dream) read Jung's *Secret of the Golden Flower* and the *Tibetan Book of the Dead.* Then came home and went to bed early – I don't know why I feel tired & listless these days, beyond a fairly mild dose of hay fever. I'm not thinking much either, though I'm thinking of beginning to think about the social and anthropological side of Jungian symbolism.[13]

In this dream, a doctor, with a certain quality of Otherness about him (not unlike Frye's colleague Emilio Goggio in the department of Italian Literature, a generous man who did not tell Frye where he could get a copy of *Ariosto* but lent him his own copy), gives Frye what he asks for by sending him a second piano. It is phrased like the arrival of a new possibility – a birth, a delivery. At first, a negative feminine figure, part mother-in-law, opposes the change, and so there's complication, a conflict. The dream ego is aware that the situation is not a logical one in the here and now: either a piano exists or it does not; either it is there or it is in the other place – how can it be both? But sympathizers now introduced into the equation (including another masculine figure who is also a familiar colleague, Ken McLean) root for the change to take place. The dream ends emphatically with the fact that the protagonist must pay: pay for the piano and pay for the delivery and even tip one of the movers. In other words, the dream ego must disidentify from a habitual prudence, from a certain small-mindedness. He must be a little extravagant, even a little reckless with the budget. (In real life, Frye may have had trouble doing this; for example, the diaries record a particularly miserly response to his wife Helen Kemp-Frye's sudden hospitalization for a uterine problem.) The dream demands a little more generosity with the psychological economy and maybe twice as much "play" as usual. The value of playing the piano gets doubled. As much as the notebooks summarize Frye's critical responses to reading Jung, the diaries record his attempts to understand himself better, and even to heal himself, by reading Jung.

In 1954, Frye wrote a very long review entitled "Forming Fours",[14] in which he declares the importance of Jung's work. He emphasizes Jung's concept of individuation as shifting psychotherapeutic treatment out of a medical analogy of diagnosis, treatment, and cure, into something more akin to creating a therapeutic alliance with the biological and teleological forces of the personality, forces that push the personality towards its own peculiar maturity. That is to say, he affirms the way in which, as he understands it, Jung practises psychotherapy. He highlights, in particular, how Jung's notion of individuation includes a collective component: "the dreams and fantasies of the individual should not be interpreted solely in relation to his personal life; they are also individual manifestations of a mythopoeic activity found in everyone".[15] Frye has taken this notion of the mythopoeic from Blake, but he finds that Jung affirms the same principle without having ever carefully studied Blake's texts.[16]

Frye praises Jung for supplementing the purely analytical interpretation of dreams with a hermeneutic study of the analogies of people's dreams to myth and romance, as argued in *Psychology of the Unconscious* (later revised as *Symbols of Transformation*). At the same time, Frye confronts what he refers to as "a complex in Jung's mind":

> His collective unconscious is actually the total mythopoeic power of humanity, and has nothing to do with ancestor cults of "racial differentiation" or groping around the windy bowels of Teutonic exclusivism. We simply have to step over such passages as the footnote in the *Two Essays* in which he says he's not anti-Semitic but . . .[17]

For the moment, Frye chooses to disregard these passages. He suspects that most psychologists would consider Jung's work of collecting images of a single dream type meaningless, but Frye wants to situate such work squarely within the orbit of literary criticism:

> Jung seems to be leading Freud's great discoveries in the direction of a first hand study of literature, whereas Freudian criticism itself, even Freud's brilliant essay on Leonardo, tends to take us away from the works of art into the biography of the artist.[18]

Essentially, he sees Jung demonstrating how archetypal criticism can function as a social science, as a potentially scientific discipline.[19]

Only now in his review does Frye come to Jung's book, *Psychology and Alchemy.* He criticizes Jung for exaggerating the extent to which, historically, alchemy was heretical or carried shadowy projections of "bad taste" for Christian orthodoxy. More important, Frye says most readers may want to hold the book up to a mirror, that is to say, reverse the orientation of the text, in which Jung works outward from his practice as a doctor, turning every mythopoetic structure into a vast allegory of his own technique of psychotherapy.[20] Frye also argues that what Jung charts in alchemy and maps out in the romantic argument of the individuation process, he could just as easily have found in biblical typology. The problem, according to Frye, is that Jung has been too influenced and misled by the idiosyncrasies of Goethe who, in his treatment of symbolism, is "brilliant, varied and ingenious", whereas Dante, Spenser, and Blake are "scholarly". (Frye's use of the term "scholarly" here is intriguing, as in many ways, it is Goethe who is precisely that: learned, but ultimately unbelieving.)[21] It is important to remember that Frye had only just demonstrated to what extent the Prophetic Works of Blake were not eccentric or particular but mapped a precise cosmology shared with *The Divine Comedy* and *The Faerie Queen*, whereas (as Frye points out) the realms explored in Goethe's *Faust*, Part 2, are peculiarly the writer's own. So Frye esteems Dante, Spenser, and Blake for working within the frame and common code of a collective cultural imagination and perhaps devalues Jung by suggesting he has been contaminated by Goethe's individualism. Still, he drops all prevaricating and closes the review with this enthusiastic statement:

> We can see that Jung's book is not a mere specious paralleling of a defunct science and one of several Viennese schools of psychology, but a grammar of literary symbolism which for all serious students of literature is as important as it is endlessly fascinating.[22]

Frye reading Blake and Vico (and not reading Jung)

But now Frye arrives at a curious turning point in his reading of Jung. In 1957, after the publication of his next major work, *Anatomy of Criticism*, Frye begins to distance himself from Jung. He turns away from Jung and toward Giambattista Vico. Why does he take up this early eighteenth-century philosopher and rhetorician rather than Jung to guide him through two decades of work toward the publication of his next important book, *The Great Code*?[23]

It is as if the objections articulated in the 1954 review increase in importance for him. First, he is no longer willing to step over the anti-Semitic footnote in *Two Essays* to get to the passages that excite him (his colleague Thomas Willard has described how, much later on, he tried to correct Frye in this regard, and Frye said warily, "Then I have no problem with Jung"[24]). Second, he sees the need to differentiate his notion of archetypal criticism from Jungian literary criticism, and his notion of archetype from Jung's psychological definition of archetype.[25] He derogates critical theorizing that employs an external framework, be it Freudian, Jungian, Marxist, or feminist, if it merely takes up a work of art in order to place it in service of that framework to justify its own tenets. Already in the 1954 review Frye notes how one needs to read *Psychology and Alchemy* with a mirror to avoid interpreting only in service of Jung's psychological theory of individuation. He progressively takes a stronger stance. In 1956, he sets up a theoretical opposition between two views of literature: "These two views are the Aristotelian and the Longinian, the aesthetic and the psychological, the view of literature as product and the view of literature as process."[26] But by 1957, he reformulates this opposition for *Anatomy of Criticism*, carefully replacing the word "psychological" with the word "creative", in order to keep Longinus's notion of the sublime and to avoid the reductive psychologizing of literature. Another way to put this might be: Frye was looking for a way to write critical theory in academic prose that would intensify the reader's experience of reading, epistemologically privileging the creative imagination and process over reason and product,[27] and he considered much of Jung's psychological prose often too self-consciously and reductively scientific for his purposes.

Most important, Frye conducts a graduate seminar and begins a paper on the mythopoeic in Blake and Jung.[28] It is his attempt to present Blake as a guide for the first half of his life and Jung as potential guide for the second half. But the seminars disappoint, and Frye never writes his paper. In his diaries, he describes how combining the elements of Blake and Jung even provoked eruptions, to which he responded with anger and perplexity:

> I think there's a jinx on my Blake and Jung paper, also on the damn course. Benton Misener is a man I should never have let into the course – an emotional lame brain who got converted to God knows what by my Milton lectures and took the Blake course for inspiration. He has been talking about his paper for weeks, but didn't turn up to do it ... I'm getting fed up with being the cynosure [that is to say, a center of attraction, a guiding star] of mental spastics. Of course the paper was too much for him, but why didn't he duck out of it in time? The last time I assigned a Blake and Jung paper was to [John] Thorburn, who not only didn't turn up, but had a

> complete nervous breakdown and became a violent homosexual. However, I'm ungrateful to destiny. I wanted to expound Jung in order to get a detached view of a possible paper on the subject. I expounded Jung beautifully, but I didn't get him related to Blake much. In the first place, Jung's later thought loses its grip on the original libido book, where he's closest to Blake, & in the second place all that stuff about types, introversion & extroversion, person and soul-image, isn't particularly Blakean.[29]

In two recent books, the Romantic scholar and Jungian thinker Ross Woodman recalls this very seminar on Blake and Jung at the University of Toronto, in which he participated as a graduate student. For his part, Woodman considers Frye's approach to Blake at the time dangerously one-sided, as rendering Blake's "Pulsation of the Artery" disembodied and falsely sane: "Coming to grips with Blake's dreamwork as the figuration of desire rather than the logocentric rationalization of it became the issue that informed my reading of Frye's Blake."[30] Woodman worried that, like Freud's materialist sanity, Frye's logocentric sanity would convert Blake's apocalypse not into art, but into an "anatomy" of apocalypse.[31] While Frye was worrying whether Jung's discourse would reduce the evidence of the collective imagination to fit a theory of a psychological process (i.e. individuation), Woodman, ironically, was wrestling with a shadowy potential in Frye's critical anatomizing that would betray Blake's corpus. I find this potential, carefully delineated by Woodman, correlative to those passages in the diaries, already mentioned, where Frye cannot cross out as completed any of the eight books of his creative "ogdoad project".

It is intriguing, then, to follow Frye's notebooks around this time, when he stops reading Jung and takes up instead Vico, the critic of the Enlightenment who developed a theory of knowledge that sees the natural sciences and the humanities as contradictory domains. Differentiating between observing the external world and understanding human experience led Vico to oppose the Cartesian bias of his time. Vico considered it fallacious to apply the rules and the language of the natural sciences to the domain of volition and feeling. Today, Vico is regarded as the first thinker to recognize the continuing underlying role of mythological motifs in Western cultures, even as these cultures have grown increasingly secularized and scientifically rationalized: Vico was the first to argue that these cultures need deliberately to privilege and rehabilitate mythopoeic language.

In the 1971 essay entitled *The Critical Path* (2009), Frye describes the affinities he discovered between Blake and Vico:

> About twenty-five years ago, I lost my way in the dark wood of Blake's Prophecies, and looked around for some path that would get me out of there. There were many paths, some well trodden and

> equipped with signposts, but all pointing in what for me were the wrong directions. They directed me to the social conditions of Blake's time, to the history of the occult tradition, to psychological factors in Blake's mind, and other subjects quite valid in themselves.... The critical path I wanted was a theory of criticism which would, first, account for the major phenomena of literary experience, and, second, would lead to some view of the place of literature in civilization as a whole.... The conventions, genres, and archetypes of literature do not simply appear: they must develop historically from origins, or perhaps from a common origin. In pursuing this line of thought, I have turned repeatedly to Vico, one of the very few thinkers to understand anything of the historical role of the poetic impulse in civilization as a whole. Vico describes how a society, in its earliest phase, sets up a framework of mythology, out of which all its verbal culture grows, including its literature. Vico's main interest is in the history of law, but it is not difficult to apply his principles to other disciplines.[32]

At the core of Vico's *New Science* (1725) is his principle of *verum factum*: truth is made, not perceived.[33] This principle leads to his perception of the difference between *certum*, knowledge from outside (such as the physical sciences), and *verum*, knowledge from inside (such as history and pure mathematics). According to Vico's epistemology, *verum* and knowledge acquired through the faculty of the imagination, through *fantasia*, are the foundation of the human sciences. Vico argues that image and narrative, rather than concept, are the primary source of philosophizing.[34] Vico acknowledges the distinction between the two traditional categories of knowledge: the deductive, which includes logic and grammar, yields truth independently of what one makes; the perceptual, derived from empirical observation, concerns matters that one perceives as natural events or external facts. However, he places particular emphasis on self-knowledge attained through the faculty of the imagination, allowing for the possibility of establishing a truth based on an inner fact. In this way, he argues, the human sciences can also posit truths, even though such truths do not rely on Cartesian-style pure and fixed ideas. Vico admits that this imaginative faculty renders humans prone to the error of anthropomorphosis, of mistakenly projecting knowledge onto the natural world and then misreading that world in human terms. But he accused Descartes of having committed the opposite error, of renouncing the epistemological function of the imagination and of assimilating the human sciences into the nonhuman realm of nature. For Frye, Vico's defence of what we today would call self-knowledge renders him a crucial precursor of Blake and his impassioned faith in the imagination.

Vico contextualizes the arguments of his philosophical contemporaries by locating rationalism in a three-stage historical cycle. Civilizations move through a mythical age of gods, a heroic age of aristocracy, and a demotic age of the people, followed by a precarious leap back to the mythical. Seeing his own times as "third-stage" allows him to acknowledge the relative merits of the Enlightenment, while, at the same time, seeing rationalism as part of an intellectual climate. Vico articulates what its viewpoint is good for, asks what is missing from its perspective, and speculates about the logical end to which it directs itself. This teleological concern leads to his mapping of *corsi e ricorsi*: advancing through time, according to Vico, a civilization either spirals progressively or merely repeats itself, depending on the quality of that leap from the third stage to the first. Paradoxically, at its very best, this leap is simultaneously a jumping forward and a jumping backward; he names it "Providentia", as if he were acknowledging that "only by the grace of God" does a civilization spiral forward into another "first stage" rather than merely regressively start over again. Leaving aside the historicism in Vico's theory of cycles, Frye admires Vico's portrayal of human culture as an intelligible, constantly changing reality that must be intuited, just as nature must be observed empirically.

Even more pertinent to Frye's purpose, Vico suggests that each age within a civilization produces its own kind of language. Thus, each culture has recourse to three kinds of verbal expression, which he calls the poetic, the heroic, and the vulgar or vernacular. In opposition to Plato and the Neoplatonists, Vico insists that poetry, not philosophical prose, underlies humanity: a culture develops out of a primary framework of mythological motifs or "imaginative universals" rather than out of reasoned principles,[35] and there are no concepts without images.[36] Vico privileges the poetic, not only because, according to his historical mapping, images and narrative precede concepts just as poetry precedes prose,[37] but also because, in order to appreciate and deftly handle concepts, one must track the genus of an image etymologically, philologically, and imaginatively, back to its original image.[38] What interests Vico are not the imaginative universals per se but the evolution of human thought and the unique style of each culture as it reveals itself in language, myth, and ritual.

The divination of "poetic logic", Vico says, forms the base upon which a first-stage culture, lacking the capacity for abstraction, constructs its more abstract "rational logic". Neither "poetic logic" nor "reasoned reflection" necessarily redeems Vico's cultures from barbarism. First-stage humans are vigorously and cruelly ignorant and third-stage humans live "like wild beasts in a deep solitude of spirit and will, scarcely any two being able to agree since each follows his own pleasure or caprice".[39] Certainly Vico's map implies that rational reflection can function as a progressive force, but *ricorsi* means that a civilization inevitably – providentially, he argues – must return to the brutality of first-stage poetic logic over and over again, that its vitality somehow resides there.

For a reader such as Frye, Vico demonstrates the inherent complementarity of poetic and rational logic, and he shows how a one-sided rationalist language endangers the human sciences by objectifying its subjects and severing self-knowledge from its cumulative phenomenological potential. Guided by Blake and Vico, in his most popular publication, *The Educated Imagination* (first given as the Massey Lectures in 1963), and in an essay entitled "The Double Vision",[40] Frye challenges academic and cultural convention by identifying literary criticism and critical theory as a social science and, at the same time, by defending myth and metaphor as crucial to the vibrancy of any society. On the one hand, clearly Vico's third-stage language marks a cultural advancement for its speakers, but, on the other hand, it also impoverishes them, rendering them increasingly subordinate (that is, *subject to*) or under the control of, the objective world. Frye picks up on this affinity between Vico and Blake when he describes a society that privileges exclusively Vico's third-stage language as subjecting itself to the tyranny of what Blake called the false gods of Bacon, Newton, and Locke. In his Notebook 19, Frye writes, "It is almost impossible not to believe that Blake had read Vico, but of course he hadn't."[41]

Frye rereading Jung

It is also almost impossible not to believe that Jung had read Vico, but no evidence exists to suggest that he had (even though, for instance, Jung's literary contemporaries, James Joyce and Samuel Beckett, made good use of Vico). James Hillman tracks Neoplatonic elements from Plotinus through Ficino to Vico in his archetypal psychology;[42] Donald Verene describes affinities between Jung's acausal principle of synchronicity and Vico's metaphysics of the self that encounters itself in repetitions of history;[43] and Leslie Gardner compares their rhetorical privileging of poetic logic.[44] I have argued elsewhere that, for Vico and Jung, the mythopoeic and the metaphorical are the raw stuff from which civilizations must distance themselves and with which they must then find ways to reconnect.[45] As a psychotherapist, Jung translated this collective dilemma into the basis for his method of treating individual sufferers: he recognized that transformative possibilities reside in moments when individuals rediscover mythopoeic imagery and metaphorical language, when they repair the broken narrative links between their creativity and their self-knowledge. In my own clinical work, particularly when it feels crucial to seal the hermetic vessel in the service of wholeness, I have learned to employ consciously Vico's three kinds of language: to look for separate moments to speak metaphorically, allegorically, and objectively about the client's experience.

How disingenuous was it of Frye to have disavowed Jung while identifying his theorizing on archetypal criticism with his readings of Blake and Vico? In case this question sounds as if it originates in my subjectivity as a reader (which could be misattributed to a kind of Jungian fundamentalism), permit me to quote a letter from Robert Denham, who edited the diaries (and many other volumes of Frye's collected works): "Like you, I've been fascinated by the Frye–Jung connections for some time. Frye always wanted to distance himself from Jung, I think, but he was much more influenced by Jung than he let on."[46] Also Michael Dolzani argues in his introduction to Frye's *Romance Notebooks*:

> Possibly the most significant figure in this area is C. G. Jung, whose influence on Frye was greater than he was willing to admit. Frye objected to Jung's deification of the void, and to his reduction of all symbolism to an allegory of the psychological process of individuation. But he also speaks of "the articulation of symbolism in modern thought, which begins in Jung".[47]

And Thomas Willard writes: "It seems likely that Frye's legacy as an archetypal critic will remain linked with Jung's. If anything, they will probably get linked more closely."[48]

In one of his late notebooks, Frye mentions in passing that he has taken up reading Jung again. About the autobiographical book, *Memories, Dreams, Reflections*, he admits:

> During the war, I had racist prejudices against Germans, feeling that there was nothing so dumb as a dumb Kraut. When Jung started talking about Jewish consciousness and the dangers of entering Oriental attitudes, the farts of a dumb Kraut polluted the air: I think he outgrew that, at least in that autobiography but (as with Spengler) I distrusted the dumb Kraut for a long time.[49]

Around the same time, Frye mordantly relinquishes hope of understanding why an apparently sane man would write such a book as *Mysterium Coniunctionis*: "I hope I don't have to crack that infernal book again",[50] although a little later, he records that he is reading Marie-Louise von Franz on alchemy, in an attempt to find an entry point back into *Mysterium.*[51] I cannot help but identify with Frye's exasperated reading response to *Mysterium Coniunctionis.* Curiously, he never lost his temper with Vico's *New Science*, which is equally encyclopedic in its range and counter-rational in its style, messy, and plodding, but, nevertheless, marked by genius.

More important, in a little-known essay entitled "Expanding Eyes",[52] Frye emphatically positions Jung as vitally important, as fundamental to his theorizing. Frye begins his argument by observing that social scientists do not (yet) understand that their subject areas, besides being sciences, are also applied humanities. Just as mathematics inform the physical sciences, so do myths and metaphors inform the social sciences. The myths and metaphors of literature inform what is specifically verbal in them, as distinct from what is quantifiable or dependent on tests for reliability and validity in experiments. Frye's diagnostic insight in this regard was verified, for instance, when G. Lakoff and M. Johnson's book, *Metaphors We Live By*[53] was suddenly rediscovered and found a niche as a textbook for cognitive scientists.

Frye insists that literary criticism should not purport to assign value to specific works and designate a literary canon, and yet, in what may seem a contradiction, he portrays any individual reader as creating a personal canon that is neither democratic nor all-inclusive. Frye writes that criticism is a form of autobiography: readers become really engaged in the study of literature when they share common elements in lifestyle with specific authors, when they find their interest is not exhausted by scholarly investigation. In this regard, Frye offers for consideration his primary enthusiasm for Blake. He explains how he became obsessed with Blake in this way very early, partly because he had been brought up in much the same evangelical subculture from which Blake had developed, and because Blake made imaginative sense out of such an oppressively narrow and reactionary subculture by reading it archetypally. Frye employs paradox to describe an element of certain creators, how their words and works expand, rather than restrict, the individuality of readers. (Elsewhere, Frye has stated that a great work of art possesses a circumference that always surpasses the sum of its readings.) Structuralism, hermeneutics, phenomenalism, sociolinguistics, cultural anthropology, the philosophy of language can all contribute to the understanding of literature, but according to Frye, these interpretative approaches still seem only incidental to literature itself, to what literature does and can do to people.

Adding to this autobiographical account of himself as reader, Frye mentions his readings of Spengler and Frazer as a student. Frye notes that he recognized very early just how extraordinarily limited and unaware of the world they both were, but by acknowledging and staying with his continued fascination with their texts, he came to understand that he was reading both of them as cultural critics who wrote, without realizing it, not history and anthropology, respectively, but literary works about the structures of the imagination. By contrast, Frye records how, as a mature reader, he discovered Vico, and again, as with Blake, found himself in a text that was intrinsically expansive. He read Vico's *New Science* as a work of revolutionary wisdom like Blake's illuminated writings: Vico, having lived at a time when there had been no permanently successful example of a democracy, concluded from his study of Roman history and law that the people cannot recover the authority they project successively onto the gods, onto heroes, and then onto others, and, hence, the third age of the people is followed inevitably by a *ricorso* that starts the cycle all over again.

Finally, in this essay, which becomes a summative reflection about the stages of his own reading life, Frye comes to Jung. At first, cautiously, he groups his reading of Jung with Spengler and Frazer. He wonders if again, without belittling Jung's achievements in psychology, it could be said that Jung's greatest significance is inadvertently as a critical and cultural theorist. But he quietly shifts and expands this argument to emphasize at the centre of Jung's vision of life a notion of progress from the "ego", from the ordinary life with its haphazard and involuntary perceptions of time and space, to the "individual" who works with more expansive modes of perception:

> I am continually asked also about my relation to Jung, and especially about the relation of my use of the word "archetype" to his. So far I have tended to resist the association, because in my experience whenever anyone mentions it his next sentence is almost certain to be nonsense. But this may actually be a reason for welcoming it.... It seems strange to overlook the possibility that the arts, including literature, might just conceivably be what they have always been taken to be, possible techniques of meditation, in the strictest sense of the word, ways of cultivating, focusing, and ordering one's mental processes, on a basis of symbol rather than concept. Certainly that is what Blake thought they were: his own art was a product of his power of meditation, and he addresses his readers in terms which indicate that he was presenting his illuminated works to them also, not as icons, but as mandalas.[54]

Frye works very hard here to prevent his argument from tumbling into the slough of the merely psychological (that is to say, into third-stage psychological discourse in which "gods" are nothing but "complexes"). For instance, he describes one student regarding poems as coming out of certain mental processes and so conceptualizing psychologically the foundations that underlie the study of literature, whereas another student sees the poems as a product of specific historical and social conditions. Frye writes that nothing has been more difficult in his career as a teacher than to advise students at such moments: "Throw that metaphor away; it's the wrong metaphor." He describes how he eventually employs the metaphor of "interpenetration" to describe how, as a critic, he reconciles himself to working comparatively with conceptual systems external to literature itself. At the same time, both in these anecdotes and within the structure of his essay, Frye alters subtly his association of Jung with Spengler and Frazer to acknowledge, instead, Jung as one of his guides to the expansive and the transformative, together with Blake and Vico.

In this context, Frye confesses that he still considers *Psychology and Alchemy* to be Jung's best book, I suspect, because in it (more than in the early *Psychology of the Unconscious* and perhaps more lucidly than in a late work like *Mysterium*), Jung found a way, argumentatively and stylistically, to honour mythopoeic language and the potential for self-transformation inherent in alchemical images – the process of bringing an immortal body (the stone) to birth within the ordinary one (the *materia prima*). Of course, we now know (since the publication of Jung's *The Red Book: Liber Novus*[55]) that *Psychology and Alchemy* was Jung's first attempt, after emerging from his then unpublished experiments with visionary writing in *The Red Book*, to write human science differently.

Frye presents the mythopoeic as it manifests in the arts and social sciences as politically charged. In any third-stage discourse, the poetic logic of myth and metaphor reads as archaic, obscure, and arcane, as requiring translation into the contemporary and the conceptual. Frye enlists Jung's distinction between ego and self to assess the potential for transformation and expansion that remains inherent in the contemporary experience of the mythopoeic, even if it is presently misunderstood and devalued:

> It is at this point that the question of the social function of the arts becomes so important. Some people find it a shock to discover, say, the commandant of a Nazi death camp can also be someone with a highly developed taste in music. If he had a thorough knowledge of organic chemistry, there would be no shock; but well, the arts are supposed to have or be based on values, aren't they? They are secondary, something to turn to when the real standards of living have been met. On that basis they become subject to evaluation, like jewels; they are enjoyed and possessed by what Jung calls the "ego", and something even analogous to price develops. The arts approached in that way can add pleasure and refinement and cultivation and even some serenity to life, but they have no power to transform it ... It would be better to think of the arts as, like physical exercise, a primary human need that has been smothered under false priorities.[56]

By the end of his essay, Frye has lined up, one beside the other, his trinity of Blake, Vico, and Jung, and offers the reader the resulting resonances of three thinkers who privilege the imagination as a key component of healing. In a lecture entitled "Literature as Therapy", given to doctors at Mount Sinai Hospital in Toronto, Frye outlines the psychotherapeutic potential of what is now called *bibliotherapy* – of employing images and narratives to facilitate and augment the healing process, based not a little on musing about how his own mother healed herself by reading through Sir Walter Scott's Waverley novels.[57] If Frye positions Freud as one of the century's greatest writers of descent – of the metamorphic fall of the gods into humankind, of humanity into the reality principle, of life into dead matter, of tragedy and Thanatos – he also credits Jung with articulating, in addition, the possibility of ascent, directed toward the romantic goal of creating a genuinely human community:

> On the ascending side there is a reversal, a disenchanting journey back to our original identity that ends when the human creator recovers his creations from his Muses and lives again, like Job, with the daughters of his memory transformed into a renewed presence.[58]

Frye positions Jung as having mapped and, in particular, described possibilities that Vico named and propitiated as Providentia and that Blake remythologized – possibilities for expansive vision and transformative healing.

Reading Frye's diaries and notebooks and this late essay makes clear that he read, disavowed, and then reread Jung's words, and grudgingly came to re-acknowledge Jung's work of stitching together with metaphor and myth the rift in Western collective consciousness, reclaiming for us imaginatively our lost humanity.

Notes

1 N. Frye, *The Diaries of Northrop Frye, 1942–1955*, *The Collected Works of Northrop Frye*, vol. 8, ed. R. Denham, Toronto, University of Toronto Press, 2001, p. 61.

2 P. B. Shelley, *A Defence of Poetry* (1821), in David Richter (ed.), *The Critical Tradition*, New York, St Martin's Press, 1989, p. 347.

3 N. Frye, *Fearful Symmetry: A Study of William Blake*, *The Collected Works of Northrop Frye*, vol. 14, ed. N. Halmi, Toronto, University of Toronto Press, 1947/2004.

4 Frye, *The Diaries*, p. 94.

5 N. Frye, *Northrop Frye's Notebooks for Anatomy of Criticism*, *The Collected Works of Northrop Frye*, vol. 23, ed. R. Denham, Toronto, University of Toronto Press, 2007, p. 267.

6 Northrop Frye, *Anatomy of Criticism: Four Essays*, *The Collected Works of Northrop Frye*, vol., 22, ed. R. Denham, Toronto, University of Toronto Press, 2006.

7 Ibid., p. 56.

8 Ibid., p. 99.

9 Frye, *The Diaries*, p. 401.

10 N. Frye, *Northrop Frye's Fiction and Miscellaneous Writings*, *The Collected Works of Northrop Frye*, vol. 25, ed. R. Denham and M. Dolzani, Toronto, University of Toronto Press, 2007.

11 Frye, *The Diaries*, p. 12.

12 Ibid., p. 59.

13 Ibid. p. 189.

14 N. Frye, "Forming fours", in *The Educated Imagination and Other Writings on Critical Theory 1933–1963*, *The Collected Works of Northrop Frye*, vol. 21, ed. G. Warkentin, Toronto, University of Toronto Press, 2006, pp. 203–13.

15 Ibid., p. 205.

16 Jung was passingly familiar with Blake's style of illuminated printing; see S. Shamdasani, *C. G. Jung: A Biography in Books*, New York, Norton, 2012, p. 120.

17 Frye, "Forming fours", p. 207.

18 Ibid., p. 209.

19 N. Frye, *The Critical Path and Other Writings on Critical Theory, 1963–1975*, *The Collected Works of Northrop Frye*, vol. 27, ed. J. O'Grady and E. Kushner, Toronto, University of Toronto Press, 2009, p. 393.

20 Frye, "Forming fours", p. 211.

21 Paul Bishop, personal correspondence, 28 March 2010.

22 Frye, "Forming fours", p. 213.
23 N. Frye, *The Great Code: The Bible and Literature*, *The Collected Works of Northrop Frye*, vol. 19, ed. A. Lee, Toronto, University of Toronto Press, 1982/2006.
24 T. Willard, "Archetypes of the imagination", in A. Lee and R. Denham (eds.), *The Legacy of Northrop Frye*, Toronto, University of Toronto Press, 1994, pp. 15–27.
25 See Denham, in Frye, *The Diaries*, p. 677, n. 21.
26 Northrop Frye, "Towards Defining An Age of Sensibility", in *Northrop Frye's Writings on the Eighteenth and Nineteenth Centuries*, *The Collected Works of Northrop Frye*, vol. 17, ed. Imre Salusinszky, Toronto, University of Toronto, 2005, pp. 7–15. The quotation is on p. 8.
27 C. N. Cotrupi, *Northrop Frye and the Poetics of Process*, Toronto, University of Toronto Press, 2000, pp. 27–31.
28 Frye, *The Diaries*, p. 53.
29 Ibid., p. 146.
30 R. Woodman, *Sanity, Madness, Transformation: The Psyche in Romanticism*, Toronto, University of Toronto Press, 2005, p. 85.
31 R. Woodman, with J. Faflak, *Revelation and Knowledge*, Toronto, University of Toronto Press, 2011, p. 31.
32 Frye, *The Critical Path*, pp. 7, 21–2.
33 G. Vico, *The New Science of Giambattista Vico* (unabridged translation of the third edition, 1744), trans. T. G. Bergin and M. H. Fisch, Ithaca, NY, Cornell University Press, 1944.
34 Donald P. Verene, *Vico's Science of Imagination*, Ithaca, NY, Cornell University Press, 1981.
35 Vico, *The New Science*, p. 143.
36 Ibid., p. 154.
37 Ibid., p. 131.
38 I. Berlin, *Three Critics of the Enlightenment*, Princeton, NJ, Princeton University Press, 2000, p. 67.
39 Vico, *The New Science*, p. 424.
40 N. Frye, "The double vision", in *Northrop Frye on Religion*, Toronto, University of Toronto Press, 2000, pp. 166–235.
41 N. Frye, *The "Third Book" Notebooks of Northrop Frye 1964–1972*, *The Collected Works of Northrop Frye*, vol. 9, ed. M. Dolzani, Toronto, University of Toronto Press, 2002, p. 86.
42 J. Hillman, "Plotinus, Ficino and Vico as precursors of archetypal psychology", in *Loose Ends: Primary Papers in Archetypal Psychology*, Dallas, Spring, 1975.
43 D. P. Verene, "Coincidence, historical repetition, and self-knowledge: Jung, Vico and Joyce", *Journal of Analytical Psychology*, 2002, vol. 47, no. 3, pp. 459–78.
44 L. Gardner, *Rhetorical Investigations: G. B. Vico and C. G. Jung*, London, Routledge, 2013.
45 C. Stephenson, "Reading Jung's equivocal language", *Harvest*, 2004, vol. 50, no. 1, pp. 75–99; and *Possession: Jung's Comparative Anatomy of the Psyche*, London and New York, Routledge, 2009.
46 Robert Denham, personal correspondence, 16 August 2001.
47 Dolzani in N. Frye, *Northrop Frye's Notebooks on Romance*, *The Collected Works of Northrop Frye*, vol. 15, ed. M. Dolzani, Toronto, University of Toronto Press, 2004, p. lvii.
48 Willard, "Archetypes of the imagination", p. 27.
49 N. Frye, *Northrop Frye's Late Notebooks, 1982–1990: Architecture of the Spiritual World*, *The Collected Works of Northrop Frye*, vols. 5 and 6, ed. R. Denham, Toronto, University of Toronto, 2000, vol. 5, p. 353.
50 Ibid., p. 332.
51 Ibid., vol. 6, p. 563.
52 First published in *Critical Inquiry*, 1975, from Frye, *The Critical Path*, pp. 391–410.
53 G. Lakoff and M. Johnson, *Metaphors We Live By*, Chicago, University of Chicago Press, 1980/2003.

54 Frye, *The Critical Path*, p. 406.
55 C. G. Jung, *The Red Book: Liber Novus*, ed. S. Shamdasani, New York, W. W. Norton & Company, 2009.
56 Frye, *The Critical Path*, pp. 409–10.
57 Frye, *The Late Notebooks*, pp. 243–4.
58 Frye, *The Critical Path*, p. 410.

7

TANGLED UP IN BLUE

A Reappraisal of Complex Theory

Betsy Cohen

To strengthen and deepen what she found useful from her years of Freudian consultation and to find a more hopeful therapy for her patients' suffering, Betsy Cohen turned to Jungian analytic training. Despite her best efforts, she could not find a way through her reading of Jung to build a solid foundation from which to address the repetitive forms of self-defeat she encountered in her patients. She was frustrated with the too conceptual terms in which Jung described his therapies. Finally, she was directed to the writings of the Jewish philosopher Emmanuel Levinas and the Torah scholar Avivah Zornberg. With them, she found a spiritual home from which she could read Jung's writing on complexes in a more interpersonally related way. Her dilemma is by no means unique, for many readers are confounded by Jung's deliberate ambiguity of expression and the multiple definitions he gives us for his basic concepts. We stumble through *The Collected Works*, eventually finding a way to uncover his deeper meanings by shining the light of yet another author's mind. Thus, we can settle into a personal way of reading with renewed confidence and a greater sense of ourselves as readers of Jung and of life.

J. K.

Bad news

A true story: I spent the 1970s in consultation with a Freudian psychoanalyst. On his left shoulder was his constant companion, a pet parrot. "What does a patient learn after a lengthy analysis?" I asked naively. "Bad news", replied the doctor. "Yup, bad news", squawked the parrot.

As the parrot parroted his master so might the therapist have been parroting his original master, Freud, who said:

> If a crystal is thrown to the ground it will break into pieces, not in a random way, but according to specific fault-lines which, although invisible, have been predetermined by the structure of the crystal. This broken structure is the structure of people with psychological illness.[1]

For the 25 years between 1970 and 1995, when I entered the San Francisco Jung Institute, I remained puzzled by the doctor's and his parrot's parting wisdom and often asked myself, "Are my patients really learning bad news?"

After entering the Jungian camp, to make it crystal clear, I discovered the answer was "no". What makes crystals beautiful are faults and inclusions that add colour; the light shining through enhances the space around them. In his song *Anthem*, Leonard Cohen reminds us that light shines through our imperfections, our cracks. Analogously, the term *complex* might describe inclusions and fault lines in the whole personality, how things are organized and affiliated, but not whether the structure is good or bad or how to deal with it.

Traditionally, if there was bad news in Jungian psychology, it fell upon complexes to take the blame. In this chapter, I explore the ambiguity, rather than the bad news; inherent in complexes is the greater enigma of our being, our relatedness, and our possible emergence beyond narrow self-definitions.

Tangled up in complex theory

"Tangled Up in Blue" is a song by Bob Dylan. How tangled up our concept of complexes has become! I will attempt a brief untangling of how the term is understood and how we collude with our patients by careless labelling of experience as complexes – a labelling, that often serves to keep important affects, associations, imagery, and thoughts at bay. As you read this chapter, hold in mind there is much more to a person than complexes; they are only part of our full subjectivity and being. I wanted to be the best analyst I could be for my patients and, to do so, wished to understand why I was so tangled up by a metaphysical concept and tripped up by my own complexes.

Where Jung opens to the spiritual and unexplainable, he brought me closer to the fundamental truth that, at the heart of it all, lies an unknowable mystery. From a passionate exploration of inner experience, Jung allows a nonlinear logic, a willingness to be imperfect, a trust in spirit and individuation. With dedication to introspection, he engages what it means to be human, the soul of the real fluid human relationship, knowing in its essence beyond words.

I have taught complex theory, as a clinical phenomenon, to the candidates at the San Francisco Jung Institute for the past decade but have remained dissatisfied with lack of clarity in this catchall notion. Within the enormous range of meaning that Jung and many post-Jungians have ascribed to it, even Soul can be a complex! "In analytical psychology, Soul does not refer to a transcendent energy in the human but to a phenomenological fact, a 'function complex'."[2] So can God. In 1945, Jung writes to Victor White, "God is *at least* a very tangible complex ... He is at least a psychological fact."[3] And, in 1960, he calls God an "autonomous complex".[4] Complexes can be anything and everything.

A complex is…

Following Jung's thought on complexes takes us on a 50-year journey, from 1902 to 1952. As early as his 1902 doctoral dissertation, he posits that the complex is an inner conscious personality[5] … or dissociated personality.[6] As late as 1935, he is consistent: "Every autonomous or even relatively autonomous complex has the peculiarity of appearing as a personality."[7]

In 1904, he describes simply a feeling tone complex of ideas (or associations).[8] In 1905, he notes that "the stronger the complex, the more vivid the emotional tone".[9] So far he is clear, understandable, and in common parlance for Jungians. But then he insists: "Every emotion produces a complex"[10] … "One's own personality is the firmest and strongest complex."[11] These statements seem simplistic and overstated.

I imagine the description of complexes as painful and unpleasant conflicts is familiar to a follower of Jung: "The complexes revealed by association experiments are either pathogenic conflicts or at least nearly such."[12] Or, complexes are "definite conflicts in his actual life … problems and difficulties which have brought the patient into disharmony with himself".[13] "Under the stress of an extreme *abaissement* the psychic totality falls apart and splits up into complexes.… It is understandable that people should get panicky."[14] Moving forward in his exploration, Jung explains complexes as instincts. "Complexes might be compared to modified instincts."[15] Perhaps he means complexes respond instinctually, without conscious intent. But is each instinct, like each emotion, a complex? Here, Jung stresses the pathological aspect of complexes: "In psychotherapy the recognition of disease rests much less on the clinical picture than on the content of complexes.… The real toxin is to be sought in this complex."[16]

What is less known is his focus on the healthy, normal, necessary, and life-affirming aspects of these mysterious phenomena.

> The possession of complexes *does not in itself signify neurosis*, for complexes are the normal foci of psychic happenings and the fact that they are painful is *no proof* of pathological disturbance.… A complex becomes pathological when we think we do not have it.[17]

Complexes are foundational to the psyche. "You deprive a man of his best resource when you help him to get rid of his complexes."[18] "Complexes are focal or nodal points of psychic life which we would not wish to do without; indeed they should not be missing, for otherwise psychic activity would come to a fatal standstill."[19]

Jung's map of the complex is creatively unclear. We now know that a complex is both positive and negative, healthy and pathological, foundational and needing to be resolved, an emotion and an instinct. It resides primarily in the unconscious, both the personal and the collective unconscious, and when it has sufficient affective intensity, it breaks through and attacks the ego in a model of combat. "The (complex) forces itself upon the conscious individual. The explosion of affect is a complete invasion ... it pounces upon the individual like an enemy or a wild animal."[20]

Confused? When you tell your patient he or she is in a complex, what are you telling him or her?

Even though Jung believes complexes are fundamental and necessary as the organizational building blocks of our psyche, an aggregate of splintered fragments, he also trusted that these both neurotic and healthy aspects of our being resolve with a hopeful outcome. "And when the complex is made conscious – which is the aim of analysis – Apparently something has been gained; the symptoms disappear, the complex is, as we say, resolved."[21] Jung, who has framed these bewildering contradictions, does not tell us why we might want to resolve what is necessary to the psyche.

Language and communication of affect

We may suppose that Jung leaves the concept ambiguous so as not to foreclose on multiple depths and breadths of meaning. When therapists announce to their patients that they suffer from an odious complex, they close down the very ambiguity that Jung had protected. Closing down the ambiguity turns therapy into bad news, and I once more see the parrot on my teacher's shoulder. I recommend we think more about the term before we use it carelessly, believing that we are saying something true.

Because of the ambiguity, I asked my Jungian colleagues: "What is a complex?" I was informed, "A way of making up the psyche.... A dissociated part.... A cluster of ideas with an archetypal core.... A splinter psyche. ... A subpersonality.... A partial personality.... Possession." Each analyst knows what he or she means, and I know what I believe, but these answers confirm that "complex" has no single dominant meaning; it eludes a simple definition. Hence, I prefer Jung's original, neutral meaning: the sum of ideas referring to a particular feeling-toned event,[22] along with his definition: "Complexes are due to passion.... Without complexes there can be no energy. They are the focus and very mother of energy."[23] This thinking does not imply a "professional" or diagnostic view that the "patient is *in* a complex". The word and concept *complex* remain essentially equivocal.

The psychological phenomenon of the complex that Jung described in his early experimental word association tests is well known. Other contemporary analytic schools have their similar constructs with their particular names, though without Jung's theory of the archetypal core, and they include: multiple self states,[24] fragmented self,[25] a repetition compulsion caused by repression,[26] unconscious organizing principles,[27] one's narrative,[28] a paranoid schizoid state,[29] splitting,[30] or pathogenic beliefs.[31] Personally, I would call it either a psychic knot or an altered lens.

By 1911, Jung emphasized that the affect in the complex is autonomous, not under conscious control, and independent in the psyche.[32] Although Jung is rarely cited by modern affect theorists, he is quite clear that "the essential basis of our personality is affectivity".[33]

At this point, I want to add to Jung's usage of the complex as an affectual experience and note that the complex emerges as a form of affectual *communication.* The communication is relational: internal (to oneself, between parts of ourselves); external (between our self and another); and spiritual (between our self and a Mysterious Other). In each case, the complex is wishing to be known, heard, and understood, often from a trapped, disquieting place.

Moving beyond Jung's language

Just as I was dissatisfied with the parrot and his master's bad news about the psyche, I found myself in an argument with Jung. I failed to find a clinical method in his writings for the "treatment of complexes" or, for that matter, an explanation that spoke to their interpersonal nature and purpose. I also failed to find in his complex theory the spiritual dimension of the psyche that I searched for. Like Jung, I turned instead to readings in philosophy and theology, outside psychology, in order to move closer to universal experiences that have meaning and growth. I wished to explore life's inscrutabilities, the very issues Jung's work points toward, to make my own beginnings more genuine and to deepen the foundations of my analytic work with patients. Something went off in my head; I grasped some of what I had been pursuing, which took me on a very long search, and now I want to share this with the reader.

A dear friend suggested I read Emmanuel Levinas, a French orthodox Jew and a phenomenological philosopher. He describes the pinnacle of interpersonal behaviour as ethics toward the other. Levinas finds the trace of God in the face of the Other and maintains that the proper stance is to serve the Other. We, of course, cannot see God, but there is a glimpse, a trace, a moment of Knowing in the face of the Other.[34]

After reading Levinas, my work with patients changed. I rarely thought of patients in terms of their complexes, but instead in a superordinate mutual seeking of their core humanity. My view – being open to the divine in my patients – altered their complexes as my patients internalized my altered experience of them. Levinas's thought had the effect of a pebble's ripples in a pond. I was able to describe what I had often felt before, but had not the words for: the sanctity of the Other.

Levinas shows, in his book *Totality and Infinity*, that conventional labels, although sometimes useful, can narrow our understanding and prevent us from moving beyond reductive formulaic models of human behaviour. They lead us away from true study and communication. *Totalizing* is his word for relating to the Other as "nothing more than", as in he is nothing more than my friend, she is nothing more than my patient, this is nothing more than a complex. When we totalize, we reduce the Other to a sameness, or to someone just like me. Levinas begs us to honour our profound differences.[35]

Some of Emanuel Levinas's thinking is compatible with Jung's view of the psyche. Jung's opus illuminates our differences: for example, valuing our different typologies, our unique individuation paths, and our particularity as humans. For Levinas, the *infinite* cannot be reduced. It is more than we can know. The infinite is found in the face-to-face encounter with the Other.[36] There are infinite possibilities for knowing the Other. What is powerful in the session is the space we leave for what we do not know. And, as Christopher Bollas reminds us, to know a patient we must also "unknow him".[37] In order to find out what we do not know, according to T. S. Eliot we must choose the path of ignorance.

As with my introduction to Levinas, my world changed after a patient introduced me to the writing of Avivah Zornberg, a Jewish scholar and student of the unconscious and the Old Testament. Zornberg, like Levinas, reminds us of the supreme otherness of the Other, our patients. Before I had been comforted with how much my patient and I had in common, even in the universality and normalcy of our complexes, but now I live more uncomfortably when I remind myself of our separateness as well as the unfathomability of our work. Zornberg reminds us that stories (our patients' stories and the Old Testament stories) are ambiguous. A story does not tell us its meaning in a literal way; instead, it may leave us in doubt. Stories remind us that all human beings stand between life and death in a fundamentally out-of-control place, ripe with insecurity. Do we bear the precariousness or do we flee? When living in a complex, do we assume we know the truth in that moment? Complexity, analysis, dialogue all invite us to search for meaning, to live in the unknown of the outcome. From Zornberg and Levinas, I enlarge my question from "Where does this complex come from?" to "Where is the mystery, where is the expanse?"

What draws me to the work of Zornberg is that she, through her understanding of the depth of Old Testament stories via psychoanalysis and literature, helps me to move beyond Jung's theoretical and conceptual, sometimes lifeless, model. She writes about the enormity of our depths – void and dense. Also of the volcano inside, which is hidden, subterranean, unknowable, and explosive. These are metaphors from nature, of the complexity of the unknown, the hot power under the surface that breaks through into our daily and nightly lives. For my own thinking and work, I prefer her language on complexes to Jung's. The self is, at the very least, double; one self to think with and one to think about. Beyond that, there is the uncanniness of an imagined future and a remembered past.... Understanding oneself becomes an aspiration at best; at worst, an illusion.[38]

Be careful in using the label

The practical, clinical value of naming a complex is that it sometimes provides an image or language for nameless experience, which might orient the analytic pair and perhaps even offer new insight. The term can diminish overwhelming affect when a patient is caught in the grip of thoughts and feelings that seem to come from nowhere, yet seem to be personally true. However, as a colleague wrote, "We are dealing with individual analyses, and therefore theory does not perform as hoped for in the *Sturm und Drang* of life."[39] While we might use the construct of "complex" as a communication tool, a new handle on painful experience, we also need to return to the actual experience and struggle of the patient, and to our own experience with the patient. Otherwise, the complex can easily become an explanation of reality, forcing a human being into a category, rather than pointing us toward richer considerations of human complexity.

Clinical application: Sam

For example, an analysand, Sam, tells me he is the poster child for a "father complex".

I listen and reply, "Tell me what you see."

"That I'm one-down to my dad. Because of his success, he never suffered the humiliations I do. And I want to stop feeling this pain." Sam wants to run away from himself, eliminate the feeling and experience, and diagnose and pathologize himself in the process. In Sam's narrative, lived out and alive, his dead dad will always be happier, richer, have more glory, and a better life than Sam.

In the same session, I ask him, "What if I had said, 'you're in a father complex'?"

He grimaces, "I'd cringe."

Rather than listening with attunement, I would have been moving toward defining him, totalizing him. I would have closed off, rather than opened up our dialogue. I would be stepping outside the relationship with him. Instead, I ask us, "What is still so alive, wanting to be known, that he returns so often to this experience of himself?"

By repeatedly locking himself into "being in a father complex", Sam organizes his reality into a small well-wrapped box. He finds certainty in answers and avoids questions. Yet when he leaves himself open, moves outside the narrative, together we are left to find its personal meaning. We may raise even larger, scarier questions with potentially disruptive affect and fear-inducing images, which may lead to deeper self-knowledge and wider possibilities.

Sometimes we talk about his drama as if we are the audience, wanting to find the narrative's purpose. Other times I question, who I am in the story and how do I re-enact or perpetuate his staying one down? Do I enjoy the imbalance between us, which perhaps his father also did? Perhaps when I'm pleased with an achievement of Sam's, does he experience me with the same insecurity he felt with his father? We must always pay close attention to how our patients hear our words.

Through our conversations, with me not being defensive when Sam thinks I am somewhat like his father, he slowly owns that he is the author of the drama and is certain of its ending. Neural pathways and wounds were laid down early in Sam's life, and together we try to change the storyline. Why did he weave this story and not another? His father was also loving, supportive, encouraging, and reliable. Who created the drama with its all (father) or nothing (Sam) theme? What would a different narrative look like? Sam's flexibility and humour about it, while owning his own reality and choices, slowly create new pathways and possibility.

The complex as relational

If we collude with our patient that she or he is in a complex and believe that we know the complex, are we using the term as a defence against uncertainty? If so, whose – ours and/or our patient's? When we package it as a complex, do we miss real relational experiences such as loss, abandonment, or love? In a *complex*, we hide from ambiguity. Even Jung, at age 81, noted that the designation "complex" had become "hackneyed".[40] To be philosophical is to keep a loving distance, to be sceptical that we have comprehended something by giving it a name.

We need to remember that the complex is a door into an interpersonal experience. We are influenced by Jung's privileging the intrapsychic, although Jung's model of transference embraces the interpersonal dimension of psyche and many, if not most, post-Jungian developments assign it equal value. Jung did not overlook the interpersonal, but it was not emphasized. However, in a 1934 letter to James Kirsch, Jung realizes that "[i]n the deepest sense, all of us do not dream out of ourselves but out of what exists between myself and the other".[41] In Jungian theory, you have a relationship with all of your internal stuff, always relating to the complexes. Can you have a real relationship with someone outside yourself or is every relationship coloured by your complexes? It is as if all your relatedness and healing happens in the inner world. That has not been my experience. For me, the complex is not only an intrapsychic other – an interrelational drama carried within, as it was for Jung – but also socially constructed. *There is no such thing as a complex until you are with someone else; it is relational, in fantasy or reality.* I see the complex as an attempt to communicate an inner experience to another.

Personal example: the hang up

For Jung, complexes are the building blocks that establish the psyche's structure. But what is their function? For Jung, their purpose is to employ Platonic universal images and concepts, such as mother, father, power, as elevators to lift unconscious contents to the personal, from the universal to the particular. At best, complexes provide containers for going deep into one's self to find hidden resources. To be in a complex is to be on the threshold of something new asking to be known.

When caught in a complex, I look for the engendering experiences and turn to the past, to childhood wounds and empathic failures, to understand its cause. Here is an example: I'm having an intimate phone conversation with my dear friend Judy. As she lives on the East Coast, we do not speak often. I surrender to the closeness of the moment, and out of the blue, she hangs up. Always in a hurry, abrupt endings have become her habit. When she is finished, she is finished. This time I feel dizzy and in a strange anguish immediately collapse on my office couch, momentarily, in a tearful heap. I have felt this before, a visceral experience, a rupture, the thud of being dropped.

Each of us has our own story of hurt and sadness. My father travelled every two weeks of the month from the time I was age one to fourteen. During those ruptures, he never called. When he was away, I was cared for by my sickly mother and a loving, robust maid named Daisy. When I was 14, my father decided not to travel for business any more. Oh, good, he's back, I thought. Not so fast. Instead of his travelling, my parents sat my brother and myself down in the den and completely surprised us by announcing, matter of factly, that they were getting divorced. This was the end of the 1950s, and I had known neither a divorced person nor the child of one. My father moved to a nearby town, and my brother and I lived in two houses during high school.

In my reaction to the abruptness of the ending of Judy's phone call, or perhaps just the ending, a profound magnet draws me to past parental ruptures, *triggers* as we call them, and I reset to hurt, helpless, and sad. I provide myself an historical explanation, that the ending of the phone call must have felt like I did as a child when my father would leave in what seemed like a broken connection. The historical explanation is known, a comfort, habitual yet incomplete, without wonder and surprise. It is a rigid, "because of this, then that" view that all analysts might guard against.

I tell myself, as I have learned to do, that I am re-creating the past in the present. But with the help of Zornberg, I am able to go deeper. "Only by turning toward the wound – the wound of reality – only from within that wound – can the event become accessible."[42] In a clinging moment, I isolated one aspect, the abrupt hang up, and lost track of the larger reality: the years of closeness with Judy, the whole of our friendship, the reality that was larger than the moment. Rather than remaining caught up in left-brain chatter, tangled up in blue, I try to use my mind: what else is going on?

I remember that the past and future come together in a moment, that I am not trapped only in the past, all tangled up in blue. I remind myself of the present and future. I try to breathe deeply, staying open to what will be and the unknown of it all. I ask, "What else is going on here?" I keep in mind the intense seduction of the complex (with its incessant repetition of past thoughts, feelings, and victimhood), along with gratitude that I now know what I know – not to block the feeling, but to go forward, knowing it will pass. Over time, many years, my immediate hurt reaction changes. By moving through insecurity and uncertainty, I gain a fuller perspective into the truth of the Other, different perspectives on my history, and a renewed inner strength. At present, if Judy thinks she might have to hang up abruptly, I ask for a warning signal. Judy listens and responds. "The history of a trauma … can only take place through the listening of another."[43] With fewer habitual perceptions, I assign new meaning to the event: "No complex is going to lock me into a pattern since that pattern changes with time." I hope to surrender to faith and remember what Martin Buber wrote: "The unique being, man, is created to be a center of surprise in the universe."[44]

I am blessed with a surprise, a positive recovered memory. Decades of analysis and life have helped, but after reading the novel *The Help*, a fresh view of my childhood wounds emerge. What I realize is that there was not as much a rupture, a hang up, as continuity. Daisy was the constant companion and firm bridge between my two parental households, present when we were with our Mom, present when we were with our Dad. We were with her and her soulful love and laughter seven nights a week. The recognition that Daisy was the constant object changed my personal myth, my historical memory. Now when Judy hangs up on me, I do not feel alone and lost inside. It's just Judy being Judy, and I can more calmly and, self-righteously, curse her for that.

Perhaps using words to describe a complex is difficult because its emotional reaction is what Wilfred Bion calls "the language of achievement", that area of mental space for which there are no words – the emotional knowing and nonverbal body processes of the psyche.[45] When we use the word *complex* to explain an emotional body reaction, the word (an example of Bion's "the language of substitution") boxes in that experience and we feel more trapped. I try to stay out of that narrow confine and feel the body sensations that transform with time and thought. The complex may convey a sense of "this is always the same and will never change", but when I allow the feelings to emerge and develop, I become a participant in their unfolding.

Emergence

Currently, I am heartened by research in emergent phenomena. We are learning that our past hurts and wounds are changed by new relationships. The bad news of the parrot and his master was wrong. We are being offered a new way of thinking about thinking.

The archetype, with its exploding energy, influences the magnetic pull to past traumas. Current thinking suggests that archetypes and, hence complexes, emerge in the moment from dialogue, the dynamic interaction of analyst/analysand, and the neurobiological activity in the brain. "Our behavior, experience, language, meaning, and affect all emerge without any precursor or predictor of the new behavior."[46] The emphasis is on what emerges rather than on a reductive conceptual model of what we thought we knew. We cannot be limited to causal connections since the elements of our self-organizing systems are too numerous and constantly reorganizing. Causality (the present as explained by what precedes it) is "complex".

David Tresan, in his 1996 foundational paper on Jungian metapsychology and neurobiological theory, describes the problems of causality, the closed system of reductive thinking:

> Reduction presumes that later events are *fully* explained by earlier ones.... The alternative to reductionism is emergence in which successively higher levels emerge from lower ones but with the understanding that, although dependent on them in some degree, the higher levels are neither caused by the lower nor are reducible to them.[47]

Not bound by my original fault lines, I am emerging in a complicated process of links and pathways and neural cell activity. With an emphasis on emergence, complexes take on new forms. The enormous capacities and processing of the brain, its plasticity, the dynamism of its memory, can re-create any known archetypal pattern, and hence complex, through self-reorganization without there having been an a priori structure of archetype, innate or not: "archetypes are seen to [re-create] themselves *de novo*, and behaviors and unconscious productions in the present are brought forward as new and unpredictable rather than renewed old truths".[48]

Rather than the complex being "static" or "fixed", words like *process*, *dynamism*, *field*, *action*, *flow* come to mind. When sitting with a patient whom we experience as inflexible or repetitious, it is important to remember that "nothing mental is immutably present in us in a definitely formed way ... we are all creating our psychic lives all the time, working to remember, working to forget, both day and night".[49] Jung reminds us of this:

> We overestimate material causation (matter) and believe that it alone affords us a true explanation of life. But matter is just as

> inscrutable as mind. As to the ultimate things we can know nothing, and only when we admit this do we return to a state of equilibrium.[50]

Jung's thinking went beyond the constraints of reductionism. Jung, through his concept of the transcendent function (which shifts us from one attitude to another, once we have developed the capacity to hold what John Perry titled "bipolar complexes"[51]), had foreshadowed modern scientific thinking in his acknowledging that new images, energy, feelings, and experiences emerge in the moment. Bound by the science of his day, he just did not have the language or the model for the science of emergent phenomena. But he was close. Tresan notes, "Emergence sounds very much like Jung's synthetic method of analysis".[52] When trying to understand the god Mercury's appearance in a patient's material, Jung wrote, "I incline to the hypothesis of spontaneous emergence, which does not eliminate the archetype but, on the contrary, presupposes it".[53] What is remarkable about emergence is that it results in new properties that could not have been anticipated based on the nature of the interacting entities. Furthermore, these new properties, according to Bruce Weber, "obey laws that arise with the novel properties" and "impose conditions on their constituents that depend on the nature of the emergent phenomena".[54]

I have become familiar with the persistent conditions imposed by the complex, with its familiar affect, its repetitious dialogue, and the behaviour it imposes on my patient and myself. As soon as certain interactional triggers appear, the complex seems to form a repeating loop in the neural circuits. We come to know these quite well, these "hot buttons" in our patients and ourselves, such as in my personal example about the "hang up" or Sam's one-down experiences with his father. These triggers are often predictable. Emergence, however, preserves a self-sameness, such as those conditions that are common to all complexes. The core formula of emergence, like that of chaos theory, is recursive in that it picks up parts from the past while, at the same time, it adds the new.

The aim for an analyst is not simply to accept these conditions but to help alter them. When you ask an unexpected question, often a more rounded picture of the scripted story emerges. Your action is motivated by the impulse to generate *new* emergent phenomena *not* conditioned by the complex. Your aim is not simply to unravel the old conditions under which the complex was generated and to stop there, thus accepting the "bad news", but to unveil new doors for your patient.

If our clinical work rests on *causality*, on predictability, rather than the emergent possibilities of the complex with its archetypal correlatives, we remain stagnant. When we ask, "Who is this unique and divine person before me now?" we open ourselves to possibility, to reverie, so new properties (attitudes) may arise as emergent phenomena.

Jung did anticipate just this clinical method when he wrote "complexes … in the conscious mind … can be corrected".[55] They respond, therefore, to dialogue and self-reflection. Consciousness is "capable of indefinite expansion".[56] With emphasis on what emerges, with the goal of expanding the personality, there is greater possibility of engagement and less fear of being stuck or overwhelmed by unwanted affects. We help free the patient from feelings of "knowing" as a defence against shame and helpless anxiety, and to attain a flexible virtuosity of thought, affect, and being. Rather than reductively looking to the past, as I was originally taught, I now ask myself (as Jung in 1954 reminded us), where are these complexes heading? What is the psyche trying to balance, expand, emerge, change? Does the energy released from emerging experience create new questions, new horizons, new quests? With a focus on emergence, we are more able to discover the interpersonal meaning in the "complex", remembering Levinas's idea of infinity.

Clinical application: Lena

My patient, Lena, who was abused by her mother, turned to alcohol and nonstop work to escape the pain of her memories, current depression, and tortured feelings about herself. She had been my patient before I knew about the brain's plasticity. When my thinking shifted toward what new can emerge, without a preconceived concept of her disturbance, her world changed.

ANALYST: Let's look at what happens when you come home. What is the feeling, the thought, the experience when you first open the bottle? When you take a drink?
LENA: Loneliness. Unbearable loneliness.

The air in the room was lead.

ANALYST: When else did you feel this?
LENA: When my mom came at me with the brush or the belt.

Jung describes qualities of the complex as similar to addiction – obsessive, possessive, unconscious, and repetitive. When I reduced her in my mind to "an alcoholic", I precluded her capacity to face the depth of her loneliness. I colluded with her that there was something wrong that needed to be fixed, changed, or stopped. In thinking I had to *do* something, to help her cut back on drinking, I shut down her experience. I tried to solve her problem behaviourally. "Can you try having only one glass a night instead of a bottle?" That got us nowhere.

When I stopped thinking in terms of addiction (complexes), she became more graphic about the details of her childhood abuse. She became better at conveying her sufferings, and I became better at letting them penetrate me. Unlike in a projective identification, I did not give back to the patient her contents to claim for herself. I could trust the pain in my stomach as representing that which she could not absorb. I moved away from my judgement that she drank a bottle a night to a more direct experience of her original and present purgatory. I could really feel hatred toward her mother. We fell in and out of each other's repulsion.

Jung did not consider as key the emotional relatedness, connection, or affect in the moment *between* our patients and ourselves. To bring out Lena's stories as if we were *both* there when the abuse originally happened, Lena depended on my willingness to be judiciously drawn into her subjective experience, to receive her in a deeper relational place. We both needed to digest and make sense and meaning. Her abuse could not become hers as long as I colluded with her to ward it off. The alcohol served to keep her pain out of consciousness, as did my, then, unconscious limited stance.

Jung believed that trauma splinters off parts of the psyche into complexes.[57] When unable to communicate the trauma, we learn to fragment. What Lena described made me feel sick and she knew it, which helped illuminate her undigested emotional life. I asked her to come more often so we could be sick together.

Like Lena, I, too, wanted to leave the feeling. I wanted to drink as I listened to her tales of being beaten and sexually assaulted and would imagine what special Sonoma County Zinfandel I would uncork the minute I dropped my keys and bag, entering my home after work. Her despair was now in both of us: a true encounter with the other.

As her memories came to life in the session and in me, I held the moment in a new way and began to see the gate between us – between our conscious and unconscious minds – opening wider. We both averted avoiding, reducing, keeping at bay, and were freer to keep her original experience alive.

From my new thinking, as we both stopped pushing the complex away, I did not see her as immutable but as emerging, like David out of Michelangelo's slab of stone. I pictured her breaking out of the imprisoning shell of her past. And she did. When I no longer thought of her as an alcoholic, she was freer to own that she had a serious drinking problem. She went to AA and quit drinking.

In remembering the words of Levinas – be hospitable to the stranger, the orphan, the widow – I welcomed the stranger and orphan in Lena (parentless, alone, stranger to herself) into the room. "The Other who dominates me in his transcendence is thus the stranger, the widow, the orphan, to whom I am obliged."[58] These fully alive parts of her had not been held in a relational field. While waiting for the opportunity to be known and understood, they had been hiding inside Lena's alcoholic behaviour.

In 1934, Jung acknowledged that "complexes are psychic agencies whose deepest nature is still unfathomed",[59] which foreshadows Zornberg. The reality of Jung's words still holds true. *Reductive thinking is a closed system, whereas emergence is an open system.* My conclusion is that rather than closing down our exploration by simply naming the complex or focusing on what caused it, we should instead remain in conversation with ourselves about what Jung's complex theory may become.

Why does all this matter to me? Because when I sit with my patients, in a state of intimate presence where the grace of our lives can unfold, I try not to think about terms, concepts, theories, or reductive causation.

> Only an unremitting openness to the unseen measure (the unpredictable) stands to affect our fate and then not with certainty. The caveat is the need to remember always that we are not our own makers and are ultimately in thrall to inscrutable powers beyond our understanding.[60]

Notes

1 S. Freud, *New Introductory Lectures on Psychoanalysis*, *The Standard Edition of the Complete Psychological Works of Sigmund Freud*, vol. 22, London, The Hogarth Press, 1933/1971, p. 80.
2 C. G. Jung, "Introduction to the religious and psychological problem of alchemy", in *Psychology and Alchemy*, *The Collected Works of C. G. Jung* (hereafter *CW*), vol. 12, Princeton, NJ, Princeton University Press, 1944, p. 9, n. 2.
3 C. G. Jung, *Letters*, vol. 1, *1906–1950*, ed. G. Adler, Princeton, NJ, Princeton University Press, 1973, p. 384.
4 C. G. Jung, *Letters*, vol. 2, *1951–1961*, ed. G. Adler, Princeton, NJ, Princeton University Press, 1975, p. 571.
5 C. G. Jung, "On the psychology and pathology of so-called occult phenomenon", in *Psychiatric Studies*, *CW* 1, Princeton, NJ, Princeton University Press, 1902/1970, p. 77.
6 C. G. Jung, *Psychology of the Unconscious: A Study in the Transformations and Symbolisms*, trans. B. Hinkle, New York, Moffat Yard and Co, 1916, p. 37.
7 C. G. Jung, "The relations between the ego and the unconscious", in *Two Essays on Analytical Psychology*, *CW* 7, Princeton, NJ, Princeton University Press, 1935/1966, p. 312.
8 C. G. Jung, *Experimental Researches*, *CW* 2, Princeton, NJ, Princeton University Press, 1904/1990, p. 72, n. 2.
9 C. G. Jung, "The psychological diagnosis of evidence", in *Experimental Researches*, *CW* 2, Princeton, NJ, Princeton University Press, 1905/1990, p. 733.
10 C. G. Jung, "The analysis of dreams", in *Freud and Psychoanalysis*, *CW* 4, Princeton, NJ, Princeton University Press, 1909/1961, p. 67.
11 C. G. Jung, "The psychology of dementia praecox", in *The Psychogenesis of Mental Disease*, *CW* 3, Princeton, NJ, Princeton University Press, 1907/1960, p. 83.
12 C. G. Jung, "On the diagnosis of complexes", in *Experimental Researches*, *CW* 2, Princeton, NJ, Princeton University Press, [1911] 1913/1981, p. 1351.
13 C. G. Jung, "The theory of psychoanalysis", in *Freud and Psychoanalysis*, Princeton, NJ, Princeton University Press, 1913, p. 408.
14 C. G. Jung, "On the psychogenesis of schizophrenia", in *The Psychogenesis of Mental Disease*, *CW* 3, Princeton, NJ, Princeton University Press, 1939/1960, p. 521.
15 C. G. Jung, "Psychological factors determining human behavior", in *The Structure and Dynamics of the Psyche*, *CW* 8, Princeton, NJ, Princeton University Press, 1937/1981, p. 255.

16 C. G. Jung, "Medicine and psychotherapy", in *The Practice of Psychotherapy*, *CW* 16, Princeton, NJ, Princeton University Press, 1945/1954, p. 196.
17 C. G. Jung, "Psychotherapy and a philosophy of life", in *The Practice of Psychotherapy*, *CW* 16, Princeton, NJ, Princeton University Press, 1943/1954, p. 179. Emphasis added.
18 C. G. Jung, "After the catastrophe", in *Civilization in Transition*, *CW* 10, Princeton, NJ, Princeton University Press, 1945/1964, p. 456.
19 C. G. Jung, *Psychological Types*, *CW* 6, Princeton, NJ, Princeton University Press, 1921/1971, p. 925.
20 C. G. Jung, "The therapeutic value of abreaction", in *The Practice of Psychotherapy*, *CW* 16, Princeton, NJ, Princeton University Press, 1928/1954, p. 267.
21 C. G. Jung, "Analytical psychology and Weltanschauung", in *The Structure and Dynamics of the Psyche*, *CW* 8, Princeton, NJ, Princeton University Press, 1931/1981, p. 710.
22 Jung, *Experimental Researches*, *CW* 2, p. 72, fn 2.
23 C. G. Jung, *Dream Analysis*, Princeton, NJ, Princeton University Press, 1929/1984, p. 416.
24 P. Bromberg, *Standing in the Spaces: Essays on Clinical Process, Trauma, and Dissociation*, Hilldale, NJ, The Analytic Press, 1998, p. 272.
25 H. Kohut, *The Restoration of the Self*, New York, International Universities Press, 1977, p. 243.
26 S. Freud, *Beyond the Pleasure Principle*, New York, W. W. Norton, 1920/1961, p. 20.
27 R. D. Stolorow, G. Atwood, and D. Orange, *Worlds of Experience: Interweaving Philosophical and Clinical Dimensions in Psychoanalysis*, New York, Basic Books. 2002, p. 45.
28 R. Schafer, *Retelling a Life: Narration and Dialogue in Psychoanalysis*, New York, Basic Books, 1992, p. 48.
29 M. Klein, *The Writings of Melanie Klein*, vol. 3, London, Hogarth Press, 1946, p. 4.
30 S. Freud, *Lectures and Addresses and Delivered Before the Departments of Psychology and Pedagogy in the Celebration of the 20th Anniversary of the Opening of Clark University. September, 1909*, BiblioLife reproduction series, Worcester, MA, 1909, p. 11.
31 J. Weiss, H. Sampson, and Mount Zion Psychotherapy Research Group, *The Psychoanalytic Process: Theory, Clinical Observation, and Empirical Research*, New York, Guilford Press, 1986, p. 79.
32 Jung, "On the diagnosis of complexes", *CW* 2, p. 1352.
33 Jung, "The psychology of dementia praecox", *CW* 3, p. 78.
34 B. Cohen, "The Trace of the Face of God: Emmanuel Levinas and Depth Psychotherapy", *Jung Journal: Culture and Psyche*, 2008, vol. 2, pp. 20–45, at p. 32.
35 E. Levinas, *Totality and Infinity: An Essay on Exteriority*, Pittsburgh, Duquesne University Press, 2004, p. 38. Originally published as *Totalité et infini: Essais sur l'extériorité*, Phaenomenologica 8, The Hague and Boston, Martinus Nijhoff, 1961.
36 Cohen, "The Trace of the Face of God", p. 36.
37 C. Bollas, *Forces of Destiny*, London, Free Association Books, 1989, p. 63.
38 When struggling to make sense of personal complexes, I marvel at the acuity of Zornberg's confession and how accurate her description is for me. A. Zornberg, *The Murmuring Deep: Reflections on the Biblical Unconscious*, New York, Schocken Books, 2009, p. 17.
39 D. Tresan, "Zabriskie's point: democracies and other systems". *Quadrant*, Summer 2008, vol. 38, no. 2, p. 3.
40 Jung quoted in J. Jacobi, *Complex, Archetype, Symbol in the Psychology of C. G. Jung*, Bollingen Series, Princeton, NJ, Princeton University Press, 1959, p. ix.
41 A. C. Lammers (ed.), *The Jung–Kirsch Letters: The Correspondence of C. G. Jung and James Kirsch*, London and New York, Routledge, 2011, p. 63.
42 Zornberg, *The Murmuring Deep*, p. 306.
43 Ibid.
44 M. Buber, *On the Bible*, New York, Schocken Books, 1968, p. 168.

45 W. R. Bion, "Attention and Interpretation", in *Seven Servants: Four Works by Wilfred Bion*, New York, Jason Aronson, Inc., 1970, p. 125.
46 G. B. Hogenson, "Archetypes: emergence and the psyche's deep structure", in J. Cambray and L. Carter (eds.), *Analytical Psychology: Contemporary Perspectives in Jungian Analysis*, pp. 32–55, London and New York, Brunner-Routledge, 2004, p. 45.
47 D. Tresan, "Jungian metapsychology and neurobiological theory", *Journal of Analytical Psychology*, 1996, vol. 41, no. 3, pp. 399–436 at pp. 402–3.
48 Ibid., p. 408.
49 Ibid., p. 421.
50 C. G. Jung, "Basic postulates of analytical psychology", in *The Structure and Dynamics of the Psyche*, *CW* 8, Princeton, NJ, Princeton University Press, 1954/1981, p. 657.
51 J. W. Perry, "Emotions and object relations", *Journal of Analytical Psychology*, 1970, vol. 15, no. 1, pp. 1–12.
52 Tresan, "Jungian metapsychology", p. 407.
53 C. G. Jung, "A study in the process of individuation", in *The Archetypes and the Collective Unconscious*, *CW* 9/i, Princeton, NJ, Princeton University Press, 1950, p. 549, fn. 61.
54 B. H. Weber, "Emergence of mind and the Baldwin effect", in B. H. Weber and D. J. Depew (eds.), *Evolution and Learning: The Baldwin Effect Reconsidered*, pp. 309–26, Cambridge, MA, MIT Press, 2003, n. 3.
55 C. G. Jung, "On the nature of the psyche", in *The Structure and Dynamics of the Psyche*, *CW* 8, Princeton, NJ, Princeton University Press, 1954/1981, p. 384.
56 Ibid., p. 387.
57 C. G. Jung, "A review of the complex theory", in *The Structure and Dynamics of the Psyche*, *CW* 8, Princeton, NJ, Princeton University Press, 1934, p. 204.
58 Levinas, *Totality and Infinity*, p. 215.
59 Jung, "A review of the complex theory", *CW* 8, p. 216.
60 Tresan, "Zabriskie's point", pp. 10–11.

8

CHINESE MODERNITY AND THE WAY OF RETURN

Shiuya Sara Liuh

Shiuya Liuh reflects upon Jung's reading of the Sinologist Richard Wilhelm's translation of *The Secret of the Golden Flower* from a postcolonial perspective. She examines Jung's and Wilhelm's arguable translations of two Chinese characters, *Hun* and *P'o*, and expands their pictographic and symbolic meaning. She also uses Jung's way of reading as a new way to approach and reread the ancient text. Marking the synchronous events of the early twentieth century that led to the transplantation of the "Golden Flower" to the West, Liuh discovers through her study of Jung a personal way back to her cultural heritage.

J. K.

In this chapter, I will share my journey through reading Jung's "Commentary on *The Secret of the Golden Flower*". Going back and forth between Jung's commentary and the original Taoist text, I experienced a different thinking process. Confused, I argued and dialogued with Jung's commentary. My inquiry into my cultural heritage and its meaning in contemporary psychotherapy opened. During this process, one interesting question arose: how can Jung help us, as non-Westerners, to engage with our old traditions in order to nourish our souls in this modern world?

The dilemma of the modern Chinese psyche

I grew up knowing my father had no religion but believed instead in science. On his deathbed, I asked him what kind of funeral service he would like to have, a Buddhist or a Catholic ceremony. He had difficulty deciding because he believed his wife (my mother), a Catholic, was in a Christian heaven and his mother, a Buddhist, was in Nirvana. Both were his dearest loves and he did not want to miss a chance to reunite with either of them. I jokingly said to him that Buddha and Christ must be neighbours in paradise, so he did not have to worry about which one he would miss. At the end of his life, my father, who had been born at the beginning of the modern Republic era in a small village in southern China, found no spiritual guidance to follow and did not know which God's home he should return to. His confusion speaks to me of a bigger reality that relates to Chinese[1] modernity: the ambiguity about where our souls belong.

In 1911, young revolutionaries successfully overthrew the old dynasty and established the Chinese Republic. My father's generation believed modernization was the only way to save China and it was their duty to make it happen. At that time, modernity meant Westernization, something opposite from the old superstitious customs and religions, which must be demolished. As a youngster, along with his brothers, my father went to a local temple and destroyed statues of gods and goddesses. Even when village elders punished him, his physical scars shone like the honourable medals of a devoted warrior fighting for Chinese modernity. His action spoke for the Chinese eagerness to restore dignity to the state through challenging the established tradition and its values. My father was one of many modern Chinese whose psyches carried the collective wounds of modern Chinese history and strived for recovery.

Chinese historians mark 1838, the year Chinese and British armies clashed over the opium import conflict, as the start of the modern Chinese era. From then on, Western powers brought the modern world to the Chinese doorway with clear and loud canon sounds. China, like most non-European countries at that time, was forced to modernize, and they came to perceive modernization as the only way to deal with aggressive foreign powers. In this process, modernity was not a value-free and emotion-free concept. It was heavily loaded with shame, humiliation, sadness, and rage. In psychological terms, modernity in the Chinese psyche can be described both as a traumatic experience and an attempt to recover the nation's wounded dignity.

To modernize, the Chinese needed to go through a transformation and initiation into a modern form of consciousness. During this process of modernization, demystifying archaic traditional culture occurred simultaneously with adapting Westernized culture. During the first half of the twentieth century, Western-educated Chinese intellectuals took the theory of social evolution to heart and believed in a unilinear trajectory of social development that, no matter how glorious Chinese culture was before, it was best to move forward. To them, clearly, their outdated culture needed to be replaced by a new, Western, and modern one. They believed the collective psyche was still locked in a primitive and mysterious mindset and needed to undergo an enlightenment similar to the European Enlightenment in the eighteenth century. Eliminating the superstitious and mystical parts of the culture and bringing the country into a new stage of development called for a rationalistic criticism of traditions on every level.

It was at this time of turmoil and confusion that *The Secret of the Golden Flower*[2] was first translated. In 1928, Jung received the German translation of this book from Sinologist Richard Wilhelm and wrote a long commentary for it. Through reading this Eastern spiritual book symbolically, Jung found a way to "build a bridge of psychological understanding between East and West".[3] This approach appears in his other readings of Eastern and Western spiritual texts. By doing so, Jung was able to cross cultures and time periods to reveal the possibility of a universal human psyche.

My initial understanding of reading *The Secret of the Golden Flower* was completely different from Jung's. It was disappointing. I only read it to understand Jung's commentary better and found it no different from other Taoist and Buddhist texts that are full of religious jargon and dogmas irrelevant to my personal life. However, I found Jung's and Wilhelm's commentaries intellectually stimulating. From the classical text of *The Secret of the Golden Flower*, read side by side with Jung's interpretation, I realized there were two completely different parallel ontologies. As a bilingual reader, I shuttled between both texts and experienced increasingly ambiguous feelings, which had not happened when reading Jung's other writings. Later, I recognized my inability to relate to the text of *The Secret of the Golden Flower* was actually a resistance – that has been, in many ways, part of the phenomenon of Chinese modernity and its ambivalence in relating to traditions.

When Jung commented on Eastern spirituality, he demonstrated a personal and creative way of engaging with an old tradition. He first read these traditional spiritual texts symbolically and then chose a psychological approach to understand them. Jung's approach has shown me a way to deal with a personal resistance innate in the collective modern Chinese psyche, from which I saw a new path of reconnecting with old tradition. Jung said:

> To understand metaphysically is impossible; it can only be done psychologically. I therefore strip things of their metaphysical wrappings in order to make them objects of psychology. In this way, I can at least get something comprehensible out of them, and can avail myself of it. Moreover, I learn psychological conditions and processes which before were veiled in symbols and out of reach of my understanding.[4]

Jung can help us find a creative way to read the old texts, both for Chinese and non-Chinese who have been unable to understand or have not been willing to accept the old Chinese ontology.

What Jung offers is not totally agreeable because his psychological approach toward Chinese spiritual texts, in many Sinologists' eyes, is a misreading and a misunderstanding.[5] Traditional Chinese literature has a long, well-established history of interpretation with unchallenged intellectual authority. Without sufficient pre-knowledge of Chinese history, any personal commentary is at risk of being harshly criticized and labelled as ignorant or arrogant. Not knowing Chinese language and not being familiar with Taoism, Jung's misunderstanding of the text is almost unavoidable, not to mention how Wilhelm's questionable translation affected Jung's understanding.[6] Jung's approach also led to his being suspected of psychologizing religious and spiritual practices. He was accused of simply appropriating Taoist ideas "for his own foreign purposes and thereby radically distorting them".[7] But in moving beyond Sinology territory, I find Jung's ability to "misread" and "misunderstand" the old texts inadvertently brought me to an exciting new understanding and avenue for Taoist study; this view is also shared by many Chinese scholars.[8] Combining this "new understanding" with the "correct understanding", which is attached to the ideology of a thousands-of-years-old tradition, could trigger ambiguous feelings in the modern Chinese psyche. Nevertheless, Jung's psychological and symbolical approach can be seen as a new tool to reach old wisdom.

The Secret of the Golden Flower is a simple, small book teaching Taoist meditation so its practitioners can reach enlightenment. As I set out to read, I shortened the name of the book in my mind to *Golden Flower*, but as I worked through its meaning, I realized that it held a secret for me – a secret that would take me back to an appreciation of my traditions. With regards to the huge collection of Chinese Taoist literature, this book has no unique status in Taoist tradition. In terms of its content, it teaches nothing new. If not for Wilhelm's translation and Jung's commentary, this book might have been buried under huge piles of similar books and been forgotten by Chinese scholars and Taoist practitioners long ago.

The book was said to come from the teaching of Lu Tung-pin, who is believed to be the founder of Taoism in the Tang Dynasty (618–907 CE) and a well-known figure in various spiritual writings, folk tales, and Chinese literature. But he is nowhere to be found in the historical records. Whether Lu Tung-pin was a real person or a fantasy figure is not important for millions of Taoist followers who believe they consistently encounter his spirit through Taoist mediums. Through the medium's mouth and hand, it is believed that Lu Tung-pin keeps giving advice, teaching, and writing books. In their writing, Taoist writers are not separated from their spiritual master. Therefore, the actual date and authorship of *The Secret of the Golden Flower* are unimportant. According to scholar Rur-Bin Yang, this book was written in the early Qing dynasty, during the time of the emperor Kangxi (1662–1721), and possibly a handwritten form circulated among a very small group of Taoist practitioners. Later during the period of the emperor Qianlong (1750–93), the book was formally published; however, only a few thousand copies were printed.[9] The later version, published in 1911 and translated by Wilhelm, was the one that circulated much more widely.[10] Interestingly, 1911 is the year the Republic was established.

The Secret of the Golden Flower starts with an explanation of Taoist ontology and establishes the fundamental reason for bodily practice to reach spiritual wholeness. Then, it progresses into teaching a method of meditation in great detail, including ways and places to concentrate as well as breathing techniques. The text describes problems and dangers that practitioners may encounter during their practice and suggests ways to avoid these pitfalls. After describing the meditation techniques, using images, the text guides practitioners through the different stages of bodily experience and spiritual development.

By quieting the mind, sitting still, focusing inwardly, and controlling their breathing, Taoist practitioners believe they are able to hear inner sounds and see inner images. Step by step, practitioners can trace back to the beginning of life as an embryo, and even beyond that to the beginning of life. The final stage is to reach the Nothingness of the universe, which is symbolized, in the text, as a golden light and golden flower.

Describing the meaningful time and space intertwined in the phenomena of synchronicity, Jung said "whatever happens in a given moment has inevitably the quality peculiar to that moment".[11] In the journey of *The Secret of the Golden Flower*, we can see how first the text was forgotten; then as Chinese modernity took hold, it re-emerged. Then Wilhelm and Jung replanted its roots in Europe and watered it where it has grown and become a beautiful flower. The emergence of *The Secret of the Golden Flower* at a time that correlated with Chinese modern history is extremely meaningful.

Jung described his core concern at the time when he received *The Secret of the Golden Flower:* "I had been seeking, striving for, thinking, and doing in my efforts to alleviate the psychic sufferings of Europeans."[12] Interestingly, at the same time and with similar concerns of alleviating the psychic suffering caused by the past, Chinese intellectuals took a different path, throwing away and eliminating the influences of those same traditional texts, which Jung praised so highly. In the process of freeing themselves from the past, the Chinese inadvertently became psychological subjects of another master. Jung in his autobiography *Memories, Dreams, Reflections*, recorded his conversation with the old African tribal shaman, who said that since the British came, they did not have "big dreams" any more, because the British knew everything.[13] Metaphorically speaking, the Chinese were in a similar psychic state as the African tribal men, even though China was never completely colonized by a single Western country. The "West" was, however, just like the "British", an over-powering object that existed in the Chinese collective psyche, representing an imaginary and practical new emperor.

The New Culture Movement started in 1917.[14] It was also called the Chinese Renaissance, and it was led by Western-educated intellectuals promoting comprehensive cultural reforms claiming that complete modernization – equivalent to Westernization – was the only way to solve Chinese problems. Around 1920, intense military and cultural battles were happening in China. Like the revolutionaries who revolted against a thousands-of-years-old political system, Chinese intellectuals also intended to totally uproot and remodel the traditional culture. At that time, Western "democracy" and "science" were the main tools for achieving cultural reforms.

Democracy and science represented modern values of individuality and rationality, which were neglected by traditional Chinese culture and so attracted the Chinese psyche's wildest imagination and desire. Intellectuals and young students passionately embraced Western culture as the Messiah coming to rescue and revive a dying civilization. With the same passion, they attacked traditional culture, specifically blaming Confucianism for people's poverty and national weakness. The movement's intent was to shake the fundamental values of traditional culture, which included the abandonment of Chinese pictogram characters to a phonetic alphabet to eliminate the ideology attached to the language.

In 1922, when the voice of cultural reforms reached its heights, Wilhelm was teaching at Peking University, the centre of the New Culture Movement. I imagine that while Wilhelm worked hard translating the I Ching, Western-educated Chinese intellectuals and youth marched just outside his small red-brick building, vowing to destroy these old texts, which they believed kept the Chinese people in ignorance and mysticism. The very texts and concepts that Wilhelm was trying to introduce to European society were believed by Chinese mainstream scholars to be the enemy of Chinese modernity. This fanatic passion to modernize one's country and culture was reflected in the humiliation caused by the failed wars against the West. Chinese intellectuals were eager to open the people's minds, which had been locked by official Confucianism for thousands of years, and let in fresh air from the West.

Wilhelm, a German minister, lived for 25 years in China where he built one of the first Western-style high schools. He befriended an old dynasty officer named Lao Nai-hsuan and together created the Institute of Honoring to preserve Confucius. Jung, in his obituary of Wilhelm, spoke of his "grateful reverence of this mind which created a bridge between East and West and gave to the Occident the heirship to a precious culture thousands of years old, a culture perhaps destined to disappear".[15] But an important question to ponder is why the thousands-years-old treasure would lose its value in the eyes of the Chinese? It is neither for Jung nor Wilhelm to answer. Jung was like a treasure hunter who found the old treaties worthy of preservation, but the Chinese wanted to destroy them as thoroughly as they could.

The crossover of cultural position between Wilhelm, Jung, and the Chinese intellectuals at the beginning of the twentieth century speaks loudly to us about the importance of each culture's different path of individuation. It appears that, at that time, the *Golden Flower* was transplanted to the West because its native homeland had neglected to nourish it.

After almost two centuries of modernization, the survival of China is no longer a burning issue, but modernity is still a sensitive issue in the Chinese collective mind. It is clear now that complete Westernization is unsuitable and unnecessary for Chinese modernity. But a return to the ways of the past is also hard to imagine. Weiming Tu, advocator of Neo-

Confucianism, points out that the problem of Chinese modernity came from only borrowing narrow and shallow instrumental values from the Western Enlightenment movement.[16] The old Chinese spiritual values were devalued and treated with suspicion due to China's humiliating past with the colonial West. Even though the Chinese claim to have a 5,000-year history, the reality is, as Tu points out, Chinese modernization is built on a shallow land of instrumental rationalism with an aggressive materialistic worldview.

The question regarding the kinds of traditions we are going to include in our process of modernity, and how this process will affect the Chinese psyche is worthy of consideration. Tu, like many contemporary thinkers, believes traditions and modernity are not incompatible categories. Rather, he believes the Enlightenment project that started in Europe has already become a part of our global heritage and needs to continue in every modern society but with its own variation of modernity. Each culture needs to reconnect with its traditions and establish its own values. Tu states, "An investigation of traditions in modernity is essential for our appreciation of modernization as a highly differentiated cultural phenomenon rather than a kind of homogeneous integral process of Westernization or more recently modernization."[17] In Jungian terms, each society has its own path to individuation. Reconnecting with traditions is one way to correct the obviously one-sided development of Chinese modernization, that is, mercantilism, commercialism, and ferocious international competitiveness.

Jung in his commentary to *The Secret of the Golden Flower* strongly emphasized the danger of imitating other cultures to solve one's own problems:

> A growing familiarity with the spirit of the East should be taken merely as a sign that we are beginning to relate to the alien elements within ourselves. Denial of our historical foundations would be sheer folly and would be the best way to bring about another uprooting of consciousness. Only by standing firmly on our own soil can we assimilate the spirit of the East.[18]

As we can see, almost a century later, modern Chinese society is suffering the consequences of what Jung warned Europeans of in imitating another culture.

Reading symbolically

Unlike most modern Chinese or Western readers, who gave up reading the old texts because of their unacceptable metaphysical concepts, Jung was able to penetrate the old symbol system to bring a new meaning. Jung's way of reading *The Secret of the Golden Flow*er can be described in two parts. First, he reads the metaphysical and spiritual content symbolically. Second, he brings a psychological interpretation to these symbols. Jung's legacy to us is a way of personalizing cultural heritage that liberates people from overarching spiritual authority, allowing each person to find his or her own way to an individualized rite of passage to cultural homecoming.

Jung may have unknowingly tapped into the Chinese unconscious with his symbolic reading. Following Jung's steps, I started my own symbolic reading of *The Secret of the Golden Flower.* For me as a Chinese, Jung's questionable reading and interpretation of some Taoist concepts in the *Golden Flower* became my way of beginning to explore the old wisdom with a modern perspective. In the text, two concepts caught my attention: *Hun/P'o*[19] and *Hui*. They are important in Taoist meditation. I decided to take these key characters as symbols and work around their images to find a personal meaning.

Chinese characters, because of their special nature, can be treated as symbols that allow our minds to expand from cognitive thinking into intuitive imagination. The oldest recorded Chinese characters are pictograms found on oracle-bone inscriptions. The later creation of new Chinese characters is still heavily based on the representation of the image and sound. Over 80 per cent of Chinese characters are created under the rule of *pictophonetic* compounds, which combine image, meaning, and sound to give Chinese characters their very distinctive features in etymology.[20] These pictorial symbols allow words not only to function for expression and communication, but also to deliver the collective understanding of phenomena from Chinese ancestors to present time. The oracle-bone inscriptions, used in the late Shang dynasty (1200–1050 BCE), were animal bones with inscribed questions that were used as divinatory tools when burned in ceremonies to communicate with the spirits. Through reading the cracks on burned turtle shells and ox bones, divine messages were received and ancient characters were used to record the divine messages on these bones. Therefore, oracle-bone characters with their pictorial nature are not just signs but are also symbols representing divine messages from the Chinese collective unconsciousness.

Jung's discussion of *Hun/P'o* and *Hui* is arguable. The possibility of his "misreading" of the Taoist concepts is not my concern here. Rather their different translations opened a door for my imagination. I see those Chinese characters carrying the potential possibility of bringing a new meaning to these collective symbols.

Hun *and* P'o

The different translations of *Hun* and *P'o* not only point out the translator's interpretation of the text but also reveal the embedded richness of the two characters. *Hun* and *P'o* are two separate characters commonly used together in Chinese language to describe the invisible essence of a person. But the various translations stimulate a big discussion. Wilhelm translated *Hun* and *P'o* as *animus* and *anima*, and Jung suggested *logos* and *anima*.[21] Later, von Franz translated them as *higher spirit-soul* and *lower body-soul*, and Cleary translated them as *higher consciousness* and *lower consciousness*.[22]

To make a better use of the "misreading" and "misunderstanding" of *The Secret of the Golden Flower*, we need to look at the ontology, origin, gender meaning, and the psychological meaning of the characters of *Hun* and *P'o*.

Hun *and* P'o *in Taoist ontology*

To understand *Hun* and *P'o*, we need to go back to Chinese Taoist ontology, which starts from the source of the universe. According to Taoist ontology, the nature of the universe is Nothingness (*Wu ji*), and from Nothingness, *Tai Ji* came out. Tai Ji has two separate and opposite forces: *yin* and *yang*. From Tai Ji, the five elements – gold, wood, water, fire, and earth – are developed, and through the five elements, heaven and earth are created. In between heaven and earth, the world of all living beings is created. The life energy flows out from Nothingness and creates and moves the world and human beings. Therefore, all sentient beings are a micro-universe, functioning according to the principle of yin and yang, Tai Ji, and the five elements. In the human psyche, the essence from the universe is called *Hun P'o*, which are two opposing principles: *Hun* represents heaven and the yang principle, and *P'o* represents earth, body, and the yin principle.

Figures 8.1 and 8.2 The original characters of *Hun* and *P'o*.

The earliest Chinese characters for *Hun* and *P'o* were found carved on bronze from the Zhou dynasty (1207–221 BCE). Both characters are pictophonetic, with combined image and sound, and have two parts. The right part of the character *P'o* means "ghost, spirit, or invisible essence", and the left part gives the sound of *P'o*, meaning "to anchor or to berth at". Together, these two parts give *P'o* its meaning of invisible spirit berths in the body that guard the physical function working according to the principle of universe. The character of *P'o* indicates the concrete nature of yin, a female, earthy, and solitary character. *P'o*, the spirit, attaches to the human body and will dissolve after death.

Hun represents the heavenly spirit inside the human being that will survive after the death of the human body. The left part of the *Hun* character means "cloud", and the right part is "ghost", representing the flowing life energy, which is fluid like clouds, not bound to earthy existence. It is guided by yang, the male principle, and leads to the development of conscious mind. *Hun* and *P'o* are paired to describe two opposite life energies and used together to represent human life striving forward. These two poles of energy dynamically compete with each other to dominate a person's life. When the physical body ceases living, *Hun* and *P'o* are released from the individual's body and go in two different directions. *P'o* goes back to earth, and *Hun* returns to the source of the universe.

In Taoist spiritual practice, controlling *P'o* and strengthening *Hun* are essential, because *Hun* is rooted in the source of universe, and it will lose its influence on people if *P'o* dominates the direction of life. *P'o* energy guards the body function and attracts, reduces, and reacts to the stimulations of the external world. Since *P'o* vanishes after the body's death and *Hun* lasts, working on one's *Hun* is working on one's immortal body. That is why Taoists believe meditation can prolong human life.

Gender meaning in Hun *and* P'o

Wilhelm's translation emphasizes the pair's relationship of yin/yang principles and, therefore, used animus for *Hun* and anima for *P'o*. Cleary based his translations on the Taoist spiritual hierarchical system and thus translated *Hun* and *P'o* as higher consciousness and lower consciousness. Jung's translation of *Hun* and *P'o* as logos and anima is the most confusing one. In Cleary's view, the difference in translation reflects Wilhelm's "Christian backgrounds and interests", and Jung "proceeds to exaggerate this distortion even further in his own disquisition on feminine and masculine psychologies".[24] Even though *Hun* and *P'o*, in Chinese, belong to the differing yang and yin principles, they have little gender indication in their common usage in terms of language. Therefore most people will agree with Cleary's translation because *Hun* and *P'o* have different values in conscious development: *Hun* is eternal and *P'o* is mortal.

Did Wilhelm's translation cause Jung to misunderstand the Taoist ontology as Cleary believes? If so, we can dismiss a big chunk of writing in his commentary about anima and logos. But if we follow Jung's thread of thought in his commentary, we may come to a very different understanding of these two metaphysical concepts. Jung said that *Hun* is "a higher, spirit-soul belonging to the yang principle and therefore masculine", and *P'o* "belongs to the lower, earth bound, bodily soul, partakes of the yin principle, and is therefore feminine".[25] Here, Jung did not use many other concepts that yin and yang represent. He only chose the gender categories – feminine and masculine – to represent yin and yang principles in order to define the meaning of *P'o* and *Hun*. From there, he developed his discourse about *Hun* and *P'o* as logos and anima, and apart from philosophical and ontological discussion, he brought psychology into Chinese spirituality.

Jung describes his reasons for translating *P'o* as anima: "Careful investigation has shown that the affective character in a man has feminine traits. From this psychological fact comes the Chinese teaching of the P'o-soul, as well as my concept of the anima."[26] Jung explains his translation of *Hun* to logos: "Although Wilhelm's translation of Hun as animus seems justified to me, none the less I had important reasons for choosing logos for a man's spirit, for masculine clarity of consciousness and reason. I prefer to translate Hun by logos."[27]

Jung has clearly used "man" instead of "person" as the subject undertaking spiritual pursuits and undergoing a total personal transformation. As he understood, the Chinese characters *Hun* and *P'o* in Taoist practice indicated a path of individuation that was, until then, a masculine path. Therefore, he said that he would reserve animus for women's inferior function, a less developed logos form. Although Jung did not say it, we can read his argument as an indication that women should have a different path of individuation, which does not appear in this Taoist text. We can read into Jung's writing in this translation that the whole ancient theory of spiritual development only considers men. The possibility of the existence of a different way for women's spiritual development had not been considered. So from my observation, when Jung suggested translating *Hun* as logos, instead of using Wilhelm's translation as animus, he was already taking an unprecedented step toward claiming that there is a need for different concepts and terms in describing men's and women's paths of spiritual development and enlightenment.

Jung was aware that the Taoist way of enlightenment is a male's way to individuation. Therefore, he kept his translation of *Hun* as logos and *P'o* as anima:

> Chinese philosophy, like all mental and spiritual activity of ancient times, is the exclusive constituent of the man's world. Its concepts

> are never taken psychologically, and have therefore never been examined as to how far they also apply to the feminine psyche.[28]

Jung was correct about the map of the Chinese psyche's development; it has no psychological and gender consideration in it. The various translations shine a new light on the text for Chinese readers familiar with Taoist ontology. People are used to nongender ontology, using a male's perspective to guard both genders' spiritual exercise. The traditional spiritual practice excludes the possibility of a different way – a female way – of enlightenment. Jung's translation quietly opens this possibility for our consideration.

Psychological meaning of Hun *and* P'o

Following Jung's psychological reading of *Hun* and *P'o*, von Franz took these two characters' interpretation to another level of understanding. Chinese ontology is known for having refined knowledge concerning body and spirit development, but the Western term *psychology* has never really existed in the Chinese psyche's map. Von Franz extended Jung's reading of *Hun* and *P'o* to see them as two aspects of the Self, the totality of the human psyche. Von Franz named *P'o* as body-soul, which carries the potentiality to be aware of the Self through body and emotional experience. This differs from the Taoist view that emphasizes controlling the power of bodily impulse, or *P'o* energy. Von Franz gave those uncontrollable sensations and emotions a very high value. *P'o* as body-soul is a lower level of soul, but *Hun* and *P'o* are direct channels for receiving archetypal messages from the unconscious. If our ego can bear the violent emotional attack, which von Franz described as "crucifixion", a resurrection can be experienced:

> when something meaningful, which can be recognized by means of a strong emotion, breaks into our life, then there is a chance for us to make its archetypal (that is, spiritual) meaning conscious. In this way a piece of something eternal and infinite is realized in our earthly existence, and that means, in a literal sense, that it has become real.[29]

Von Franz, in her Jungian psychological way, redescribed the relationship of *Hun* and *P'o*: that *Hun*, spirit-soul, carries archetypal meaning through *P'o*, the bodily emotional sensation, to reach the conscious ego and to realize the eternal meaning of the universe.

In *The Secret of the Golden Flower*, the concept of "overcoming *P'o*" can be read, in von Franz's way, as, instead of avoiding or controlling our bodily sensations for spiritual enlightenment, we should consciously confront those bodily impulses and emotions to overcome their overwhelming bodily and emotional influence to find the deeper meaning within. "Overcoming *P'o*" to reach wholeness in the Taoist way is achieved through meditation and, in the Jungian way, through analysis. As von Franz says:

> This, in the last analysis, is the meaning of the cross in Christianity, or of the crucifixion; complete endurance of the conflict between violent emotions and their spiritual meaning. This spiritual meaning, however, reveals itself only when one confronts the conflict without reservation.[30]

Jung's and von Franz's readings of *Hun* and *P'o* have given the old Chinese concept a modern meaning. An individual's gender psychology can be considered when reading Chinese spiritual texts. Also, like von Franz, we can redefine the meaning of "overcoming *P'o*", which is not meant to suppress bodily sensations and emotions, but rather to hold the tension coming from the unconscious through the body so it can emerge and have a spiritual meaning. So body and spirit, *P'o* and *Hun*, can come together and create a new meaning in our modern life. In that way, the traditional attitude in Chinese religion that suppresses women and the body can find a new place in modern consciousness.

*Return (*Hui*)*

Like *Hun* and *P'o*, the character *Hui* has been misread and misunderstood and created a maze of disagreement and confusion to work through.

The main concept of *The Secret of the Golden Flower* is to teach people to recognize the need to reverse the flow of life energy and the method for reversing it. The life libido, which naturally flows outward, needs to be guided inward to bring life back to the source of universe. Only through reversing the natural way can universal wisdom be received, and personal life be prolonged or even become immortal. Therefore, the core of the Golden Flower can be described by using one Chinese character *Hui*, meaning "return". *Hui* is not the only character that has repeatedly appeared in the text; other characters, with similar meaning, were also used frequently throughout the whole text, such as the Chinese character *Ni* (against) and *Fain* (going back). The first chapter of the text states that the method for finding the true self "depends entirely on the backward-flowing movement".[31] The strong emphasis on the inward and return concept is related to the centre, which reflects the Taoist spiritual concern for preserving human life. According to Taoism, the natural way of life, completely attached to the external world, exhausts one's energy and brings sickness, ageing, and death. This can be avoided if people practise the meditation of reverting life energy.

Hui in Chinese can have many different meanings, but the two most commonly used are (1) "to return, to go back to", which emphasizes reverse

Figure 8.3 Hui.

motion; and (2) "to wind, to circle, to rotate", which emphasizes the continuing circulation of movement. Interestingly, Wilhelm and Cleary each chose different meanings for *Hui* in their translations of the *Golden Flower*.[32] Wilhelm chose "circulation", and Jung followed this concept, bringing "mandala" into his reading and elaborating it beautifully in his commentary.[33] And Cleary chose "return and reverse" representing the regression movement of the life flow.

If we trace the ancient form of *Hui*, its earliest representation was found in oracle-bone script. Later, this pictographic character changed little in its form. It appeared as two circles,  or , representing swirls of water. It is the original meaning of "circulation". *Hui*, from the image of a swirling river or pond indicates a circulating motion and that motion's continuing nature. The character is also related to water and cloud, which gives it the meaning of "eternity". The *Hui* character is not only a word with its corresponding meaning but also one of the most commonly carved patterns used in ancient decoration for crockery. From *Hui*'s strong connection with the water image, we can read its symbolic meaning related to human unconsciousness. No matter how far we go, to return to the source of life, the Self, and the Golden Flower, we need to follow the water way, the path of the unconscious to reach its eternal truth.

Figure 8.4 Echo.

In the latest study of oracle-bone scripts, Chinese researcher Qiang Hua[34] identifies one character that was later included in one of the multiple meanings of *Hui*. This character was created to emphasize the circulation of sound. This form of *Hui* can be directly translated into English, meaning "echo". This pictographic character is a combination of a cliff on the left part, and an ear on the right part. The picture represents a person standing in front of a high rocky cliff, listening.

In *The Secret of the Golden Flower*, the importance of hearing is mentioned. The function of the ear is not to hear the sound from outside; rather it is used to hear the sound from inside. The text calls this kind of hearing "the Light of the ear".[35] In meditation, practitioners are trained to do attentive hearing in order to regulate their breathing. By concentrating on their hearing, practitioners can reach the level of no breathing sound, which is regarded as the highest level of hearing. By listening to the inner no-sound, the highest goal of hearing is reached, which is the meaning of the illumination of the ear.

In the symbol for *Hui*, I found the translation of echo especially meaningful. My experience of studying this Taoist text has corresponded with what this character represents. I was like that primordial man who stood in front of a high cliff, listening attentively. He extended his ears and tried to determine the source of the sound. It might be from something behind or around him or from inside himself.

The word "echo" symbolizes my experience of reading Jung's reflection on *The Secret of the Golden Flower.* The huge echo swam through space and time across thousands of miles and years. In between modern Chinese reality and Jungian depth psychology, I suddenly stood in the same position as my ancestor in 1400 BCE when this word was created. I extended my ears to hear the sound echoing from the high cliff of Jung's writing. Where is the source of the sound? It is from me, or from my ancestors whom I left behind for a long time in order to find my own way of being in the modern world. Now I hear the echo, so I turn my hearing inward, trying to hear the sound of no-sound, the sound from remote antiquity, coming from my ancestor's spirit.

Reading Jung sheds light on old texts and has brought me to new ways of understanding. He drew nuances from these old texts, making them personally relevant. Between completely Westernized and traditional mentality, Jung demonstrated a modern, individualized, personal, and psychological way to understand the old knowledge. China, the central kingdom, had its soul moved out from its centre in the process of modernization. A personal journey that returns to one's cultural heritage can help the collective soul to go back to its centre. It is also how I return home.

Notes

1 In this chapter, *Chinese* indicates a shared cultural heritage that includes mainland China, Hong Kong, Taiwan, southern Asia, and overseas Chinese communities.

2 Richard Wilhelm, *The Secret of the Golden Flower: A Chinese Book of Life*, trans. Carly F. Bayners, London, Routledge & Kegan Paul, 1957.

3 C. G. Jung, "Commentary on *The Secret of the Golden Flower*", in *Psychology and the East*, pp. 3–58, trans. R. F. C. Hull, Princeton, NJ, Princeton University Press, 1978, p. 57.

4 Ibid., p. 51.

5 J. J. Clarke, *The Tao of the West: Western Transformation of Daoist Thought*, London & New York, Routledge, 2000; Thomas Cleary, *The Taoist Classics – The Collected Translations of Thomas Cleary*, vol. 3, Boston, Shambhala, 2003; Caifang Jeremy Zhu, "Analytical psychology and Daoist inner alchemy: a response to C. G. Jung's 'Commentary on *The Secret of the Golden Flower*' ", *Journal of Analytical Psychology*, 2009, vol. 54, pp. 493–511.

6 Cleary, *The Taoist Classics.*

7 Clarke, *The Tao of the West*, p. 127.

8 H. Jing, "An analysis on the significance of Jung's commentary on *The Secret of the Golden Flower*", *History of Chinese Philosophy*, 1999, vol. 3, pp. 102–12; H. Y. Shen, "Jung and China: the continued dialogue", *Academic Studies*, 2004, vol. 11, pp. 23–5; L. Y. Zhang, "The Daoist cultural origin of Jung's analytical Psychology", *Journal of Hengyang Normal University* (Social Sciences), 1999, vol. 20, no. 5, pp. 19–27.

9 Rur-Bin Yang, *The Secret of the Golden Flower – Introduction of Taoist Alchemy*, Taipei, Shundin Publisher, 2002.

10 This version of *The Secret of the Golden Flower* includes Liu, Hua-yang. *Hui Ming Ching (The Book of Consciousness and Life)*, translated into German by L. C. Lo, *Chinesische Blatter*, vol. 3, no. 1, published by Richard Wilhelm.

11 C. G. Jung, "Foreword to the I Ching", in *Psychology and the East*, trans. R. F. C. Hull, pp. 189–208, Princeton, NJ, Princeton University Press, 1978, p. 192.
12 C. G. Jung, "In memory of Richard Wilhelm", in Wilhelm, *The Secret of the Golden Flower*, p. 151.
13 C. G. Jung, *Memories, Dreams, Reflections*, recorded and edited by Aniele Jaffé, New York, Random House, 1963/1989, p. 265.
14 Some Chinese historians trace the start of the New Culture Movement to 1915, based on the movement led by Chang Du Shua who started his cultural discourse in his magazine published in 1915. Y. S. Ling, *The Creative Transformation of Chinese Tradition*, Peking, Joint Publishing Company Limited, 1996.
15 Jung, "In memory of Richard Wilhelm", p. 139.
16 Weiming Tu, "The Confucian world", presented at Colorado College 125th Anniversary Symposium, "Cultures in the twenty-first century: conflicts and convergences", Colorado, 1999.
17 Ibid.
18 Jung, "Commentary", p. 51.
19 The translation of Chinese characters in this article is based on Wilhelm's version.
20 Hua Qiang, *Comparative Research of Oracle-bone Inscriptions*, China, Shanxi Publishing Group, Sei Chin Company, 2011.
21 Jung, "Commentary"; Wilhelm, *The Secret of the Golden Flower*.
22 Cleary, *The Taoist Classics*; Marie-Louise von Franz, *On Dreams and Death: A Jungian Interpretation*, Chicago, Open Court Publishing Company, 1998.
23 The calligraphy in this chapter was drawn by calligrapher Yi Tun Chan.
24 Cleary, *The Taoist Classics*, p. 328.
25 Jung, "Commentary", p. 114.
26 Ibid., p. 115.
27 Ibid., p. 116.
28 Ibid., p. 116.
29 Von Franz, *On Dreams and Death*, p. 119.
30 Ibid., p. 119.
31 Wilhelm, *The Secret of the Golden Flower*, p. 24.
32 Ibid.; Cleary, *The Taoist Classics*.
33 Jung, "Commentary", p. 96.
34 Qiang, *Comparative Research*.
35 Wilhelm, *The Secret of the Golden Flower*, p. 45.

9

PHILOSOPHY, THE THINKING FUNCTION, AND THE READING OF JUNG

George B. Hogenson

The invitation to contribute an essay for this book stimulated George Hogenson to reflect upon how he originally began his reading of Jung and how his reading has developed since the early 1970s. While preparing to write a doctoral dissertation, Hogenson drew on Jung's late work on synchronicity to better understand Leibnitz's interest in alchemy. He discovered, however, that Jung's work must be regarded as a coherent whole. Consequently, he returned to Jung's early work and wrote his dissertation on Jung's struggle with Freud. Currently, he sees Jung as an ongoing intellectual challenge and provocation. Jung does not propose a complete and finished theory of the psyche, but rather presents observations and hypotheses that ask later thinkers to take his theoretical constructs – such as archetypes, synchronicity, and the psychoid unconscious – as points of departure for further investigation. Hogenson urges us to bring Jung into a dialogue with both the history of science and ongoing scientific research.

J. K.

Sustained engagement with a single figure or text, particularly if it extends over the better part of a person's life, raises questions about the person's deepest intellectual commitments and passions. Early in my own work on Jung, my friend and teacher George Schrader may have come as close as anyone as to why I was embarking on what has been my life project ever since. George was, at the time, one of the leading Kant scholars in the world, and I had spent a great deal of time with him working on Kant's *Critique of Pure Reason*,[1] but now I was beginning to write my dissertation on Jung under the direction of George's colleague Rulon Wells, who was professor of both philosophy and linguistics. At a departmental party, George asked me what I was working on, and when I told him I had started on the Jung work with Rulon, his response was immediate: "That's just what I would expect from you two; you are the most rational human beings I know, so you spend all your time working on these irrational subjects." I doubt that anyone has made a more succinct formulation of the compensatory theory of the psyche and the notion of the unity of opposites, which are so central to Jung's system. George's comment, however, is also indicative of a point of view on typology, particularly the thinking function. Rulon Wells and I may have appeared uncommonly rational to George Schrader – a somewhat ironic state of affairs given that he had devoted his career to Kant's *Critique of Pure Reason* – but it is also the case that the thinking function, at least as I conceive of it, can be characterized by its openness, without prejudgement to virtually any subject or phenomenon that presents itself. This is in contrast to the feeling function, which, while also identified by Jung as a rational function, that is a function that can give an account of its form, practice, and conclusions, is nevertheless characterized by the distinctions and value-judgements it places on subjects and phenomena. As I consider my reading of Jung, beginning with my work with Rulon Wells, I believe the dominant point of view I bring to the enterprise is precisely this: the point of view of the thinking function. The phenomena, be they the relationship between Jung and Sigmund Freud or understanding the nature of the archetypes, present problems and occasions for thinking, but I rarely feel compelled to make value judgements as part of my response. Another sideways George Schrader comment, involving Rulon, further illustrates the point. Again, he was chiding me for undertaking the work on Jung, and I remarked in response that part of the pleasure of working with Rulon was that, as Bart Giamatti, at the time President of Yale, had remarked when I told him about my work, "Oh, well of course, Rulon knows everything." "Yes", George replied, displaying more than a little feeling function, "Rulon knows everything, but he can't tell the difference."

Notwithstanding George's occasional comments, Rulon Wells was known for his work on the philosophers Gottfried Wilhelm Leibniz and Charles Sanders Peirce, as well as the semiotics of Ferdinand de Saussure, on whom he wrote one of the first major studies in English. He also had an encyclopedic knowledge of esoteric materials ranging from medieval astrology to *glossolalia* – speaking in tongues. He had worked for years trying to decode the Voynich Manuscript in Yale's Beinecke Rare Book and Manuscript Library, and with his colleague Robert Brumbaugh he had compiled a definitive index of the oldest existing manuscripts of the works of Plato. As a linguist he was a fierce opponent of Noam Chomsky's generative linguistics, remarking to me once that if Chomsky was right his theory "would constitute a proof for the existence of God". Rulon Wells was and continues to be the single most important intellectual influence on my life.

Reading Jung I: from Leibniz to Freud

My own work with Wells, and also with Jung, began in a graduate seminar on Leibniz. In 1975 I returned to Yale's Graduate School after four years in the United States Air Force, moving from the Department of East Asian Languages and Literatures, where I had worked on Buddhism and modern

Japanese philosophy, to the Department of Philosophy proper where my work moved more directly into the Continental European tradition from Nicholas of Cusa to the phenomenologists and existentialists. It was in this context that I first encountered Jung as anything more than a passing acquaintance. My seminar paper on Leibniz dealt with his metaphysics of the "windowless monads". In the course of preparing the paper, I came upon evidence of Leibniz's association with the Nuremburg chapter of the Rosicrucians, a group associated with alchemical practices. This was an aspect of Leibniz's life that was almost universally ignored in philosophical circles, much as Newton's involvement with alchemy was ignored. I had recently read Betty Jo Teeter Dobbs's book on Newton's alchemy[2] and its role in his scientific thinking, and wondered whether there was any corresponding influence on Leibniz. Indeed, once I began to examine actual alchemical texts, it became evident that windows, open or closed, play an important role in the art. Foremost among the window metaphors in alchemy is the window on eternity or *fenestra aeternitatis*, associated by alchemists like Gerhard Dorn with the philosopher's stone but also, theologically, with the Virgin Mary as mediatrix. The issue in both instances is a notion of some direct means of access to the eternal or transcendence of the temporal world. What was striking about Leibniz's metaphor, therefore, was what appears to be a foreclosure of direct access to the transcendent or eternal dimensions of experience that had figured prominently in medieval mysticism.

As I continued to examine Leibniz's relation to the esoteric traditions of the Renaissance, his philosophical and mathematical investigations revealed other unexpected aspects. The term *calculus*, which Leibniz likely borrowed from Albertus Magnus (*c.*1200–80), is also a veiled reference to the philosopher's stone. Similarly, Leibniz's development of the binary number system, which eventually became the basis for the digital computer and the entire digitization of our culture, was first conceived of by Leibniz as a proof for God's creation of the world out of nothingness. The motto on a medallion that he used to announce the number system was "*Omnibus ex nihilo ducendis sufficit unum*" ("To derive everything from nothing, unity suffices").[3] What is important about this background in seventeenth- and early eighteenth-century philosophy is that it marks a genuinely decisive transition in relation to both God – or the eternal/spiritual – and the world. What one most commonly hears in discussions of modern philosophy is that the dissolution of the classical worldview lies with Descartes and his separation of *res cogitans* from *res extensa*, in other words, the separation of the mind from the body. But an equally important move derives from Leibniz and his notion that the monads first of all contain representations of the totality of the world – albeit in varying degrees of clarity and distinctness all the way up to God, who perceives with perfect clarity and distinctness – and second that the monads are closed or windowless. What happens here is that we get the first concerted argument that leads to an inquiry into interiority and the foreclosure of the eternal. Despite Leibniz's deep religious commitments, after his metaphysics has been put in place, mind turns in upon itself.

Roughly 60 years after Leibniz's death, Immanuel Kant took Leibniz's intuition to its logical conclusion when he argued in the *Critique of Pure Reason* that our knowledge of the world is a function of what we would now call *cognitive structures* in the brain.[4] Additionally, while modernity may have started with Copernicus, Kepler, and Galileo, who mathematized the heavens, with Leibniz we begin to see the mathematization of the mind as well – at least that would be the consequence of his binary number system once it was applied to a thinking machine by John von Neumann. What you have, in other words, is the emergence of an argument to the effect that the analysis of the world rests on an analysis of interior states, that is to say, the beginning of a depth psychology. You also have the beginning of what will appear to many, by the end of the nineteenth century, as a profound crisis in the Western or European comprehension of the world brought on not only by the mechanization of the material world but also by the mechanization of the interior world.[5]

Where does Jung fit into this, and why does this story provide reasons for reading Jung? First of all, in what was in retrospect perhaps a bit of hermeneutical sleight of hand, I proposed that Leibniz's windowless monads represented a closure of the *fenestra aeternitatis*, the window on eternity. By cutting human experience off from access to the eternal, he opened up a new way of thinking about the problematic of time, the ancient question of the relationship of time to eternity. It was at this point that I first engaged Jung – naively, but instructively. I felt I needed some source from outside the existing philosophical commentary on Leibniz to act as a reference point for the argument I was constructing, and I knew just enough about Jung to be familiar with his paper on synchronicity[6] and the fact that he had worked on alchemy. I also came upon a copy of Maria Louisa von Franz's *Number and Time*,[7] which is an attempt at an explication of Jung's very late work within a framework of Jung's – and von Franz's – relationship with Wolfgang Pauli. What was clear to me in both these sources was the centrality of the problematic of time in Jung's thinking. Jung claimed that his theory of synchronicity was prefigured in Leibniz. Therefore, Jung provided a valuable counterpoint and perspective on the question of time in Leibniz and thereby within the modern tradition.

The next step in my own reading of Jung was my dissertation, which was directed by Wells and prompted George Schrader's ironic comment. My first inclination was to go no further with Jung, but in conversations with Rulon, it became clear that a dissertation on Jung was plausible and, in particular, of interest to him. Rulon had already directed dissertations on Freud and on Jacques Lacan, and as he put it to me, he wanted to learn Jung. By this time, I was fascinated with the alchemical texts I had found in the Beinecke

Library, and Rulon and I first thought it was possible to take up Jung's relationship to the alchemists and to Gnosticism, essentially skipping over earlier materials. This was, needless to say, a mistaken notion, and we soon abandoned it. What was important about this misstep, which has informed my understanding of Jung ever since, is that Jung really needs to be read as a whole; it is deeply misleading to see him as segmented in some way at critical transition points, such as the writing of *The Red Book*.

What did develop in the writing of the dissertation, and its subsequent publication as *Jung's Struggle with Freud*,[8] was the importance of Jung's contentious relationship with the founder of psychoanalysis. Sonu Shamdasani has argued, correctly, that Jung's background and many of his theoretical proposals originated independently of his relationship with Freud.[9] Although this is undoubtedly true, the case can also be made that, for both Freud and Jung, the relationship they had between 1906 and 1913 was pivotal for their future development. My argument in the dissertation was built on this premise, which, in my reading of the relationship, devolved on the question of how to define the nature of the unconscious and particularly what I argued were several critical points of controversy between Freud and Jung on fundamental issues regarding the nature of the psyche. The major questions I identified at this early point involved the relationship of the unconscious to time; the relationship between images, such as dream images and language; and the relationship between repression and projection as the principal mechanism of unconscious activity.

These three issues actually fit together, rather like matryoshka dolls, and inform one another in important and intricate ways. One of the more startling claims made by Freud, and with which Jung partially concurred, is that the unconscious is, in some sense, timeless. Freud argued that drives or desires that are repressed at an early age do not change over time once they are resident in the unconscious. This argument forms the basis for his larger theoretical and clinical assertions regarding repression and the analytic process of releasing repressed drives. Freud's model, or topography, of the unconscious, particularly his early model that includes the censorship, demands that in order to seek discharge these repressed drives first express themselves as images. It is the analyst's task to bring them to language in order to comprehend their meaning fully. Jung, at the time of his relationship with Freud, accepted Freud's contention that the unconscious was in some sense timeless, but where Freud saw the unconscious as only the repository of repressions from the past, Jung, as early as his dissertation, posited a teleological dimension to the unconscious. In other words, for Jung, the timeless unconscious contained potential developmental trajectories in addition to repressions of past desires and drives. Similarly, this teleological aspect of the unconscious relativized Freud's argument for the primacy of repression in the psychic economy and posited the workings of a kind of projection that was not dependent on prior repressions. Jung's view on this matter was much closer, in fact, to a position that would be argued 20 years later by Martin Heidegger in *Being and Time*,[10] in which the individual – *Dasein* – projects him- or herself into the future. Finally, for Jung, due to his rejection of Freud's arguments for the censorship and the essential distortion of dream materials and myths, the image came to enjoy its own autonomy and integrity. Eventually, Jung would bring all of these elements together in his mature system, in which he argued that the collective unconscious contains, in the form of the archetypes, essentially atemporal patterns that give rise to the symbolism of dreams and cultural phenomena such as the great religions. This makes the unconscious into something akin to a realm of the eternal without God.

Looking back on this early period of my reading of Jung, it is clear that the larger issues that shaped the philosophical and cultural discourse of European philosophy into the 1970s and 1980s significantly influenced my point of view. In 1971, as I was about to leave Yale to enter the Air Force, I had stopped by the offices of Yale University Press to see what new works were available and walked out with Paul Ricoeur's just published Terry Lectures, *Freud and Philosophy*.[11] This extraordinary work became one of my most closely read texts in the four years I was away from Yale, and reading it was probably instrumental, in ways I did not at the time understand, in opening me up to the possibility of working on psychoanalysis more broadly. Ricoeur, however, completely neglected the relationship between Freud and Jung, confessing in a footnote that he could not make sense of Jung. Nevertheless, the problem that Ricoeur addressed in relation to Freud centred on the function of the symbol, particularly in relation to the understanding of religion in modernity. As I began to understand more about Jung in relation to Freud, I saw these issues as central to their relationship, going so far as to argue that both men were, in effect, proposing competing cosmologies, complete visions of the nature of reality and the human ability to inhabit and understand reality.

Additionally, it seemed to me, as it still does, that Freud was proposing a particularly closed system of understanding that rested on his self-analysis in ways that were scientifically illegitimate and essentially authoritarian in nature. For Jung, it seemed to me, as it still does, that Freud's closure of the unconscious, his insistence that the insights of his personal journey were normative for all others, notwithstanding contrary data and experience, was inimical to both the scientific understanding of the unconscious and successful understanding of the vicissitudes of modernity. At the same time, it seemed that wherever one looked Freud was being hailed as the great liberator of modernity, the hero who had revealed the dark underbelly of repression. Whether in the form of Jürgen Habermas or Jacques Lacan, Freud was the touchstone for liberation. The deeper I delved into Freud's own work, and into his relationship with Jung, the more convinced I became – and remain – that this view of Freud was among the most deeply misguided intellectual constructs of the twentieth century. To be clear, this point of view is not intended to relieve Jung of his personal responsibility for actions he took, for example, in the 1930s, or for his frequently disturbing comments on events and people. The argument lay at the time, and still does, in the nature of the systems of interpretation and the view of the psyche proposed by the two men, not necessarily the particulars of their personal lives. It is the case, however, that during the rise of the Nazi party in Germany, it was not only Jung who became engaged with that particular evil in order to advance personal and institutional interests, but also Freud himself, working through Ernest Jones, who attempted to use the Nazis to pursue political objectives within the psychoanalytic movement.[12]

This overview might be called, "Why I Still Read Jung, Part 1". It does seem to me that the history of psychoanalysis, regardless of one's ideological commitments, is unintelligible without carefully working through the relationship between Freud and Jung. The dimensions of this relationship, brief though it was, were of singular importance for the further development of Freud's work, as we can see in a careful reading of the papers on metapsychology, and on Jung's further development. I argue in my book on their relationship that Jung's break with Freud compelled Jung to establish new foundations for his own work and self-understanding, and I believe the recent publication of *The Red Book* points to precisely this undertaking on his part.[13] Further, I would argue that, insofar as Freud is one of the most dominant figures in the development of late twentieth-century psychological, philosophical, and even political theory, it is essential, again, to understand the full scope of the relationship he had with Jung and the challenge to traditional readings of Freud that an appreciation of that relationship presents.

Interlude

I completed my PhD in 1979, an unusually bad employment year for aspiring academics, particularly philosophers who had just written dissertations on Jung and Freud. Fortunately, my four years of active duty in the Air Force, as well as four years as a reserve officer in the Office of the Secretary of Defense at the Pentagon while I was in graduate school, provided a different set of credentials and opportunities, and I took a position as assistant professor of management in Yale's School of Organization and Management, teaching courses on organizational politics and general management. My military experience had initially involved working directly with nuclear weapons and then moved into first theatre and later strategic planning. Shortly after joining the faculty at the School of Management, I was also given a joint appointment at Yale's Institution for Social and Policy Studies, where I formed and chaired the faculty research seminar on international security policy and arms control. This seminar was prompted in large part by the recently arrived Reagan administration's decisions regarding the placement of a new generation of medium-range ballistic missiles in Europe – the Pershing II – and the concern among many strategic thinkers that this was a singularly dangerous escalation of the arms race. Although I was able to rework my dissertation on Jung and Freud for publication in 1983, my teaching responsibilities and work with the arms control seminar preempted further formal work on Jung, although I continued my reading of the *Collected Works* and other Jungian materials.

In 1986, I left Yale to become Assistant Director of the Program on Peace and International Security at the John D. and Catherine T. MacArthur Foundation in Chicago. In this role I found myself, among other responsibilities, administering much of the initial funding for the recently established Santa Fe Institute, under the guidance of the physicist Murray Gell-Mann, a member of the Foundation's board of directors. This brought me into direct contact with the still relatively new fields of complex adaptive systems, the somewhat misnamed "chaos theory", artificial life, and other related innovations in analysis and modelling. The work being done on artificial life was particularly interesting to me, as it appeared to hold the promise of insight into living systems that are intrinsically very complex, nonlinear – that is without simple linear causal links – and developmental in a new and provocative way. These systems displayed "emergent" properties. Significant new research and theorizing related to evolutionary theory was also on the agenda at the Institute, and I found myself reading extensively the work of theoreticians such as Stuart Kauffman.[14] It appeared to me that it was at least possible that some of this material could inform psychology, and that it would be worth investigating the degree to which the entire field of complexity studies might shed light on Jung's work.

In 1989, my friend William Borden, who had worked on me for some time to move beyond my historical and theoretical interest in Jung and Freud, finally persuaded me to take a clinical course at the University of Chicago's School of Social Service Administration. I, therefore, took an evening course on adult psychopathology and became immediately fascinated with the actual clinical application of psychological theory. Shortly thereafter I left the Foundation and completed my degree in clinical social work at the University. In 1994, I was admitted to the Analyst Training Program at the C. G. Jung Institute of Chicago and completed my training in 1998. My thesis at the Institute, "The Baldwin Effect: A Neglected Influence on Jung's Evolutionary Thinking" marked my first sustained attempt to address Jung in 15 years. Much of the inspiration for the thesis derived from further reading in the literature regarding emergence, including papers by the Jungian analyst David Tresan[15] and the anthropological neuroscientist Terrence Deacon.[16] That same year, while on my way to attend the Congress of the International Association for Analytical Psychology in Florence, Italy, I spent a week at the Eidgenössische Technische Hochschule (ETH) in Zurich, attending a conference of the International Society for Adaptive Systems, which is one of the leading organizations for the study of artificial life, including robotics, where I was able to observe closely some of the latest research demonstrations in this developing field. It was also at this conference that I first encountered the work of Horst Hendricks-Jansen, whose meticulous work on theoretical robotics and cognitive science continues to influence my own thinking.[17] This experience would crystallize much of my thinking about Jung and set the path for further work.

Reading Jung II: Jung, science, and the psyche

In 1906, Jung initiated his correspondence with Freud by sending a copy of his recently published papers on the word association test.[18] What was important about these papers, and initially established the relationship between the two men, was that Jung's experiments appeared to provide evidence for Freud's controversial theory of repression. Freud and his followers often maintained that it was his proposals regarding infantile sexuality that first prompted objections to his theories, but at least within the medical community of the time, the manifest sexual curiosity and behaviour of children were hardly a mystery. It is important to keep in mind when reading Freud that the idea of "infancy" extended to about age five at this time, rather than being confined to the first year or so of life as is more common today. What did present a problem was repression as Freud conceived of it. Jung, in his experiments, was finding evidence of significant distortions in response to the word association test, but more to the point, on questioning his subjects about the words that had caused the greatest distortion, he uncovered forgotten memories and associative patterns that had many of the qualities of some form of repression. At the same time, as Jung remarked to Freud, he was finding evidence that seemed to contradict the univocally sexual etiology of the neurosis. Freud, of course, was undeterred by Jung's contrary findings, and assured Jung that he would eventually understand that he, Freud, was correct in his arguments. Nevertheless, Jung's research into the word association test had already established his reputation as the rising young star in psychiatry, which was also enhanced by his position at the prestigious Burghölzli hospital in Zurich. As John Kerr argued in his detailed study of the relationship between Jung, Freud, and Sabina Spielrein, at the time of their meeting Freud needed Jung more than Jung needed Freud.[19]

The word association test, however, is important for reasons other than the relationship between Freud and Jung. In the context of Jung's early development, the test stands as a counterpoint to his dissertation on somnambulistic phenomena[20] and as a bridge to his later work, beginning with his study of dementia praecox.[21] The notoriety that Jung's work on the test enjoyed was also a tribute to the rigour Jung and his colleagues applied to the test and to Jung's extension of the test beyond the simple study of associations into a much larger set of indicators and a more sophisticated interpretation of the test results as diagnostic indicators. Jung's own commitment to the significance of the test can be measured by his quite detailed review of his findings almost 20 years later in the first of his Tavistock Lectures.[22] In a comprehensive review of the history of the word association test, Manfred Spitzer outlines in detail the contribution Jung made to the development of the test and the degree to which he moved the test to a high level of precision.[23] Spitzer notes that Jung's work on dementia praecox and the word association test likely had a significant impact on Eugen Bleuler's development of his understanding of schizophrenia as a disorder of the associative process,[24] which can also be seen in Jung's study of the disorder.

What is also important about the word association test, however, is the role it plays in defining Jung's attitude toward research in analytical psychology. The test, and its refinement, in terms of its scope and precision – both in administration and in the analysis of results, which was statistically quite sophisticated for the time – point to Jung's deep commitment to rigorous, genuinely scientific research in addition to the acute observational – phenomenological – studies of specific individuals and disorders as in his dissertation and the dementia praecox study. In terms of why I still read Jung, and how I read him, this aspect of his approach has influenced much of my thinking and work for the last 10 to 15 years.

Jung had begun his career while still a student with his critical comments in the so-called Zophingia Lectures on the mechanistic psychology of the late nineteenth century,[25] and as Anne Harrington has clearly spelled out, Jung was largely committed to the ideals of those late nineteenth- and early twentieth-century German thinkers who sought a "reenchantment of science".[26] But this ideal did not preclude rigorous research, and among those Harrington reviews were the early ethologists and several important psychologists, some of whom Jung knew personally. Seeing Jung in this context opens the door to understanding his quite consistent, albeit often frustrating attempts to underwrite parts of his theoretical development with references to possible natural scientific foundations. This effort on his part includes a variety of references to possible biological or evolutionary explanations for such phenomena as archetypal images and culminates late in his life with the extended correspondence with the quantum physicist Wolfgang Pauli.[27]

Beginning with reflections on Jung based on the work I was doing with the Santa Fe Institute, while at the MacArthur Foundation, and coming to fruition first in my thesis at the Chicago Institute, my own reading of Jung has been strongly oriented to the questions of whether and how one can make sense of Jung's theoretical constructs, such as archetypes, synchronicity, and the symbolic, within a contemporary scientific framework. Probably the most noteworthy instance of this process came at the Congress of the IAAP in Cambridge, England, in 2001, where I debated with the British analyst Anthony Stevens on the question of how to view Jung's work in terms of biology and evolution.[28] Stevens was, at the time, the leading exponent of a strongly evolutionary reading of the theory of archetypes, based on his own reading of what was then called *socio-biology*, a term coined by the Harvard entomologist, E. O. Wilson. I had read Stevens's book, *Archetype: A Natural History of the Self* when it first appeared in 1982[29] and found it to be a very interesting and provocative argument. By 2001, however, I had become quite sceptical of what by then was called *evolutionary psychology*. The essential elements of this scepticism derived not only from straightforward critiques of evolutionary psychology, of which there were a number, but also from my growing understanding of the interaction among various disciplines regarding neuroscience, linguistics, complex systems, theoretical robotics, and artificial life.

This catalogue of disciplines points to a particular problem in reading not only Jung, but also psychoanalysis in general, that I think is important to highlight. If there is a single book I would recommend reading before embarking on any attempt to explicate Jung in terms of the natural sciences, it would be Patricia Kitcher's *Freud's Dream: A Complete Interdisciplinary Science of Mind*.[30] Kitcher is professor of the philosophy of science at Columbia University, and her book is not really intended to be a study of Freud so much as a commentary on the rise of interdisciplinary research generally. Freud, however, provides, as Kitcher argues, a singular test case for her analysis. To oversimplify a quite detailed examination of Freud's sources, Kitcher argues that Freud fell into a trap by assuming that the sciences upon which he drew for theoretical purposes were relatively stable in terms of their essential findings and formulations. Unfortunately for Freud, this was not the case, pretty much across the board. The most striking example of Freud's dilemma as time passed was his commitment to a Lamarckian view of evolution. Jean-Baptiste Lamarck, of course, had proposed a theory of evolution based on the inheritance of acquired characteristics, and Freud relied on this notion to underwrite several essential elements of his theory, most notably to establish the foundations for the theory of repression in *Totem and Taboo*.[31] It is important to understand that Freud's acceptance of Lamarckian principles was hardly extraordinary at the time, as even Darwin had a Lamarckian element in his theory. It was only around 1900, with the work of the embryologist August Weismann and the rediscovery of Mendel's work on genetics, that Lamarckism was finally forced out of theories of inheritance and evolution, but by then, Freud was so deeply dependent on Lamarckian principles that he could not retreat from them without jeopardizing his entire system. Kitcher's analysis of Freud's theoretical debts to the other sciences extends this problem to almost all aspects of his system, calling into question most of Freud's theoretical propositions.

The real issue, however, and the purpose of Kitcher's cautionary tale, is that whenever one ventures into interdisciplinary work, which is essentially what we do when we read Jung or Freud through the prism of one or another of the natural sciences, we are venturing into territory that is inherently ambiguous to the non-specialist and probably highly unstable. I would add to her argument the increasing degree to which the sciences themselves have become interdisciplinary. This feature of a movement such as evolutionary psychology is one of the reasons Anthony Stevens and I came to have the debate we had. Evolutionary psychology is not a simple science along the lines of physics, but is rather an amalgam of evolutionary theory and cognitive science. Cognitive science, as it was conceived at the time evolutionary psychology appropriated it, was largely based on early research on artificial intelligence (AI) and adopted a model of information processing derived from computer science, the key element of which was the execution of computational algorithms to solve problems, a point of view based on the work of the mathematician Alan Turing. But by the mid-1980s, theoreticians such as Rodney Brooks[32] and Rolf Pfeifer[33] were questioning the algorithmic AI models for at least some functions, particularly functions that actually modelled behaviour, such as getting robots to move through natural environments, rather than pure information processing as in AI systems for medical diagnosis.

In my debate with Anthony Stevens, my contention was that the ground had shifted so irrevocably under the evolutionary model of the archetypes as specifically proposed by Stevens that his position was no longer sustainable. Needless to say, he saw the matter differently, and, in one form or another, the debate has continued ever since. For a sense of how the debate progressed immediately after the Cambridge Congress, I recommend reading my exchange with Alan Maloney and Raya Jones concerning my paper on the Baldwin effect.[34] But the basic issue remains, in that a field like evolutionary biology and the collateral disciplines that depend on it are constantly undergoing revision, and unless one is willing to continually update one's understanding of those revisions, one is likely to end up like Freud when he was told by his followers that Lamarckism had been totally rejected by the biologists. "So much the worse for the biologists" is reputed to have been his response. The net result, however, as Kitcher makes clear, was that his metapsychology largely disappeared from psychoanalytic discourse after his death.[35]

In my own reading of the Jungian literature, my concern, which arises from this point of view on the sciences and psychoanalysis, is what I call *Jungian apologetics.* There is a class of Jungian literature, and I would include my own work in this, that seeks quite explicitly to ground Jung's theories in the larger frame of the natural sciences. This project began with Jung himself, as already noted, and continues today with a considerable array of researchers. However, the shadow side of this enterprise appears in those works where the author has basically cast about in the larger literature for a point of view that underwrites their preconceived interpretation of Jung, rather than survey the field sufficiently to understand the controversies and competing arguments that might alter their point of view. A common example of this was to point at Noam Chomsky's notion of innate grammatical structures as an argument for the innateness of archetypes, not realizing that Chomsky's theory was far from universally accepted in linguistics and had been attacked at an early point by some of Chomsky's own students, such as George Lakoff.[36] More recently, the work of Steven Pinker[37] has taken on a similar role in some attempts to put an evolutionary foundation under Jung's theories.[38] But again, Pinker's work has many critics with at least equal claim to an understanding of the details of evolution and language.[39]

While it is clearly important to remain in dialogue with the larger scientific community, as Jung himself sought to do, one essential feature of the dialogue has to be openness to the flux and change within that larger community. The shadow of Jungian apologetics is to try and link Jung to some favoured bit of research in the larger scientific community at the expense of careful and thorough examination of the field in question. This will only, in the end, diminish our own understanding of Jung and the value of his insights in the larger scientific discussion.

Why do I still read Jung?

Jean Kirsch's invitation to contribute to this volume presented one of those disquieting moments when one has to actually reflect on what one has taken for granted for a very long time. Why do I still read Jung? Of course, Jung has become part of my professional identity, at least since I finished training as a Jungian analyst and now make my living by trafficking in the Jungian approach to psychotherapy, but that is not in itself sufficient to explain the fascination that Jung does exercise on me. At the same time, I can say with some confidence that I do not find in Jung something like the answer to life's mysteries in some quasi-transcendent sense. My first reading of Jung did not have the revelatory impact some Jungians report, and I find discussions of Jung as some sort of epochal guru possessed of unique insight into resolving the travails of modernity deeply off-putting. On the other hand, I do think that George Schrader was probably on to something in his assessment of Rulon Wells and myself and why we would end up reading Jung in the first place, although I would modify his comment in some important ways.

First of all, I do not think that to study Jung is to study an irrational subject. Frankly, one of the striking features of Jung in my reading of him is how rational he actually is. What is curious about Jung is closer to what disturbed late nineteenth- and early twentieth-century psychologists about the late work of William James after James started his research into spirituality and other "occult phenomena". Even G. Stanley Hall, who had been James's student at Harvard, was fearful that James was going to end up discrediting academic psychology by way of these exotic investigations. James, on the other hand, argued that he was simply investigating phenomena that were manifestly present as psychological phenomena, regardless of their "metaphysical" status, and, therefore, worthy of investigation by psychologists. Jung's dissertation on so-called occult phenomena follows the same path, as is the case with many of his other observations.

The problem that Jung presents is not that he is irrational but that he does not really propose a complete and closed theory of the psyche. Rather I would argue that Jung presents a set of observations and hypotheses that are all too often taken to be final statements in a theory. This characteristic of Jung's work can be both intensely frustrating and intensely provocative at the same time, but I would suggest that it represents a continuation of Jung's attitude toward psychological research that was evident from the beginning in his relations with Freud. From the outset, Jung criticized Freud for imposing doctrine rather than proposing hypotheses and developing research programmes. Perhaps the best example of Jung's approach to the question of how hypotheses can be proposed and researched in analytical psychology is his discussion of synchronicity. While Jung had been thinking about synchronicity at least since the late 1920s, the most sustained discussion of the topic in Jung's work went on in the correspondence with Wolfgang Pauli[40] and their joint publication on synchronicity and the Kepler/Fludd debate.[41] Investigation of the problem of synchronicity continues to prompt new interpretations.[42] Joseph Cambray, in particular, shows how discussions of Jung's hypothetical proposals can undergo re-examination in the light of new findings, even in the area of quantum physics to which Jung and Pauli appealed in their correspondence, so long as they are taken to be hypotheses and not doctrines that require some sort of a priori justification – another way of framing the problem of apologetics. Cambray is one of the Jungian theoreticians who are associated with what can best be called the emergence model of interpreting Jung, among whom I count myself but also such theoreticians as Jean Knox, John Merchant, Maxson McDowell, and others. This group tends to take Jung's theoretical constructs – hypotheses – such as synchronicity, archetypes, and the psychoid unconscious, as points of departure for further investigation into the nature of the psyche. Many differences exist among these theoreticians, but the consistent element in all of them, I would suggest, is a greater emphasis on process or structure rather than definition of stable propositions. To that degree I would argue that the emergence model of Jungian theory is closer to Jung's own approach to research regarding the psyche.

With all of this in hand, I have to conclude that I am still reading Jung very much in the spirit with which I began, when Leibniz, perhaps one of the most disciplined and, if you will, rational philosophers suddenly showed another side to his carefully crafted metaphysics. Placing Jung in dialogue with Leibniz was my point of departure. I still believe that Jung in dialogue with both the tradition and ongoing scientific research is a constructive and worthwhile undertaking. Jung started his work at a critical moment of crisis in the history of the European sciences, to use Edmund Husserl's expression,[43] and as much as Freud, Husserl, Wittgenstein, or Heidegger warrant our detailed attention as we continue to sort out the nature of modernity, Jung will remain a compelling and essential figure.

Notes

1 I. Kant, *Critique of Pure Reason*, New York, Macmillan, 1929.
2 B. J. T. Dobbs, *The Foundations of Newton's Alchemy: or, "The Hunting of the Greene Lyon"*, Cambridge, Cambridge University Press, 1975.
3 F. Cajori, "Leibniz's image of creation", *The Monist*, 1916, vol. 26, pp. 557–65.
4 Kant, *Critique of Pure Reason*.
5 A. Harrington, *Reenchanted Science: Holism in German Culture from Wilhelm II to Hitler*, Princeton, NJ, Princeton University Press, 1996.
6 C. G. Jung, "Synchronicity: an acausal connecting principle", in *The Structure and Dynamics of the Psyche, The Collected Works of C. G. Jung* (hereafter *CW*), vol. 8, Princeton, NJ, Princeton University Press, 1952, pp. 419–519.
7 M.-L. von Franz, *Number and Time: Reflections Leading Toward a Unification of Depth Psychology and Physics*, Evenston, IL, Northwestern University Press, 1974.
8 G. B. Hogenson, *Jung's Struggle with Freud*, Notre Dame, IL, University of Notre Dame Press, 1983.
9 S. Shamdasani, *Jung and the Making of Modern Psychology*, Cambridge, Cambridge University Press, 2003.
10 M. Heidegger, *Being and Time*, Oxford, Basil Blackwell, 1967.
11 P. Ricoeur, *Freud and Philosophy: An Essay on Interpretation*, New Haven, CT, Yale University Press, 1970.
12 J. E. Goggin and E. B. Goggin, *Death of a "Jewish Science": Psychoanalysis in the Third Reich*, West Lafayette, IN, Purdue University Press, 2001; G. B. Hogenson, "Roazen, Paul. 'The exclusion of Erich Fromm from the IPA' ", *Journal of Analytical Psychology*, 2003, vol. 48, pp. 127–30; P. Roazen, "Psychoanalytic ethics: Freud, Mussolini and Edoardo Weissmann", *Journal of the History of the Behavioral Sciences*, 1991, vol. 27, pp. 366–74; and "The exclusion of Erich Fromm from the IPA", *Contemporary Psychoanalysis*, 2001, vol. 37, no. 1, pp. 5–42.
13 C. G. Jung, *The Red Book: Liber Novus*, ed. Sonu Shamdasani, New York, W. W. Norton & Company, 2009.
14 S. A. Kauffman, *The Origins of Order: Self Organization and Selection in Evolution*, New York, Oxford University Press, 1993.
15 D. I. Tresan, "Jungian metapsychology and neurobiological theory", *Journal of Analytical Psychology*, 1996, vol. 41, pp. 399–436.
16 T. W. Deacon, *The Symbolic Species: The Co-evolution of Language and the Brain*, New York and London, W. W. Norton, 1997.
17 H. Hendricks-Jansen, *Catching Ourselves in the Act: Situated Activity, Interactive Emergence, Evolution, and Human Thought*, Cambridge, MA, MIT Press, 1996; and "The epistemology of autism: making a case for an embodied, dynamic, and historical explanation", *Cybernetics and Systems*, 1997, vol. 28, no. 5, pp. 359–415.
18 C. G. Jung, *Diagnostische Assoziationsstudien. Beiträge zur experimentellen Psychopathologie*, Leipzig, J. A. Barth, 1906.

19 J. Kerr, *A Most Dangerous Method: The Story of Jung, Freud, and Sabina Spielrein*, New York, Knopf, 1993.
20 C. G. Jung, *On the Psychology and Pathology of So-called Occult Phenomena*, Princeton, NJ, Princeton University Press, 1900/1970.
21 C. G. Jung, "The psychology of dementia praecox", in *The Psychogenesis of Mental Disease*, *CW* 3, ed. W. McGuire, Princeton, NJ, Princeton University Press, 1907/1960, pp. 3–152.
22 C. G. Jung, "The Tavistock Lectures", in *The Symbolic Life*, *CW* 18, ed. W. McGuire, Princeton, NJ, Princeton University Press, 1935/1976.
23 M. Spitzer, "Word-associations in experimental psychiatry: a historical perspective", in M. Spitzer, F. A. Uehlein, M. A. Schwartz, and C. Mundt (eds.), *Phenomenology, Language and Schizophrenia*, New York, Springer-Verlag, 1992.
24 Ibid., p. 173.
25 C. G. Jung, *The Zofingia Lectures*, Princeton, NJ, Princeton University Press, 1983.
26 Harrington, *Reenchanted Science*.
27 S. Gieser, *The Innermost Kernel: Depth Psychology and Quantum Physics. Wolfgang Pauli's Dialogue with C. G. Jung*, Berlin, Springer, 2005; C. G. Jung and W. Pauli, *The Interpretation of Nature and the Psyche. Synchronicity: An Acausal Connecting Principle*, New York, Pantheon Books, 1955; C. A. Meier (ed.), *Atom and Archetype: The Pauli/Jung Letters, 1932–1958*, Princeton, NJ, Princeton University Press, 2001.
28 A. Stevens, G. B. Hogenson, and D. Ramos, "Debate: psychology and biology", in R. Hinshaw (ed.), *Cambridge 2001: Proceedings of the Fifteenth International Congress for Analytical Psychology*, pp. 367–77, Einsiedeln, Daimon Verlag, 2003.
29 A. Stevens, *Archetype: A Natural History of the Self*, New York, William Morrow, 1982.
30 P. Kitcher, *Freud's Dream: A Complete Interdisciplinary Science of Mind*, Cambridge, MA, MIT Press, 1995.
31 S. Freud, "Totem and taboo", in *The Standard Edition of the Complete Psychological Works of Sigmund Freud*, vol. 13, ed. J. Strachey, pp. 1–161, London, The Hogarth Press, 1913.
32 R. A. Brooks, *Cambrian Intelligence: The Early History of the New AI*, Cambridge, MA, MIT Press, 1999.
33 R. Pfeifer and C. Scheier, *Understanding Intelligence*, Cambridge, MA, MIT Press, 1999.
34 G. B. Hogenson, "The Baldwin effect: a neglected influence on C. G. Jung's evolutionary thinking", *Journal of Analytical Psychology*, 2001, vol. 46, pp. 591–611; R. A. Jones, "On innatism: a response to Hogenson", *Journal of Analytical Psychology*, 2003, vol. 48, pp. 705–18; A. Malony and G. B. Hogenson, "Archetypal theory, evolutionary psychology and the Baldwin effect: a commentary on Hogenson's paper", *Jounal of Analytical Psychology*, 2003, vol. 48, no. 1, pp. 101–16.
35 In "Moses and Monotheism", Freud wrote, regarding the rejection of Lamarckism, "This state of affairs is made more difficult, it is true, by the present attitude of biological science, which rejects the idea of acquired qualities being transmitted to descendants. I admit, in all modesty, that in spite of this I cannot picture biological development proceeding without taking this factor into account." S. Freud, "Moses and monotheism: three essays", in *The Standard Edition of the Complete Psychological Works of Sigmund Freud*, vol. 23, ed. J. Strachey, London, The Hogarth Press, 1939, p. 100.
36 G. Lakoff and M. Johnson, *Metaphors We Live By*, Chicago, University of Chicago Press, 1980.
37 S. Pinker, *The Language Instinct: How the Mind Creates Language*, New York, William Morrow, 1994; *How the Mind Works*, New York, Norton, 1997; and S. Pinker and P. Bloom, "Natural language and natural selection", *Behavioral and Brain Sciences*, 1990, vol. 13, pp. 707–84.
38 J. R. Haule, *Jung in the Twenty-first Century*, New York, Routledge, 2010.
39 Deacon, *The Symbolic Species*; Hendricks-Jansen, *Catching Ourselves in the Act*; J. Fodor,

"Review of Steven Pinker's *How the Mind Works* and Henry Plotkin's *Evolution in Mind*", in *Critical Condition: Polemical Essays on Cognitive Science and Philosophy of Mind*, Cambridge, MA, MIT Press, 1998, pp. 203–14.

40 Meier, *Atom and Archetype*.

41 C. G. Jung and W. Pauli, *Naturerklärung und Psyche. Synchronizität als ein Prinzip akausaler Zusammenhänge*, Zurich, Rascher, 1952.

42 J. Cambray, *Synchronicity: Nature and Psyche in an Interconnected Universe*, Lubbuck, TAMU Press, 2009; G. B. Hogenson, "The self, the symbolic and synchronicity: virtual realities and the emergence of the psyche", *Journal of Analytical Psychology*, 2005, vol. 50, pp. 271–84; R. Main, *The Rupture of Time: Synchronicity and Jung's Critique of Modern Western Culture*, London and New York, Brunner-Routledge, 2004; and *Revelations of Chance: Synchronicity a Spiritual Experience*, Albany, State University of New York Press, 2007.

43 E. Husserl, *The Crisis of European Sciences and Transcendental Phenomenology: An Introduction to Phenomenological Philosophy*, Evanston, IL, Northwestern University Press, 1970.

10

JUNG

Respect for the Non-literal

David Tacey

> An archetypal content expresses itself, first and foremost, in metaphors.
>
> C. G. Jung[1]

Through reading Jung as a young man, David Tacey discovered a path between the literal religious belief in which he had been raised and the only alternative he had previously seen open to him, atheism. In this passionate essay, he gives a brief historical account of literalism in Christian dogma and argues on behalf of a non-literal reading of Christian scripture, speaking in concert with Jung's insights and views on the reality of psychic experience of the Resurrection.

J. K.

"All thinking people are atheists"

I am drawn to Jung for religious insight as much as for psychological knowledge. For a period of time in my early adulthood, I was tossing and turning between going back to my childhood faith or accepting, with some reluctance, the seemingly inevitable fate of atheism. My sister, a few years older than me, had already made the leap into atheism. I found it audacious and startling. She told me that our family was behind the times to the tune of 150 years, and that "all thinking people are atheists now". She did not know it at the time, but she was quoting Mark Twain and Ernest Hemingway who had both said essentially the same thing. Would I, too, she asked, join her in jumping ship? When I was 16, she gave me numerous books to read on the subject, including works by Freud and Nietzsche, and *Irrational Man* by the existentialist William Barrett. I was impressed by this literature and wondered where my sister had found this material. My parents were not readers, did not belong to libraries, and discouraged reading because, my father said, "If you read too much you lose your faith". I think he was right in a way, and here I was, reading my sister's books and losing my religion. But my sister had not come across Jung.

Beyond belief vs. disbelief

I read Jung as a student at university, and he seemed to offer a way beyond the dilemma of believing versus disbelieving. The first paper I ever read by Jung was his "Two Kinds of Thinking",[2] which outlines the differences between *directed*, or conscious thinking, and *undirected*, or fantasy thinking. It struck me at the time that the second kind of thinking related directly to the language of myth and religion, and this gave me my first clue as to the language in which the gospels were written. I wanted to share this new point of view with my sister, but by the time I had developed enough facility with Jung to explain his approach to others, she was locked inside a mental illness and unable to engage me or anyone else in communication. She has stayed that way for many years, and I often feel bereft in this regard; we began a journey but she fell by the wayside and has been unable to continue. Sometimes I feel I am continuing the journey for her, even though she refuses dialogue on religious matters. She thinks religion is part of a worldwide conspiracy against good citizens and common sense, even though her own "sense" has, technically speaking, departed. So here am I, 40 years later, writing essays to share my knowledge with others. I write to maintain the dialogue that I have been unable to have with family members who were either too rigidly religious or else not religious enough. Religion is a wound in the psyche of the family, and I sense it is a wound in a great many people and families. I find that the wound heals over a little if I pay it respect and attention, as I shall try to do here.

Jung points to a third way beyond the clash of believing or disbelieving. His response is a surprising mixture of the two, but he sides with neither. Rather, he resolves the conflict at another level. He takes the "belief" factor of religion and the "critical questioning" of atheism and brings them together in a new synthesis, which might be called *critical spirituality*.[3] The statements of religion are, for him, not literally true, so he thinks the atheists are right on that score, but the statements are neither empty nor meaningless either, as atheists imagine. The statements of religion are to be read as symbols and metaphors, pointing to the reality of the spirit. Spiritual reality does not always express itself in physical acts or historical events, and so to this extent the literal-minded believers are wrong. Spiritual reality is not visible on the surface; it is the invisible deeper significance of what happens, which can only be expressed indirectly in symbol and image. The believers have lost their literalism, but would they take up the consolation prize of non-literal truth? More often than not, the answer is no.

Believers are often too strong-minded to be able to distance themselves from their beliefs to contemplate a non-literal approach. They are mesmerized by the archetypal images, and these hold them in a spell, which is, at the same time, a spell of concrete thinking. Being "under the influence" means they cannot imagine how they can be true apart from their literal meaning. That is why it often takes a dose of unbelief or atheism to get the symbolic function working. We have to lose our beliefs in order to find them. Unless we find a certain level of detachment and lose our magical thinking, we remain stuck in literalism, or, as Jung would put it, we remain unconscious of our beliefs. In the literal state, this business about a symbolic approach, or what Jung calls psychic reality, is just too intellectual by half. It is not even a consolation prize for the loss of literalism; it's a booby prize. For many of my religious associates and acquaintances, Jung is actually an atheist who dares to challenge the revealed Word of God. Jung might as well be Freud or Nietzsche, and he is coming from the same place. But for me, he is not. Jung knows his Freud and Nietzsche, and he respects these "great destroyers"[4] – and why they had to destroy so much. But he is aiming for a new approach to the gospel narratives, an approach through symbol and myth.

Jung considers the symbol far more than a consolation prize for those who discover that the virgin birth and physical resurrection are not literal events as is claimed. The symbol, for him, is the royal road to the sacred. It is "the best possible description of a relatively unknown fact",[5] "an expression for something that cannot be characterized in any other or better way".[6] Moreover, "whether a thing is a symbol or not depends chiefly on the attitude of the observing consciousness",[7] so here is a conundrum: unless we maintain reverence for the images, they no longer transport us to the places to which they point. This is why the loss of literalism is a potentially disastrous experience for many people: when the spell is broken, nothing is left. Images can only function as icons if we give them value, and in the post-literal state, value is often absent. The believer feels let down, deflated, and inclined to go into reverse, claiming that he or she has been duped by religion. Therefore, we have to work with diligence on educating the imagination, on restoring sacredness to the images independently of any claim to historicity.

Archetypes and hyperbole

Archetypes are the organs of myth, the elements that "link us back" to the primordial mind and ancient past. They are hampered by such literary modes as realism and naturalism and can only express themselves in florid and hyperbolic modes. In recent times, they have found expression in such styles and modes as surrealism, expressionism, primitivism, neo-romanticism, imagism, science fiction, magic realism, and mythic realism. It is the archetypes, and their need for expression, that keep the creative arts alive and looking for new ways to express psychic realities. In the time of Christ, the preferred literary modes were parable, miracles, and wonders, all of which are ancient forms of metaphor. This metaphorical style infuriates the literal-minded, but it will always keep doing so:

> It is not the world as we know it that speaks out of the mythical imagination, but the unknown world of the psyche, which moulds the empirical world in accordance with its own assumptions. The archetype does not proceed from physical facts, but describes how the psyche experiences the physical fact, and in so doing the psyche often behaves so autocratically that it denies tangible reality or makes statements that fly in the face of it.[8]

When statements are made that "fly in the face" of tangible reality, we know that archetypes are present, and we are in the presence of the holy. Thus, the virgin birth or physical resurrection are statements to be viewed in this way. To take them literally is absurd, according to Jung, and a sign of a poverty of imagination.

Religion as mythos

For Jung, the two kinds of thinking had already been discovered by the ancient Greeks. *Logos* is directed thinking, controlled by consciousness and used to describe reality in its outward, historical, and factual manifestation. *Mythos* is undirected thinking, which arises from the unconscious and spontaneously forces itself upon inspired writers and storytellers. The symbolic attitude derives from mythos, and it is this attitude that allows us to see the virgin birth and physical resurrection, for instance, as entrances into the mystery of being. To view these events as symbols does not close down faith but opens it up. It does not destroy religion, as many suppose, but allows it to return to its true basis in mythos. In "Answer to Job", Jung writes, "What is the use of a religion without a *mythos*, since religion means, if anything at all, precisely that function which links us back to the eternal myth?"[9]

Religion, he reminds us, derives from the Latin *religio*, meaning to link back. "This original form of *religio* ('linking back') is the essence, the working basis of all religious life even today, and always will be, whatever future form this life may take."[10] What religion links us back to is the sacred, the holy, that which is beyond awareness: "Religion is a vital link with psychic processes independent of and beyond consciousness, in the dark hinterland of the psyche."[11] We can only know this deeper reality indirectly, through metaphor and symbol. It is not that metaphors try to obscure or distort the real, but they seek to bring out its deeper dimension. As Jung put it, "The archetype does not proceed from physical facts, but describes how the psyche experiences the physical fact."[12] This is why metaphor is indispensable; it describes how the soul experiences a fact. This is the perspective we have lost today, which is why for us metaphors are said to hide the truth, and only historical facts reveal it.

But it actually works the other way around. We have confused the nature of the real by trusting far too much in logos. It is an overdose of logos that has made us unreceptive to the sacred and its symbolic languages. Religion and myth perform the vital function of reconnecting consciousness to its source, to a life independent of itself: "If this link-up does not take place, a kind of rootless consciousness comes into being no longer oriented to the past, a consciousness which succumbs helplessly to all manner of suggestions and, in practice, is susceptible to psychic epidemics."[13]

To lose our sacred myths and images is to lose our psychological health and well-being. Without them, we become rudderless, lacking purpose and direction in the universe. We become strangers to ourselves, and our life and identity suffer from this spiritual alienation. If governments understood how much our psychological health depends on the cultivation of a symbolic life, they would put far more emphasis on exploring the connections between mind and body, psyche and society, and cultural attitude and well-being.

But the problem we face is that myth is heavily discounted and not valued enough for its role in maintaining well-being. People say myth is "nothing but" illusion or myth is "merely" a product of the mind. As Jung puts it, "Where, exactly, does this immense prejudice come from?"[14] If we say that a myth or miracle is "nothing but" a symbol, this means we do not comprehend its meaning. The "nothing but" indicates our ignorance before a mystery that has not been discerned. Mythos is so undervalued that many see it as synonymous with lies, deception, or make-believe. It is, however, the genuine basis of all religions, but in the Christian West, it was removed from this basis around the third and fourth centuries. At that time, religious authorities tried to bolster the new faith, depriving it of its mythic qualities and changing it into history and fact. As a result, Jung writes:

> It has been assumed, perhaps as the result of a growing impatience with the difficult factual material, that Christ was nothing but a myth, in this case no more than a fiction. But myth is not a fiction: it consists of facts that are continually repeated and can be observed over and over again.[15]

This statement can be confusing for readers because Jung is talking about psychic facts, not physical facts. For him, psychic facts are real, and it is the psychic reality of the Christ story that interests him and that, he believes, has inspired so many human souls throughout the ages.

The mystery of incarnation and divine filiation

In Jung's view, Christianity was torn from its roots in mythos and placed, bleeding and wounded, on a platform of logos, as an incentive for people to adopt the new faith. In the third and fourth centuries, people had stopped believing in the gods of the Greco-Roman world, and the new religion wanted to present itself as factual. No more mythical gods on Mt Olympus;

here was a god who had become a man. Jung saw this claim as right and wrong. It was right insofar as God wanted to enter into closer relationship with the human and thus further the process of incarnation. It was inevitable that the divine would be brought closer to consciousness and not kept away from us in otherworldly figures. Jesus seemed to Jung a perfectly good example of this growing intimacy between humanity and God. In "Psychology and Religion", Jung refers to this increasing intimacy in these terms:

> The gods at first lived in superhuman power and beauty on the top of snow-clad mountains or in the darkness of caves, woods and seas. Later on they drew together into one god, and then that god became man. But in our day even the God-man seems to have descended from his throne and to be dissolving himself in the common man.[16]

But Christianity was wrong insofar as the process of incarnation was felt to be limited to *one* human, who was turned into an idol. This served the all-too-human need to project archetypal contents onto a charismatic figure, but it did not further the need to evolve a new consciousness in which each one of us is seen as the locus of the divine and, therefore, the "sons" and "daughters" of God.

Jung feels, however, that this transference of the God-image to Jesus served a historical purpose, because the realization that the divine is within reach of all of us was too great to be shared and known at the time. Consciousness would have burst its bounds, and the populace would have become terribly inflated. The Christian aeon was thus a "holding pattern", and this provisional condition, he feels, is necessarily falling apart in our time. We have had enough time to grow up; and even if we are not ready for it, a new era is dawning. God is "coming, ready or not" as children call in the playground. The Gnostics had foreshadowed this process all along, but they had been vilified and suppressed by Christianity. After the Gnostics, alchemy had kept the dream alive of the divine being born in the soul of the individual. Jung sees his own depth psychology in this lineage or tradition: an outcast tradition that now has to be brought into the scientific and intellectual mainstream.

In its early context, the literalism of the incarnation appealed to the desire to find a *better* religion, one which involved historical events rather than stories. The Roman empire was collapsing, and many wanted something to hold on to. A time of major cultural upheaval, of the "passing of the gods", is fraught with anxiety and fear. Because so much is collapsing and falling into ruins, people naturally look for solace and hope. Jung argues that Christianity dressed itself up as historical fact, and this phase lasted a remarkably long period of time. Even though it claimed to be historical, it was the "power of myth" that kept it alive, that held people entranced and caught by its spell. The mythic images were seductive, and

Jung refers to the "suggestibility" of the archetypes, which binds people to them with almost irrational force. The spell has broken in our time, but it lasted until the late Middle Ages. By the time we got to Meister Eckhart in the thirteenth century, the notion that the incarnation was exclusively limited to Jesus was blown to pieces. Eckhart was an early version of Jung to the extent that he called for all human beings to accept responsibility for their personal relationship to the divine. The literal phase of the Christian faith was over.

After the collapse of literalism

The historicized mythos of Christianity lasted while a number of things worked in its favour: the masses were uneducated; the religious authorities were unassailable and supreme; and science was in its infancy. It lasted, that is, so long as proponents of science and philosophy were able to be disciplined and punished by the authority of the church. But then there was a colossal shaking of the foundations. When people became educated, they could no longer swallow myth dressed up as history. When science blossomed and grew, it was the end of religion in its literal form. Like the *Titanic*, the ship of religion (mythos) hit the iceberg of reason (logos) and was ripped apart. There have been many casualties and few survivors. Over the last 200 years, people have deserted religion in prodigious numbers, with no intention of going back. As I look around at my colleagues at university, I see time and again the same pattern: those who had a religious upbringing, usually Jewish or Christian, have been forced to throw it out on attaining what could be called the "university mind", with its empiricism and devotion to reason. I can think of numerous colleagues who have traversed this pathway and who found that the religion of their background was devoid of meaning and utterly implausible.

In particular, I am conscious of a number of my colleagues who were former Catholic priests, and they often seem more aggressively antireligious than many of the others. Jung has an interesting insight on the ex-Catholic priests and their newly discovered atheism: "The Catholic who has turned his back on the Church usually develops a secret or manifest leaning toward atheism … the absolutism of the Catholic Church seems to demand an equally absolute negation."[17] Having read this, I thought: Jung seems to know some of my university colleagues, without even having met them! The "absolute negation" is indeed the tell-tale sign, indicating that somewhere beneath the resistance, such people are still bound to the past, if only through rancour and hatred. But many of the people around me on campus who were once hardened believers are now hardened atheists. This reversal seems to be a sign of the Heraclitian principle of *enantiodromia*, a contrariwise running to the opposite position.

Personally, I cannot afford an enantiodromiac response; it does not suit me. I am more interested in returning religion to its basis in the loamy, dark earth of mythos, and, hopefully, in finding new life and vitality for religion as it is returned. I see honour and reward in the process of returning religion to its original home in mythos. The soil is good there, and the great exotic plants of religion are gladly received back into this ground and given nutrients and sustenance for continued growth. Christianity is languishing and dying because it is prevented from growing in the glaring, solar light of logos, where it has been subject to too much ratiocination. I recognize, as Jung did, that this de-literalizing path is lonely and isolated. The religious see only heresy and betrayal; the atheists also see heresy and betrayal. It is not a pathway for anyone whose identity and esteem relies on institutional support because that simply will not happen. Jung's last wish in his memoirs is for Christianity to be allowed to grow and develop:

> This myth remained unassailably vital for a millennium – until the first signs of a further transformation of consciousness began appearing in the eleventh century. From then on, the symptoms of unrest and doubt increased ... until [we arrive at] the twentieth century, [which] revealed to what extent Christianity has been undermined.[18]

Growth in the Christian mythologem will require, as all growth requires, a giving up of certain cherished illusions of the past. To grow up, Christianity will have to sacrifice false elements in its previous character. Many Christians will refuse to grow up, and they stymie the growth of this tradition. Jung commented: "In contradiction to the saying of Christ, the faithful try to *remain* children instead of becoming *as* children. They cling to the world of childhood."[19] In a later passage, he elaborated on this remark:

> Faith tries to retain a primitive mental condition on merely sentimental grounds. It is unwilling to give up the primitive, childlike relationship to mind-created and hypostatised figures; it wants to go on enjoying the security and confidence of a world still presided over by powerful, responsible, and kindly parents.... In this way the faithful remain children instead of becoming as children, and they do not gain their life because they have not lost it. Furthermore, faith collides with science and thus gets its deserts, for it refuses to share in the spiritual adventure of our age.[20]

Like Jung, I am interested in participating in a faith that shares in the "spiritual adventure of our age". That adventure has to engage science and philosophy in their various forms, and current indications suggest that science and philosophy are waiting for the Christian tradition to enter into the dialogue that they have tried to start. It is hard, however, having a one-way dialogue; science is engaged in a monologue until religion gets on board. As

Einstein famously said, "Science without religion is lame, religion without science is blind."[21]

Jung's insights for those who can receive them

Jung's five-page preface to "Answer to Job", "Lectori Benevolo" or "To the Kind Reader", is probably the best and clearest account of the problem of religious literalism in his collected writings. Therefore, I would now like to turn to this short essay. Perhaps the title of this piece is a form of propitiatory magic or wishful thinking because Jung is aware that many of his readers will be far from kind. In fact, he opens this preface admitting that he runs the risk of being "torn to pieces by the two parties who are in mortal conflict about [religion]".[22] He is referring to believers and nonbelievers. The first take the statements of scripture literally, and the second assume they are illusory. The conflict between them, he asserts, "is due to the strange supposition that a thing is true only if it presents itself as a physical fact". He explains:

> Some people believe it to be physically true that Christ was born as the son of a virgin, while others deny this as a physical impossibility. Everyone can see that there is no logical solution to this conflict and that one would do better not to get involved in such sterile disputes. Both are right and both are wrong. Yet they could easily reach agreement if only they dropped the word "physical". "Physical" is not the only criterion of truth: there are also *psychic* truths which can neither be explained nor proved nor contested in any physical way.... Beliefs of this kind are psychic facts which cannot be contested and need no proof.[23]

He then goes on to present probably his clearest case about the nature of religious truth:

> Religious statements are of this type. They refer without exception to things that cannot be established as physical facts. If they did not do this, they would inevitably fall into the category of the natural sciences. Taken as referring to anything physical, they make no sense whatever, and science would dismiss them as non-experienceable. They would be mere miracles, which are sufficiently exposed to doubt as it is, and yet they could not demonstrate the reality of the spirit or *meaning* that underlies them, because meaning is something that always demonstrates itself and is experienced on its own merits.[24]

Our concept of truth and reality is defective if we believe that only physical facts are true. Jung is aware that the typical "believer" is unable to comprehend this point of view since the religious traditions have conditioned its followers to believe that something is "true" only if it happened as a fact in time and space. Jung becomes impatient with religious traditions at times and wonders whether they are generating more ignorance than awareness. If they are not enabling people to enter into the spirit of a critical spirituality, but merely into a credulous or blind faith, Jung doubts that such traditions deserve to continue into the future. He is quite unsentimental about this possibility, and, to some extent, he personally seals the fate of such traditions by indicating they are fraudulent.

I can feel a certain tension in his mind as he casts judgement on Christianity. He wants to slough off its infantile traits, yet, at the same time, he wants to preserve what is good and noble in Christianity. He says that a literal understanding of the miracles is not needed to get the message of the gospels. That message comes through in other ways, in the moral and spiritual values that are apparent in Christ's ministry. We do not need pyrotechnics or supernatural acts to demonstrate the worth of his ministry:

> The spirit and meaning of Christ are present and perceptible to us even without the aid of miracles. Miracles appeal only to the understanding of those who cannot perceive the meaning. They are mere substitutes for the not understood reality of the spirit. This is not to say that the living presence of the spirit is not occasionally accompanied by marvellous physical happenings. I only wish to emphasize that these happenings can neither replace nor bring about an understanding of the spirit, which is the one essential thing.[25]

This is a major point: regardless of whether miracles and wonders are literally true, they cannot "bring about an understanding of the spirit". The mere existence of miracles does nothing to change the consciousness of the reader of scripture; it does nothing to bring the believer into a relationship with spirit. It merely satisfies the somewhat primitive human desire for a sign and that, according to scripture, is unholy and unreliable. In Matthew, we are told "It is an evil and unfaithful generation that asks for a sign!"[26] The gospels, therefore, confirm Jung's argument that miracles do not bring a person into a relationship with spirit. Only faith can do that, or what we might today call "intuition". Miracles delight the need in us for supernatural displays, the same kind of delight that we gain when, for instance, looking at acts performed by a stage magician. But none of this concerns the living reality of the spirit, but merely that part of us that seeks the spectacular.

Jung is at pains to convince his readers that psychic facts are not nothing and cannot be dispensed with lightly. He knows his argument has to contend with an age-old prejudice about what constitutes "reality", and that is why he keeps trying to approach the reality of the psyche from different angles:

> The fact that religious statements frequently conflict with the observed physical phenomena proves that in contrast to physical perception the spirit is autonomous, and that psychic experience is to a certain extent independent of physical data. The psyche is an autonomous factor, and religious statements are psychic confessions which in the last resort are based on unconscious, i.e., on transcendental, processes. These processes are not accessible to physical perception but demonstrate their existence through the confessions of the psyche. The resultant statements are filtered through the medium of human consciousness: that is to say, they are given visible forms which in their turn are subject to manifold influences from within and without.[27]

The psyche, like the spirit, is ultimately a "transcendental" factor, and as such there are no ways of accessing the psychic process apart from symbolic images. Moreover, the metaphors of the psyche are not "invented" arbitrarily by gospel writers or poets but are impressed on their consciousness by the creative imagination. As Jung says later in his preface to "Answer to Job":

> Ideas of this kind are never invented, but enter the field of inner perception as finished products, for instance in dreams. They are spontaneous phenomena which are not subject to our will, and we are therefore justified in ascribing to them a certain autonomy. They are to be regarded not only as objects but as subjects with laws of their own.[28]

Here Jung seems to be exaggerating to make a point. I do not agree that religious ideas enter the minds of scripture writers as "finished products" from an internal cosmic source. Surely those ideas are suggested to such writers by tradition, training, and cultural and historical factors. I doubt that the ideas come to writers "finished", as if they were taking divine dictation. I cannot see Jung's argument being damaged by suggesting, for instance, that apostles and scribes are inspired by seed-ideas and images, but that such raw materials have to be worked on and shaped by the conscious mind before they find their final expression.

Respect for a God unknown

Jung goes on to raise an argument about the unknowable nature of God and spirit. He also points to one of his preoccupations in all his writings about religions: whether discussing the character or nature of our metaphorical expressions has any bearing on the sacred itself:

> [W]henever we speak of religious contents we move in a world of images that point to something ineffable. We do not know how

> clear or unclear these images, metaphors, and concepts are in respect of their transcendental object. If, for instance, we say "God", we give expression to an image or verbal concept which has undergone many changes in the course of time. We are, however, unable to say with any degree of certainty – unless it be by faith – whether these changes affect only the images and concepts, or the Unspeakable itself. After all, we can imagine God as an eternally flowing current of vital energy that endlessly changes shape just as easily as we can imagine him as an eternally unmoved, unchangeable essence.[29]

According to Jung, all statements about God are metaphorical and provisional. Despite what religions may believe about their own revelations, Jung insists that such revelations are not absolute. In this way, he introduces a note of relativity into all discussions of a religious nature. This is what makes many religious people nervous. He is saying that the so-called Word of God is not definite, beyond challenge, or eternally valid, but that it is simply the "best possible expression of something as yet unknown". The consolation to religious advocates is that it is our "best" chance at knowing God, but Jung believes it is neither our only chance, nor is it beyond reproach. He is a relativist when it comes to religious phenomena; no single revelation is binding, though all revelations have relative significance. Jung's relativism does not, however, extend to uncertainty about the very existence of God:

> There is no doubt that there is something behind these images that transcends consciousness and operates in such a way that the statements do not vary limitlessly and chaotically, but clearly all relate to a few basic principles or archetypes.[30]

This important point is often lost on his religious critics. He is relativistic only in terms of our human knowing, not in terms of the existence of the objects of our knowing. In this way, Jung demonstrates his indebtedness to the philosopher Kant, who was the first to make the distinctions clear between what we can know and the object to which our knowing points.

Jung is aware that most believers are not philosophically sophisticated. It is asking a lot of those believers to think in terms of a philosophical difference between religious statements and the objects to which they point. Jung says "the naïve-minded person has never separated [religious symbols] from their unknowable metaphysical background".[31] Such people "instantly equate the image with the transcendental 'x' to which it points".[32] Nietzsche referred to this as *word magic*, but the technical term is *hypostatization*, that is, treating something conceptual as if it were real. Religious traditions encourage such thinking because it shores up their status and serves to strengthen, they think, the faith of their followers. In my experience, however, it serves to alienate followers, especially those who are educated and understand that the relation of signifier to signified is arbitrary at best. As Jung puts it, a religious image "does not posit" the transcendental object to which it points.[33] In this regard, he was about 35 years ahead of the postmodernists, who boldly announced this "disconnect" between sign and signified as if no one had heard of it before.

The mystery of the resurrection

Finally, I would like to turn to Jung's approach to the resurrection. In a note written specifically for members of his seminar on *Aion*, Jung said, "Indubitably resurrection is one of the most – if not the most – important item in the myth or the biography of Christ and in the history of the primitive church." He continues:

> To the primitive Christians as to all primitives, the Resurrection had to be a concrete, materialistic event to be seen by the eyes and touched by the hands, as if the spirit had no existence of its own. Even in modern times people cannot easily grasp the reality of a psychic event, unless it is concrete at the same time. Resurrection as a psychic event is certainly not concrete, it is just a psychic experience. It is funny that the Christians are still so pagan that they understand spiritual existence only as a body and as a physical event. I am afraid our Christian churches cannot maintain this shocking anachronism any longer, if they don't want to get into intolerable contradictions. As a concession to this criticism, certain theologians have explained St Paul's glorified body given back to the dead on the day of judgment as the authentic individual "form", viz., a spiritual idea sufficiently characteristic of the individual that the material body could be skipped. It was the evidence for man's survival after death and the hope to escape eternal damnation that made resurrection in the body the mainstay of Christian faith. We know positively only of the fact that space and time are relative to the psyche.[34]

It is stated in the dogmas of the traditions of Christianity that "the faith" rests on the reality of resurrection. St Paul emphasized that resurrection is the cornerstone on which all else rests: "If Christ has not been raised then our preaching is useless and your believing it is useless."[35] But significantly, Paul was not thinking in terms of a physical resurrection, which is what is stressed in church doctrines. This has always struck me as a serious anomaly. If we look closely at the gospels, we see that there is no physical resurrection in Mark, the earliest of the gospels, as his testament ends with the empty tomb.[36] In the fourth gospel, John's Jesus is already transcendent and

God-like at the beginning of the story; there is no need of a physical resurrection to demonstrate the divinity of Jesus. And if we look closely at the letters of St Paul, as Jung suggests we do in the previous quotation, we do not find support for a physical resurrection. On the contrary, Paul seems to castigate those who think about the resurrection in literal terms.

Paul suggests that the resurrection has to be understood symbolically, and he rails against those who want to see it as a merely physical event:

> Someone may ask, "How are dead people raised, and what sort of body do they have when they come back?" They are stupid questions. Whatever you sow in the ground has to die before it is given new life and the thing that you sow is not what is going to come.... The thing that is sown is perishable but what is raised is imperishable.... When it is sown it embodies the soul, when it is raised it embodies the spirit.
>
> If the soul has its own embodiment, so does the spirit have its own embodiment.... Or else brothers, put it this way: flesh and blood cannot inherit the kingdom of God, and the perishable cannot inherit what lasts for ever.... When the last trumpet sounds, the dead will be raised, imperishable, and we shall be changed as well, because our present perishable nature must put on imperishability and this mortal nature must put on immortality.[37]

There is nothing here to support the church's doctrine of the physical resurrection. Paul shows impatience with the idea of a physical resurrection and does not see it as central to the new faith. Questions about a physical resurrection, he says, are "stupid questions" and to reduce the resurrection to a literal, physical event is to lose the true nature and meaning of the risen Christ.

I have quoted from the Jerusalem Bible, but the King James Version gives an even clearer depiction of the distinctions Paul is trying to make:

> All flesh is not the same.... There are celestial bodies, and bodies terrestrial: but the glory of the celestial is one, and the glory of the terrestrial is another.... So also is the resurrection of the dead.... It is sown a natural body; it is raised a spiritual body. There is a natural body and there is a spiritual body.[38]

In this version, Paul does not refer to "stupid questions" but says that those who ask such questions are "fools".[39] Paul is uncompromising about the fate of the physical body, including the body of Christ: "What you sow does not come to life unless it dies."[40] The body is a "seed", he says, and the seed must die. "What is sown is perishable, what is raised is imperishable."[41] He continues: "It is not the spiritual which is first but the physical, and then the spiritual."[42] How much clearer can he be? He adds, "Flesh and blood cannot inherit the kingdom of God."[43] There is no doubt in Paul's mind about the body's fate: it is, like the first Adam, "a man of dust", and, "as was the man of dust, so are those who are of the dust".[44] The link is to Genesis: "for dust thou art and unto dust shalt thou return".[45]

For us, the confusion arises when we face Paul's metaphorical language to describe the nature of the spirit. As was common practice in ancient times, spirit is described as a subtle body. Paul uses the language of "bodies" to refer to all three elements: the physical body, the soul, and the spirit, and this is where the complications arise. Some have misread his comments about "celestial bodies" as a reference to physical bodies. For Paul, however, the physical body is cast aside as a husk, and a new "spiritual body" is put on. The trouble is that we no longer think of the immortal spirit as a "body", but as a presence, or in Jungian terms, as an archetype, and I would suggest that this stands at the heart of the centuries-long confusion about the nature of the resurrection. Paul makes it clear that resurrection does not mean a *resuscitation* of the human body. When he refers to a celestial, glorified, or spiritual body, he is not referring to the body as we know it.

Paul's "glorified body" is synonymous with spirit, which means that a physical resurrection is not even on his agenda. When he says that resurrection is the basis of faith, he is not thinking in physical terms. Paul's Greek word for the resurrected body is *pneumatikos* (spiritually), and Northrop Frye asserts that "whatever else the word means, it means 'metaphorically'".[46] Christ rose from the dead "metaphorically". It is not metaphorical in the sense that it is make-believe or did not really happen. It is metaphorical in the sense that nothing physical occurred, and hence we must resort to metaphor and symbol to talk about it at all. An event took place, yet it can only be known, and communicated, in faith. If we expect to see the resurrection with our physical eyes, Paul would accuse us of being foolish and stupid. The Pauline testament is thus completely at odds with the church's traditional insistence on the physical nature of the resurrection.

The apostle Paul is no primitive thinker, but a sophisticated one, even if his language about different kinds of "bodies" has created confusion. Paul and Jung are saying the same thing when it comes to the interpretation of miracles. The real mystery is that spirit neither experiences a common birth, nor does it suffer a common death. The real mystery is that spirit is immortal and everlasting, and after his death, Christ rises in spirit and acts as source and inspiration for those who wish to follow in his spirit. This mystery is not unique to Christ, as the churches insist, but a natural mystery experienced by all of us, all of the time. Jung is clearly not impressed by the cult of Jesus:

> The gospel writers were as eager as St Paul to heap miraculous qualities and spiritual significances upon that almost unknown young

> rabbi, who after a career lasting perhaps only one year had met with an untimely end. What they made of him we know, but we don't know to what extent this picture has anything to do with the truly historical man, smothered under an avalanche of projections. Whether he was the eternally living Christ and Logos, we don't know. It makes no difference anyhow, since the image of the God-man lives in everybody and has been incarnated (i.e., projected) in the man Jesus, to make itself visible, so that people could realize him as their own *homo*, their self.[47]

Jung accepts that archetypal figures such as the saviour or redeemer need to be projected on to historical beings so the archetype becomes visible and discernible. This projection of unconscious contents is inevitable; what he criticizes is the extent to which this projection takes place, its intensity and obsessive quality, so that the archetype of the Self projected onto Jesus is no longer accessible to the common person because it is entirely externalized. We need to take some of the burden of "Christ" from Jesus and take it on ourselves, so we too can suffer a spiritual passion and transform our lives. I have shown, I hope, that one can be an intensely religious person without being a literal thinker, and one can even be a Christian and refuse the literal doctrines of the church.

Notes

1 C. G. Jung, "The psychology of the child archetype" (1940), in *The Archetypes and the Collective Unconscious*, *The Collected Works of C. G. Jung* (hereafter *CW*), vol. 9/i, London, Routledge, 1968, p. 267.

2 C. G. Jung, "Two kinds of thinking" (1912/1952), in *Symbols of Transformation*, *CW* 5, London, Routledge, 1967.

3 The term *critical spirituality* has been developed by several Australian writers, including Fiona Gardner, Marcus Bussey, and Ivana Milojevic. The term seems to have arisen in response to so much unreflective and uncritical spirituality in recent years. As the term *spirituality* has become more popular, it has been used loosely and vaguely. Therefore, it has become necessary to subject it to critique and discernment. For Bussey, critical spirituality is "the critical engagement with the soul" and is "a condition of continuous becoming through objective adjustment" (Marcus Bussey, "Critical spirituality: toward a revitalized humanity", *Journal of Future Studies*, 2006, vol. 10, no. 4, pp. 39–44). For Gardner, critical spirituality is reflexive, open, diverse, and capable of being adapted to varying historical, cultural, and social conditions (Fiona Gardner, *Critical Spirituality: A Holistic Approach to Contemporary Practice*, Farnham, Ashgate, 2011).

4 Jung refers to Freud and Nietzsche as "great destroyers" in "In memory of Sigmund Freud" (1939), in *The Spirit in Man, Art, and Literature*, *CW* 15, London, Routledge, 1966, p. 69.

5 C. G. Jung, "Definitions", in *Psychological Types*, *CW* 6, London, Routledge, 1921/1971, p. 14.

6 Ibid., p. 816.

7 Ibid., p. 818.

8 Jung, "The psychology of the child archetype", p. 260.

9 C. G. Jung, "Answer to Job" (1952), in *Psychology and Religion: West and East*, *CW* 11, London, Routledge, 1958, p. 647.
10 Jung, "The psychology of the child archetype", p. 271.
11 Ibid., p. 261.
12 Ibid., p. 260.
13 Ibid., p. 267.
14 C. G. Jung, "Symbols and the interpretation of dreams", in *The Symbolic Life*, *CW* 18, London, Routledge, 1961, p. 606.
15 Jung, "Answer to Job", p. 648.
16 C. G. Jung, "Psychology and religion (The Terry Lectures)" (1938/1940), in *Psychology and Religion: West and East*, *CW* 11, London, Routledge, 1958, p. 141.
17 Ibid., p. 34.
18 C. G. Jung, *Memories, Dreams, Reflections*, London, HarperCollins, 1963/1995 p. 360.
19 C. G. Jung, "Psychological Commentary on 'The Tibetan Book of the Great Liberation' ", (1939/1954), in *Psychology and Religion: West and East*, *CW* 11, London, Routledge, 1958, p. 762.
20 Ibid., p. 763.
21 Albert Einstein, "What I believe", in Alan Lightman (ed.), *Ideas and Opinions*, New York, Modern Library, 1994.
22 C. G. Jung, "Lectori Benevolo", in "Answer to Job", p. 553.
23 Ibid., p. 553.
24 Ibid., p. 554.
25 Ibid.
26 *The Holy Bible*, *The Jerusalem Bible*, Garden City, NY, Doubleday, 1966, Matthew 16:4.
27 Jung, "Lectori Benevolo", p. 555.
28 Ibid., p. 557.
29 Ibid., p. 555.
30 Ibid.
31 Ibid., p. 558.
32 Ibid.
33 Ibid.
34 C. G. Jung, "On resurrection", (1954), in *The Symbolic Life*, *CW* 18, London, Routledge, 1961, p. 1574.
35 1 Corinthians 15:14.
36 The Gospel of Mark ends at 16:8, but an addendum has been added by church authorities.
37 1 Corinthians 15:35–53.
38 *The Holy Bible, Authorized King James Version*, Oxford, Oxford University Press, 1976, 1 Corinthians 15:39–44.
39 Ibid., 15:36.
40 *The Holy Bible, The Revised Standard Version*, New York, Collins, 1952, 1 Corinthians 15:36.
41 Ibid., 15:42.
42 Ibid., 15:46.
43 Ibid., 15:50.
44 Ibid., 15:48.
45 KJV, Genesis 3:19.
46 Northrop Frye, *Northrop Frye's Notebooks and Lectures on the Bible and Other Religious Texts*, ed. Robert D. Denham, Toronto, University of Toronto Press, 2003, p. 435.
47 Jung, "On resurrection", p. 1570.

11

A LIFELONG READING OF JUNG

Thomas B. Kirsch

From the vantage point of age, Tom Kirsch shares his experience of first coming to and reading Jung, beginning in his late teens and then extending through the years of his early development as a Jungian analyst to the present, some 50 years later. His essay includes an impressive meeting with Jung himself as well as an account of his early encounters with some of Jung's written works. Just as, at the start of a personal analysis, the powerful images and affects of an initial dream may continue to reverberate for decades and become a living symbol in the psyche of the dreamer (a symbol that is never fully unpacked), so Kirsch's initial experience of reading Jung as a young man seems to go on living vividly within his psyche.

J. K.

All my life I have been attracted to the study of Jung, yet have felt an equally strong resistance. I began reading him when I was 17 and have continued to do so for nearly 60 years. Growing up with two Jungian analysts, whose primary analyses were with Jung, he loomed as a larger than life figure in our household. My father, who had been educated in the classical European manner along with the Jewish tradition of study, spent many hours every day studying Jung's texts. My mother lacked a formal education beyond high school, but she, too, studied Jung intensely and respected the Jewish tradition of scholarship. Both parents expected that I would become a Jungian scholar and follow in my father's footsteps. While I could sense the importance of Jung for my parents and even for myself, their desire put me in conflict with my desire to belong in our Jewish neighbourhood of post-war Los Angeles and to become part of the American culture of the 1950s – a powerful lure for my extroverted, social, and athletic temperament. My father, especially, was distressed and disappointed by my interest in tennis and Hollywood musicals instead of opera and serious studies. I vividly remember driving along Sunset Boulevard through Beverly Hills with my dad in his 1949 silver Chrysler. I was 15 and not terribly interested in what he had to say. I still remember what he said on that ride: "You'll see! People will read Jung and appreciate him more 50 years from now!"

Though I passed it off with "Yeah, Dad", his words have come back to me many times over the years.

My father read Jung avidly and asked Jung for copies of everything he wrote as soon as it was published; sometimes, and always with Jung's approval, he translated them from German in order to pass along the latest essay to his growing number of students in Los Angeles. The most significant example was his translation of "Answer to Job".[1] Although he knew that the Bollingen Foundation had arranged for a translation of *The Collected Works* by R. F. C. Hull, he also knew about the time lag for Jung's other books to appear in English, and he considered "Answer to Job" crucial at that moment, so he made a translation. Subsequently, there was some discussion about what should be done with it. Finally, the publisher decided to use Hull's translation for the sake of uniformity, with acknowledgement that my father's translation had been consulted. Actually, Hull and my father met for several days in Ascona, Switzerland, to go over the translation word by word. Still, my father was disappointed that he never got the recognition that he rightly deserved, but to his credit he did not put up a fuss.

As *The Collected Works* were published in English, my father gave weekly seminars on all of Jung's alchemical texts. They were all recorded, with the expectation that one day I would transcribe, edit, and eventually publish the tapes. Alchemy was my father's love, not mine; studying and writing about alchemy is not a natural thing for me. So, for my own individuation I felt that I needed to put those tapes aside for someone else to attend to.

It was my mother who facilitated my first reading of Jung; in fact, she was the pivot for a major turning point in my life. In June 1953, I turned 17 and had just graduated from the American public school system. She had gone to Zurich in the early spring to analyse with C. A. Meier, not realizing the importance of those final months for an American teenager. Alone with my father and an older cousin, I had to face the anxieties of a high school senior without her guidance, and I became ill. She pushed me to return to Europe after graduation, to the place of my birth and to the spiritual centre of my parents' psyches – Zurich, Switzerland. That summer I left Los Angeles with my father, mainly wanting to be united with her, not to see Europe. We travelled via New York, where we stopped to see my father's old friend Werner Engel, and thence to London, where we visited my mother's brother and his family. Then we travelled by train and boat from London to Paris, where we scoured the city on foot, eight hours a day, for a week. My father was indefatigable in his hunger for culture and desire to influence me! When at long last we arrived in Zurich, I found the warmth I had been missing desperately, especially after seeing war-torn London, where its population was still digging its way out of the rubble and where food was still in short supply. I was enormously relieved to be with my mother after five months with my father, who was not the most related of characters, for all his intellect and his caring for me. I took in the beauty of the Swiss landscape, along with her presence; ever since Switzerland has been a second home for me. The contrast with Los Angeles in the 1950s, with its glamour and reliance on the automobile, was striking. I appreciated the public transport system in Switzerland. More directly, I experienced a desire to immerse myself in European culture, which I had so strongly resisted, and I suddenly wanted to study the French and German languages. In this context, my mother gave me a book she thought would be a basic introduction to Jung: *Introduction to Jung's Psychology* by Frieda Fordham.[2] It was easy to read, and I still have the book, although nothing about it stands out in my mind. A week of travel south through war-torn Italy with my mother and my cousin Peter completed my introduction to the world of Jung and my parents' origins – or as close to their homeland, Germany, as they dared go emotionally or physically. Switzerland and Jung had become their homeland. After that trip, I was prepared for college and ready to read Jung seriously.

Shortly after returning to Los Angeles, I bought the first paperback edition of *Modern Man in Search of a Soul*,[3] which I carried to Reed College to read during my freshman year. In the dawning era of paperbacks, that was the one book of Jung's available in paperback for the cost of $1.35. I still have that book, too. What struck me about this reading was Jung's common sense, which appealed to me deeply. I knew that I wanted to study more of Jung from reading *Modern Man.* I hate to admit it, but at college I was a naïve and callow youth and had been puffed up by life in proximity to the movie industry. My father was the analyst of many well-known movie stars and studio executives, and it had been more than gratifying when my friends were blown away by the sight of one of them sitting in the dining room, which served as the waiting area for my parents' home offices. I was swept up by the importance of our lives in Los Angeles, and when I went to Reed College, I had classmates who were from rural parts of the country. As a consequence, I bragged about my parents' connections and became known as a superficial, Southern-California, Jewish smart-ass. Though it was painful, my classmates' reaction shocked me into a new level of self-realization. Ever since that painful college experience, I have been much more modest, inhibiting myself from speaking candidly, being specific, and elaborating my observations and reflections. I neither wanted to suffer more rejection, nor did I want to make my parents look bad.

The next important experience for me in reading Jung came three years later between my junior and senior years at Reed. Again, my parents were making their annual pilgrimage to Switzerland, but this time I went with them. In 1956, Scandinavian Airlines had opened their polar route from Los Angeles to Copenhagen, with stops in Winnipeg and Greenland. It was a 24-hour journey. By this time, *Two Essays on Analytical Psychology* had been published in paperback.[4] Throughout that night and day, to the constant drone of the plane's four engines, I read this seminal work. Jung's comprehensive view of the psyche, relating his own psychology to that of Freud and

Adler, and also tracing his psychology back to the roots of psychoanalysis, made eminent sense to me. We travelled to Salzburg, Austria, where we attended five operas in five days, with chamber concerts in between. I heard Mozart and appreciated his music as never before. Later that summer, I had the opportunity to visit Jung with my father, who wanted to pay a call to express his condolences, for Emma Jung had died the previous winter. We sat in the garden beside the lake. Jung was subdued and in mourning.

One of Jung's statements in *Two Essays* was that "all knowledge was relative".[5] In my sophomoric way, I questioned Jung about that statement, asking him if that was not an absolute statement. I cannot remember his answer, but I do recall that I did not feel shamed or made to feel uncomfortable by his response. The curious thing is that in two recent readings that I have given this book in preparation for teaching I have not been able to find this statement. That idea itself does not mean too much to me now; I only look upon it as symbolic of my immaturity. In fact, talking to Jung and experiencing his quiet wisdom had a profound effect, especially having just read his work. Jung's depth of perspective, which for me was more a matter of his feeling for life than what he thought about it, made a deep impression on me and has shaped both my personal and professional development.

When I returned to Reed for my senior year, I was crammed with undigested experience, which I unloaded on my unsuspecting roommate, Bob Hertzberg, who to this day thanks me for opening his "Los Angeles frame of mind" to a world he has since explored for himself. I think that my entire life has centred around the assimilation and recapitulation of my experiences that summer in Europe. Reading Jung is my touchstone in that process.

Two years later, I was between my first year at Albert Einstein Medical School and about to transfer to Yale, where I ultimately graduated. That summer in 1958 I had an individual hour with Jung. My father was teaching at the Jung Institute in Zurich during the hour Jung had made available, and I was allowed to go in his stead. I was prepped by my Zurich analyst, C. A. Meier, about what would interest Jung, who was then 83 years old. The growing circle of Jungian students and analysands in Zurich, well aware of Jung's importance to the world, felt it was their responsibility and privilege to assist his research by contributing material. At the time, Jung was working on his monograph on *Flying Saucers*,[6] and Meier helped me select dreams that might interest him. Jung cut through that veneer by announcing as we sat down, "So you want to see the old man before he dies!" I was totally taken aback by his directness, but over the years I have come to appreciate it.

Six years later I began my psychiatric residency and also began working with a Jungian analyst whom I chose, not one my parents had chosen. In the course of this analysis, it gradually became clear that I am an extroverted intuitive feeling type. I had grown up with the belief and expectation that my typology was introverted thinking intuitive, like Jung's. This realization came with a tremendous feeling of relief. I no longer had to be a Jungian scholar, which meant that I did not have to read everything in the Jungian literature. Since this time, reading Jung has been deeply embedded in my psyche, and even though I have never been able to judge how "deep" my reading is, I believe that I took Jung in from my inferior and profoundly unconscious side, that is, through my introverted thinking and sensation functions. My Jung lives inside me like a dark, swift underground river, accessible at any point of contact in time and place in the form in which I originally took it in. Reading Jung feels like an authentic part of my being. The result has been that I am often described, somewhat accusingly, of being a true-blue Jungian.

At the time of Jung's death in 1961, his alchemical writings had been translated and published by the Bollingen Foundation as his *Collected Works.* Many Jungians at that time did not read the alchemical texts but focused on his earlier work on psychotherapy and psychological types. Maybe, like me, they had not caught up with Jung's late-life developments and were still trying to absorb his earlier material. Maybe, again like me, they were caught up in collective movements of the era and needed also to become conversant in the dominant psychoanalytic theory and method if they were to gain legitimacy as psychotherapists or psychiatrists.

Apart from *The Collected Works*, two of Jung's books were published posthumously in the early 1960s, both of which proved to be popular and widely read. *Memories, Dreams, Reflections* (*MDR*), Jung's so-called autobiography, traced his inner life as related to Aniela Jaffé.[7] The second book, *Man and His Symbols*, was a project initiated by John Freeman of the BBC, who had interviewed Jung in March 1959 for the television programme *Face To Face.*[8] The book, written by various authors, was assembled in order to meet the growing need for a general introduction to Jungian thought. Jung wrote an introductory chapter; the man who became my personal analyst, Dr Joseph Henderson, also contributed a chapter. Both texts were especially meaningful to me and continue to hold their wider value. Jung's respect for and emphasis on the inner world in the face of increasingly extroverted societal norms has provided validation and a path to follow for those who seek to build a deeper and more meaningful way of life than is ordinarily modelled for us.

Of the many chapters in *Memories, Dreams, Reflections* that were personally meaningful, several stand out. In the first chapter, "Early Years", Jung recounts his earliest dream from age four in which he experiences the underground Phallus. That dream made a lifelong impression on me. The dream phallus was to Jung the underground god-not-to-be-named, and it was an affect/image that strongly influenced his development; he called it the source of his creativity. Reflecting on its impact on my developing relationship to the unconscious, I wonder whether I had made a partial identification with Jung. His dream included the enigmatic statement by his mother, "Yes, just look at him. That is the man-eater!"[9] At the age of four, I, too, had had an encounter with the powerful forces of the unconscious as they were laid out before my young eyes. We lived near Hampstead Heath in London, where the sight of a downed fighter airplane or an unexploded bomb was not uncommon; air-raid sirens sounded at night, sending us to the basement of a local school, where I learned to sleep in a chair beside my mother, who always managed to make me feel safe there. My mother had mediated my experience of the war – an archetypal phenomenon, *par excellence* – and the impetus to study Jung and to become a Jungian analyst primarily came through her.

The chapters in *MDR* that Jung devotes to his choice of psychiatry as a profession and his relationship to Freud were especially significant to me. In the mid-1960s, when I first read it, I was just beginning my own career in psychiatry. The question that loomed for me was how was I going to find my place in contemporary psychiatry as a Jungian? Jung's work had been marginalized, and at that time there were few psychological or psychiatric training programmes where Jung was considered worth teaching. To choose a Jungian training meant that, in many respects, I, too, would be marginalized, although people were also attracted to me because of my Jungian ideas. During my psychiatric residency at Stanford University Medical Center, I was specifically told by my professors that a Jungian identity would definitely limit the academic positions to which I might aspire. Since my primary identity up to then had been as a successful and academically competitive student, it was a source of great anxiety. Yet, after having accepted an important academic position at the National Institute of Mental Health, I finally turned it down to continue my personal analysis and pursue Jungian analytic training. That decision changed my life. Making the choice to become a clinical Jungian analyst meant, as it had for Jung, sacrificing all academic ambition. This had tremendous ramifications for my personal life as well, for my wife at the time, who was also a physician, did end up pursuing an academic career, which in many ways divided us.

An important chapter for me in *MDR* was Jung's account of the visionary experience in which he realized himself as a rabbi.[10] Jung had broken his leg in 1944 and subsequently had a heart attack and nearly died. His central vision, during this period of near death, of the Mystic Marriage in the Garden as it appears in the Kabbalistic tradition transformed him and seems to have erased any ambivalence he felt toward Jews in the aftermath of his relationship to Freud, whom he had seen as unwilling or incapable of realizing the mystery of numinous phenomena, which was central to his vision of spirituality. Although I was unable to understand the dimensions of meaning to which Jung pointed, I was able to grasp the significance of the event intuitively. It also fully satisfied my need, as a Jew, to make Jung acceptable. I had felt accepted as a Jew by Jung through my parents' feelings of his acceptance.

In 1963, after my first year of residency in psychiatry at Stanford, I began analytic training at the C. G. Jung Institute of San Francisco; reading Jung now was a requirement. My personal analyst Dr Joseph Henderson gave the first seminar, and he chose to base it on a lecture that Jung had given in January 1934 at the Eidgenössische Technische Hochschule (ETH), the premier engineering university in Switzerland. Between 1933 and 1941, Jung gave lectures on psychology to engineering students; shorthand notes were made of the lectures, which were translated into English, privately printed, and distributed with Jung's approval among his English-speaking students.[11] In the lecture that Henderson discussed, Jung used a diagram to show and validate both sides of the psyche, the extroverted and the introverted.[12] For me, this diagram and lecture affirmed my psychological type in a way that no other writing of Jung's had done, for I had always received the message that only the introverted life was worth living! There were very few extroverts in the Jungian world, and generally we were judged to be superficial and not really "Jungian".

When I was both a psychiatry resident and a candidate in analytic training, I read and reread *Two Essays on Analytical Psychology*. Even though it had been published as Volume 7 of *The Collected Works*,[13] I studied the paperback edition published in 1956.[14] The text was discussed in an analytic training seminar offered by Dr Mel Kettner, whose own life had been changed by the book. Mel reports that in 1953, on his way to a year of post-graduate work in a cardiology lab in Geneva, Switzerland, he accompanied a travelling companion on a visit to the Manhattan apartment of John Farrar, head of the publishing company, Farrar, Straus, and Young, Inc. Mr Farrar began telling him about a most interesting book he had just read by a Swiss psychologist named Carl Jung, who thought that spiritual needs were as instinctual as the sexual. When Dr Kettner showed interest and said he would buy a copy before he sailed, Mr Farrar gave him the book, saying it was not yet available for sale since it was an advance copy. The book was *Two Essays on Analytical Psychology*, the second volume of Jung's writing to be published for the Bollingen Foundation by Pantheon Books (which then became Volume 7 of *The Collected Works* when published by Princeton University Press). Reading this book during his Atlantic crossing struck a resonant cord and changed the course of his professional life and personal identity, for a year later he enrolled as a student in Zurich at the Jung Institute.[15]

Two Essays is a complex text and somewhat confusing. It is a book in four parts, with two main chapters – the essays – and two lengthy appendices. To read the appendices first and then the two essays makes great sense, for in that order, one can see most clearly how Jung built his psychology. The first appendix, "New Paths in Psychology", was written in 1912 in German for a yearbook of Swiss art and culture and was later revised to become the first of the two essays. Here, one finds Jung most under the influence of Freud, explaining, by way of clinical examples, Freud's 1895 text *Studies in Hysteria*, written with Josef Breuer, in which they set forth their original trauma theory of neurosis.[16] They later discarded this theory and followed it with the sexual theory of the origins of the symptoms. This, Jung proclaims, is real knowledge of the human soul required of the medical doctor who is called on to treat the psychological ills of his suffering patients. The second appendix, "The Structure of the Unconscious", is dramatically different in tone and content. It was written in German and translated into French for publication in *Archives de Psychologie*, vol. 16 (1916); since the original manuscript was no longer available, the English edition was translated from the French. During the period in which it was written, we know that Jung was still deeply engaged in making sense of his profound psychological experiences of 1913–14, which he described so compellingly in *Memories, Dreams, Reflections* in the chapter called "Confrontation with the Unconscious".[17] Publication of Jung's *The Red Book*[18] in 2009 has given us a wider perspective on this period of Jung's life. Here, we see Jung becoming Jung, making a clear distinction between the personal and the impersonal unconscious, elaborating the phenomena one may observe in the person who begins to connect with and assimilate material from the impersonal unconscious, introducing his hypothesis about the opposition and tension between the two levels of unconsciousness, describing the persona and its function, citing the negative effects of ways in which one may attempt to deal with an upsurge of image and affect-laden material from the collective (impersonal) level of the psyche, and outlining his form of treatment, so that a synthetic solution may be found to one's internal conflict. Here, Jung is setting out to make his unique and powerful impact on the development of depth psychology.

The *Two Essays* proper are the result of several revisions of the originals, which Jung subsequently made; for a full understanding, reading the prefaces he wrote to each revision, also published in Volume 7 of his *Collected Works* is worthwhile. The first essay, which he calls "The Psychology of the Unconscious", was most extensively revised in 1916, 1918, 1926, and 1942. In the first part of the essay, Jung adds a description of Adler's theory of the will to power and Freud's sexual theory. He then reflects upon the similarities and differences he sees between the two theories, or hypotheses, as he prefers to call them; in this essay, one may see the formulations that led to his later work on typology. In the last three sections of the first essay, he expands on his own hypotheses and methods.

The second essay, "The Relations Between the Ego and the Unconscious", is a 1934 revision of the original 1916 paper included in the appendices. He tells us in his preface that in its present form it represents an

> expression of a long-standing endeavour to grasp and – at least in its essential feature – to depict the strange character and course of … the transformation process of the unconscious psyche. This idea of the independence of the unconscious, which distinguishes my views

> so radically from those of Freud, came to me as far back as 1902, when I was studying the psychic history of a young girl somnambulist.[19]

This essay was an important aid to me in defining my own Jungian and psychiatric identity. It was an era when psychoanalytic theory and methods were the dominant influence in both the collective and the psychiatric worlds. I needed to be able to relate to my psychiatric colleagues and be conversant with their thinking, yet to do so from a Jungian perspective. Because these clinical languages were so different, I had, in a sense, to become bilingual. Through reading, I could see the value of other approaches and treat them respectfully. Also, I could recognize in Jung a man of independent thought, able and willing to assert his own vision in the face of strong cultural countercurrents.

Two Essays also is one of the few places in which Jung gives us a clear view of how he actually worked. In "The Synthetic or Constructive Method", section VI of the first essay, he describes his method, relates the patient's dream of a crab and her associations and gives us the causal-reductive interpretation that he does not give to the patient. He tells us why he did not offer his interpretation to her; he then demonstrates his own synthetic-constructive interpretation.[20] In the next section, "Archetypes of the Collective Unconscious", he further amplifies the dream image and illustrates his way of drawing out and relating to his female patient's transference fantasies. This level of detail is rare for Jung, who seldom revealed so much of his analysand's personal history. I think this is because he simply was not interested in writing about that level of analytic work. His mission was to explore the archetypal psyche. My mission was to explore my own unconscious through my dreams and my work with my personal analyst. Reading Jung amplified my understanding of what I was discovering within.

One Sunday during my residency training, I sat down and spent the entire day reading "General Aspects of Dream Psychology".[21] At that time, Freud's *Interpretation of Dreams*, first published in 1899, still dictated the standard interpretive treatment of dreams, which were basically seen as wish-fulfilments, with the unconscious operations of disguise and condensation producing the manifest content, the analysis of which invariably led to a reductive interpretation, designating an early infantile origin for the dream's latent content.[22] Things were about to change in the San Francisco Bay area, which was transformation central for a revolutionary new movement toward a humanistic approach to the psyche. Harry Wilmer (later to become a Jungian analyst) had brought a new model of treatment for mental disorders, which he had been introduced to by Maxwell Jones in the UK, to the therapeutic community at Oak Knoll Naval Hospital in Oakland. The National Institute of Mental Health had given a huge grant to nearby San Mateo County Hospital's psychiatry department to develop a model programme for community mental health. The newly opened and beautifully designed Stanford Hospital and medical school, planted among the oak forests and golden hillsides of a vast ranch that had become Leland Stanford Junior University, was setting its sights on becoming one of the nation's leading research centres. Teaming with the San Mateo Hospital and the Palo Alto Veterans Hospital as training sites for its medical students and resident physicians, Stanford instituted the forward-thinking, democratic model of the therapeutic community in its mental health programmes. William Dement, whose pioneering work in EEG studies of sleep at the University of Chicago led to the discovery of the rapid-eye movement phase associated with dreaming, had joined its faculty. Timothy Leary and Richard Alpert, later to take the name Ram Dass, were doing their research on LSD in Stanford's psychology department. Ken Kesey was living at the edge of the Stanford campus, working at the Palo Alto Veterans Hospital, one of Stanford's sites for educating medical students and resident physicians, and writing his novel, *One Flew over the Cuckoo's Nest*.[23] Many of the psychiatry residents were experimenting with LSD and dipping into the wild affect-imagery of the collective unconscious without the benefit of any form of psychological guidance.

I discovered my own way of approaching the same material through my dreams and personal analysis, and this path was affirmed most dramatically the weekend when I read Jung's "General Aspects of Dream Psychology". That weekend my then wife was on-call, which meant that she spent from Friday afternoon through Sunday evening at the hospital. I was serving on Stanford Hospital's small in-patient unit but was not on-call that weekend, and its staff, dedicated to the concept of the therapeutic community, had organized a party at someone's home that Saturday evening. I attended to join the group spirit that animated the unit and found myself becoming too intimate with one of the young nurses. I was probably slightly drunk when I left the party, feeling guilty. Maybe my decision to read Jung all the next day was my penance. I do remember having a lot of energy for the reading! I have no recollection of what dictated my choice of texts. Perhaps I chose it out of curiosity and the need to understand what was happening between me and my analyst, whose fearless and wide-ranging treatment of my dreams was so impressive and helpful. Having an analyst not chosen by my parents from among their intimate colleagues was a relief; I felt I was just getting started. I had been seeing him twice weekly for several months and wanted to see what Jung had to say about dreams. Perhaps it was synchronicity at work, guiding my hand to the one volume that would strike me most solidly at that moment, for soon I was personally and profoundly engaged and felt as though Jung were speaking directly to me. Imagine my shock when Jung began to analyse a dream that reflected in its imagery and affect the inner situation of a young man who was guilt-filled over an illicit erotic encounter! Jung analysed it by Freud's causal method of interpretation and introduced his own additional (but not to be substituted for the causal) final method, which asks us to consider to what purpose the dreamer produces a dream.

> All psychological phenomena have some such sense of purpose inherent in them, even merely reactive phenomena like emotional reactions. Anger over an insult has its purpose in revenge; the purpose of ostentatious mourning is to arouse the sympathy of others, and so on.[24]

And the purpose of being drawn by Eros? I was edified by Jung's lengthy elaboration of my inner status. The apropos nature of this text impressed its content and meaning indelibly on my mind. I *knew* now what Jung meant by the symbol and the compensatory function of the dream. I *knew* what he meant when he said that the dream contains the subliminal material of a given moment and grasped his formulation of its purposive impulse. Intuitively, I *knew* what Jung meant when he said that the whole situation of the dreamer needs to be taken into account to make an adequate interpretation. I *understood* what it meant to differentiate the conscious realization of a psychological fact from its fully conscious integration through direct personal experience.

As Jung wound toward the conclusion of his essay on dreams he reflected on the criticism that he had received for venturing into material that he was told was not the purview of the psychologist, but belonged to the philosopher or theologian. He responded:

> If the patient's view of the world becomes a psychological problem, we have to treat it regardless of whether philosophy pertains to psychology or not. Similarly, religious questions are primarily psychological questions so far as we are concerned.[25]

Jung went on to say that medical doctors were least apt to understand his psychology, for they were trained to act, not think, and would not understand his ideas or his methods. True as this was for most doctors, at the time I first read this I had the opposite problem. From childhood, I was on intimate terms with Jung's psychology, so I had no trouble with his basic ideas, which had been a subtle part of what shaped my mind; rather, I had struggled to adapt to the expectations of my medical education and often wondered whether it was worth my while to learn all that I had to learn, when I knew, more or less from the beginning, that I wanted to become a Jungian analyst. So although what Jung said struck me as true of the medical profession, I saw promising signs in the kind of psychiatry I was being taught in the liberal era of the 1960s and 1970s. However, the direction in which psychiatry was headed abruptly shifted in the political climate of the late 1970s and 1980s and, subsequently, with the development of powerful psychoactive medications and the phenomenal rise of the psychopharmacology industry. What Jung observed of psychiatry (what he called *medical psychology*) in 1948, the date of his most recent revision of this essay, is even more true today, when any form of psychotherapy is eschewed in favour of a prescription.

In retrospect, though, I am grateful for two aspects of my medical education that set me apart from my nonmedical Jungian colleagues and gave me a solid foundation from which I still approach each patient in every encounter. First, I developed a clinical attitude. This is a subtle attribute and not easy to describe. Through learning the patterns in which the doctor approaches his or her patient, carefully listening and observing during the process of obtaining a history of the presenting problem "as if" a physical exam were to be the culmination of the encounter, I developed habits of appraising the whole person and the presenting problem that I believe are unique to the physician. Recently, I had occasion to be examined by a senior physician in one of the medical specialties, who had a young medical student at his side; I smiled inwardly as I listened to his careful explanation of my physical condition as revealed by a CT scan, illuminated on the computer monitor before all three of us, as he pressed his stethoscope to my body and urged her to listen here, compared to there, preparing her to recognize by physical examination alone what was visible on the screen. He was inculcating in her a particular attitude, a stance toward the human organism, which will become so deeply integrated into her personality that she will, over time, be transformed into a doctor. It is this imperceptible function for which I am grateful, this way of apprehending and perceiving, with which I appraise the patient's well-being or non-well-being. Quietly, it was integrated into me and became second nature to my being.

The second is the ability to look at death. A medical student's first patient is a cadaver to be dissected over the course of the first year of medical training. The memory of that single individual who surrendered his or her body for my education is indelible, and it was the first of many opportunities to know the reality of death and dying, to observe the way in which people died and the reactions of those around them, to listen carefully to the ways in which my teachers related to the dying person and the family members, and to participate, assuming some of the responsibilities attending the event on my own. I could easily recognize those among my teachers whose abilities I wanted to emulate and make part of my own character, and I am grateful for their capacity to allow me to align myself with them and thus acquire those attributes for myself. This familiarity with death lends gravitas to the serious business of inviting the approach of other human beings for my participation in their intimate emotional lives.

Of course, the personally directed meanings that filled me on that Sunday afternoon were submerged in the course of time, but not before setting me straight, outwardly as well as psychologically, along the Jungian path. I felt I neither needed LSD to explore the unconscious, nor required further sexual experimentation to know that side of my shadow. (I also knew I did not want to be like my dad, whose protracted self-discovery through Eros had been the source of so much pain in my family.) I did, however, become an enthusiast for the inner way of self-realization. I began to proselytize for Jung like crazy and got myself into trouble. Stanford was aimed at medical science and research and here were all these students and psychiatry residents taking LSD and clamouring instead for Jungian analysis! Little did any of us know that our education was coincident with the first stirrings of a cultural revolution. The early 1960s was a very interesting time to be in the Bay Area. My whole situation fitted together like two halves of a seed that weekend, my outer experience of partying on Saturday and then drawing back from outer enactment to read all day on Sunday, paired with my inner experience of temptation/guilt and my conscious realization of the power of the unconscious. Subsequently, I have taught Jung's essay "General Aspects of Dream Psychology" in many venues and still believe that it retains its freshness for every reading. It is one of Jung's clearest, most straightforward, and least equivocal texts.

Reading Jung deeply and why we do so are the primary questions raised by the editors of this book. The short answer is a resounding yes – we do need to read Jung deeply now because his message is more relevant today than when he was writing in the first half of the twentieth century. What my father told me when I was a teenager about his importance has proved true. My father was a difficult man to be around because he followed his own wishes without much consideration for the rest of his family. In the 1950s, Freud and psychoanalysis were at the peak of their influence, and many believed that through psychoanalysis the world's problems would be solved. Jung's concepts of complex, archetypes, collective unconscious, individuation, and synchronicity were poorly understood, whereas his psychological type theory had taken hold and introvert and extrovert had become part of everyday language. Generally, Jung was seen as a "woolly mystic" and more or less a kind of guru figure, a description that, from personal experience, I knew that he rejected!

Over the past half century many of the issues that Jung raised have become much more relevant. His interest in the religious experience, the numinous, and transcendence as it was expressed in different cultures led him on broad explorations. He was the first modern psychologist to study Oriental philosophies, having been invited in 1928 by the German sinologist, Richard Wilhelm, to comment on his translation of *The Secret of the Golden Flower*, an ancient Chinese alchemical text.[26] The publication of Wilhelm's translation of the *I Ching or Book of Changes*, a 3,000-year-old Taoist philosophical treatise, by the Bollingen Foundation in 1950, with a lengthy introduction written by Jung, was a landmark that allowed this ancient text of wisdom to have an increasing influence in the West.[27]

Modern man is *still* in search of soul food, as I am reminded daily in my clinical work. It is increasingly the task of individuals buffeted by the world of technology and our contemporary culture of instant communication, with its sense of *anomie*, a term borrowed from anthropology and sociology that describes our growing sense of alienation. Our traditional religions no longer contain the spiritual urges that are a natural part of the human psyche, and we are tempted by the media to substitute its opposite, materialism, whose value is fleeting and always demanding of greater novelty and excess. But it cannot last. Our search for meaning will always find a voice and Jung's psychology, developed out of his own courageous exploration into the depths of his psyche, can help us in our quest for a deeper understanding and wisdom. This is why I think his oeuvre has become essential for us to read and assimilate. I offer my own early experience with the hope that another beginner might find that following in my footsteps provides him or her with assistance into some of Jung's most accessible work.

Notes

1 C. G. Jung, "Answer to Job", in *Psychology and Religion: West and East*, *The Collected Works of C. G. Jung* (hereafter *CW*), vol. 11, Princeton, NJ, Princeton University Press, 1952/1958, pp. 355–470.
2 Frieda Fordham, *Introduction to Jung's Psychology*, London, Pelican Books, 1953.
3 C. G. Jung, *Modern Man in Search of a Soul*, New York, Harcourt, Brace, 1933.
4 C. G. Jung, *Two Essays on Analytical Psychology*, New York, Meridian Books, 1956.
5 Ibid.
6 C. G. Jung, "Flying saucers: a modern myth of things seen in the skies", in *Civilization in Transition*, *CW* 10, trans. R. F. C. Hull, Princeton, NJ, Princeton University Press, 1958/1968.
7 C. G. Jung, *Memories, Dreams, Reflections*, recorded and edited by Aniela Jaffé, trans. Richard and Clara Winston, New York, Pantheon Books, 1961.
8 Interview by John Freeman, *Face to Face*, BBC Television, March 1959; C. G. Jung and M.-L. von Franz (eds), *Man and His Symbols*, Garden City, NJ, Doubleday, 1964.
9 Jung, *MDR*, p. 12.
10 Ibid., pp. 288–299.
11 These lectures will be republished by the Philemon Foundation.
12 C. G. Jung, "Notes on lectures given at the Eidgenössische Technische Hochschule, Zurich, by Prof. Dr C. G. Jung", October 1933 to July 1935, in *Modern Psychology*, vols. 1 and 2, 2nd edn, Zurich, privately published by the C. G. Jung Institute, 1959, p. 47.
13 C. G. Jung, *Two Essays on Analytical Psychology*, *CW* 7, New York, Pantheon Books for the Bollingen Foundation, 1953.
14 See note 4.
15 I am indebted to my friend and colleague, Mel, for sharing the details of his story, which will appear in the memoir he is preparing for publication.
16 Sigmund Freud and Josef Breuer, *Studies in Hysteria*, *The Standard Edition of the Complete Psychological Works of Sigmund Freud*, vol. 2, London, Hogarth Press, 1895.
17 Jung, *MDR*, 170–99.
18 C. G. Jung, *The Red Book: Liber Novus*, ed. Sonu Shamdasani, New York, W. W. Norton & Co., 2009.
19 Jung, *Two Essays*, p. 133.
20 Ibid.
21 C. G. Jung, "General aspects of dream psychology", in *The Structure and Dynamics of the Psyche*, *CW* 8, New York, Pantheon Books for Bollingen Foundation, 1960, pp. 237–81.

22 Sigmund, Freud, *The Interpretation of Dreams*, *The Standard Edition of the Complete Psychological Works of Sigmund Freud*, trans. James Strachey, London, Hogarth Press, 1961/1899.
23 Ken Kesey, *One Flew over the Cuckoo's Nest*, New York, Viking Press, 1962.
24 Jung, "General aspects of dream psychology", p. 456.
25 Ibid., p. 526.
26 C. G. Jung "Commentary on the *Secret of the Golden Flower*", in *Alchemical Studies*, *CW* 13, Princeton, NJ, Princeton University Press, 1967, pp. 1–56.
27 Richard Wilhelm, *I Ching or Book of Changes*, with an Introduction by C. G. Jung, Princeton, NJ, Princeton University Press for the Bollingen Foundation, 1950.